Studies in Christiani
and Judaism / Études sur le
christianisme et le judaïsme: 4

Studies in Christianity and Judaism/
Études sur le christianisme et le judaïsme

Studies in Christianity and Judaism / Études sur le christianisme et le judaïsme publishes monographs on Christianity and Judaism in the period 200 B.C.E. to 400 C.E. with
a special interest in studies of their interrelationship or the
cultural and social context in which they developed.

STUDIES IN CHRISTIANITY
AND JUDAISM

Number 4

# LAW IN RELIGIOUS COMMUNITIES IN THE ROMAN PERIOD

## THE DEBATE OVER *TORAH* AND *NOMOS* IN POST-BIBLICAL JUDAISM AND EARLY CHRISTIANITY

Peter Richardson
and
Stephen Westerholm
with A. I. Baumgarten, Michael Pettem
and Cecilia Wassén

Published for the Canadian Corporation for Studies in Religion / Corporation Canadienne des Sciences Religieuses by Wilfrid Laurier University Press

1991

## Canadian Cataloguing in Publication Data

Richardson, Peter, 1935-
  Law in religious communities in the Roman period

(Studies in Christianity and Judaism,
ISSN 0711-5903 ; 4)
Includes bibliographical references and index.
ISBN 0-88920-201-X

1. Religion and law − History.  2. Religious
communities − Rome − History.  3. Jewish law −
History.  4. Christianity and Law − History.
5. Christianity and other religions − Judaism −
History.  6. Judaism − Relations − Christianity −
History.  I. Westerholm, Stephen, 1949-
II. Canadian Corporation for Studies in Religion.
III. Title.  IV. Series.

BL65.L33R52 1991        291.8′4        C91-093547-5

© 1991 Canadian Corporation for Studies in Religion /
    Corporation Canadienne des Sciences Religieuses

Cover design by Michael Baldwin, MSIAD

Order from:

Wilfrid Laurier University Press
Wilfrid Laurier University
Waterloo, Ontario, Canada   N2L 3C5

Printed in Canada

# Contents

# Contributors

ALBERT I. BAUMGARTEN is Associate Professor of Jewish history at Bar Ilan University in Israel; he was previously associated with McMaster University in Hamilton, Ontario, where he was co-director of the "Normative Self-Definition" project, co-editing *Jewish and Christian Self-Definition*, Volume 2: *Aspects of Judaism in the Greco-Roman Period*.

MICHAEL PETTEM has recently defended his dissertation on "Matthew: Jewish Christian or Gentile Christian?" at McGill University's Faculty of Religious Studies in Montréal. He has been *chargé de cours* for several years at the Université de Montréal, and has also taught at Carleton University in Ottawa and at McGill University.

PETER RICHARDSON is Professor of Religious Studies in the University of Toronto. His books include *Israel in the Apostolic Church, Paul's Ethic of Freedom, From Jesus to Paul* (editor, with John Hurd), and *Anti-Judaism in Early Christianity*, Volume 1 (editor).

CECILIA WASSÉN (a graduate of the University of Uppsala) is a doctoral student at McMaster University in Hamilton; the present contribution is part of her Master's Thesis at McMaster.

STEPHEN WESTERHOLM is an Associate Professor of Religious Studies at McMaster University. He has published *Jesus and Scribal Authority* and *Israel's Law and the Church's Faith*.

# Introduction

Law in post-Biblical Judaism and early Christianity continues to be a matter of prime importance. As the present volume shows, the history of scholarship on the place of *torah* and *nomos*, and of their relationship, is very rich. A seminar of the Canadian Society of Biblical Studies worked on these issues from 1983 to 1988, and collectively its members became convinced that, despite the recent flurry of interest in the place of law, the question has not yet been put in a sufficiently broad context. Indeed, no one scholar can tackle the range of problems connected with law: its textualizing in the post-exilic period, the development of an oral alongside a written *torah*, the shaping of various Jewish groups by discretely different attitudes to *torah*, the complex attitudes to "law" — to *nomos* and to *nomoi* — in the classical world, the views of Jesus and earliest Christianity on Judaism's law, the influence of classical law on Christianity and Judaism, the place of different attitudes to *nomos* in the separation of Christianity from Judaism, the conservative group's withdrawal from mainstream Christianity over matters of *torah*, and so on.

It was this range of questions — semantic, legal, sociological, anthropological, historical and theological — that constituted the mandate of the CSBS seminar. This volume, reviewing the scholarly debate over the past century or so, has been produced by five scholars; one of those has borne the lion's share of the burden. In the planning stages of the seminar it was thought essential to review the previous debates, since these have continued to shape current views significantly. Stephen Westerholm (McMaster University) agreed to take on this daunting task, and Chapters 2 to 5 of the present volume are his contribution to the group's understanding of its intellectual inheritance. He was to stand back and provide a broad overview of the major developments, without special reference to subordinate features of the debate or sub-sets of questions. We are all in his debt.

To this Michael Pettem (Montréal) has contributed Chapter 6 on the way in which scholarship has looked at Christian groups and their various reactions to *torah*. Al Baumgarten (Bar Ilan University in Israel, formerly of McMaster University) has done somewhat the same task for Judaism in Chapter 7, focussing on the Pharisees and two of the major contributors to our understanding of that influential group with its distinctive views on *torah*. And Cecilia Wassén (McMaster University) has reviewed the state of scholarly assessment of the Sadducees in Chapter 8.

Finally, I have contributed a brief piece in Chapter 9 on some of the published contributions of the members of the seminar to date; I have also introduced the whole in Chapter 1, both with a summary of the main lines of debate in the past 10 years or so and with a sketch of the intellectual origins of the connection between religion and law, particularly as that was developed in the middle of the 19th century among writers who have subsequently been looked upon as the founders of anthropology. As the organizer of the seminar I was enormously impressed with the enthusiasm of the members both for the topic and for the collective activity. More than that, I have been impressed with a growing sense of vitality of Biblical studies in Canada.

The volume tries to be consistent in the use of *torah* ("law," "instruction," "direction," etc.) for the linguistic term or for specific legal issues. Torah (with a capital and no italics) is used for "the whole Law," the "Law of Moses," and the like — general or whole as opposed to the particular. In this, it stands close to the word "Law" (with a capital), and when "law" generally is meant, or not specifically implying the whole of Torah, a lower case "l" is used.

I should like to acknowledge the early encouragement of Harold Coward, formerly President of the Canadian Corporation for Studies in Religion, and of Sandra Woolfrey, Director of Wilfrid Laurier University Press.

This book has been published with the help of a grant from the Canadian Federation for the Humanities, using funds provided by the Social Sciences and Humanities Research Council of Canada.

Peter Richardson
University College
November, 1989                                    University of Toronto

# Chapter 1

# Law and Religion: Origins and Present State

The last 25 years have witnessed a fascination with law in religious and theological circles.[1] This attention – described in parts of what follows but much larger than even this account would suggest – has not been much noticed, nor has its significance been carefully addressed within religious studies circles. A sociologist of knowledge would have much to say about it in a detailed fashion, but even an interested bystander can begin to see that it is not entirely accidental that law should become a prominent topic among scholars concerned with post-Biblical Judaism and early Christianity.

In this first chapter I will argue that the roots of the recent flood of studies on law and the religion of post-Biblical Judaism, including Jesus and Paul among others, are in fact quite remote. They go back to the middle, or perhaps even the early part, of the 19th century. But first some demonstration is needed of the seriousness of this issue in recent study, for some of the evidence post-dates the writing of the following chapters. Westerholm's, Pettem's and Baumgarten's contributions were all completed before it was quite so apparent that the work of the seminar in the Canadian Society of Biblical Studies which generated these analyses was a part of a larger ground-swell of scholarly activity.

## Turning Points: Sanders and Neusner

The work of E. P. Sanders represents a modern turning-point in the study of post-Biblical Judaism, and it is apparent in the analyses of the last dozen years that it has been so viewed by others. His examination of *Paul and Palestinian Judaism*[2] has been very influen-

Notes to Chapter 1 appear on pages 14-18. This chapter was prepared by Peter Richardson.

1

tial, not so much in connection with Paul as with its assessment of Palestinian Judaism. His own way of describing its contents refers to "patterns of religion"; its main effect, however, is to call into question the ways in which Judaism has been viewed by Christian scholars; and its creative contribution is to suggest a new kind of category for interpreting crucial aspects of Judaism's self-understanding: "covenantal nomism." Though not universally accepted, this term is increasingly commonly used; its importance for us lies in the way the phrase highlights two important claims about post-Biblical Judaism: it is focussed on law — *nomos* in Greek or *torah* in Hebrew — but it focusses on law in a particular way that emphasizes the societal context in which *torah* or *nomos* operates, a society that presupposes a "covenant" between itself and God.

Sanders has not described at length the social and religious characteristics of this society that claims it is founded on a covenant. He has described rather the various documents that contribute to an understanding of Palestinian society in the post-Biblical period, and then gone on to extend this analysis by applying the same set of concerns to Paul. This latter portion of the work seems to many less substantial and more open to questioning, but this observation does not detract from the book's signal importance. It marks — even though it might not have created *de novo* — a modern turning-point.[3]

There is a second turning-point of even more substance and significance than that marked by Sanders' work, though it is not so much a point as a period: the work of Jacob Neusner. Its influence has been less clearly acknowledged, in part because of the sheer bulk of his scholarly output and in part because its central attention lies in an extensive body of texts not easily accessible to scholars whose primary interest lies elsewhere than in Mishnah and Talmud. Neusner's significance can, however, hardly be exaggerated. Virtually single-handedly he has created a sub-discipline of religious studies: he has set the agenda, laid out the guidelines and erected the edifice. His corpus includes a still rapidly growing list of contributions, but its prime characteristics are, in my opinion, the following: (1) he focusses on the legal traditions of Judaism in the second Temple and post-destruction period, and provides a careful analysis of how those legal traditions have been developed and modified;[4] (2) he is conscious of the importance of the social sciences for our understanding of post-Biblical Judaism, so that he frequently draws important insights against that background, and he has stimulated many of his students to explore further and more deeply these connections;[5] (3) he has shown how *torah* in Judaism is of a piece with the fabric of society; he has woven a picture of the complexities of that society that are effectively a new portrayal;[6] (4) he has demonstrated the importance of individuals in the larger picture of society that he has drawn, giving full value to the creativeness of both persons and groups;[7] and (5) he has set out the main theological lines that need to be taken into account by subsequent scholars of Mishnah and Talmud.[8]

## Studies in Religion and Law

There have been other important and provocative studies of law in the last decade or so, following those of Neusner and Sanders. These have covered the whole range of subjects—though in very unequal quantities—in the post-Biblical period: intertestamental literature, the Essenes and the Dead Sea scrolls, Pharisees, Sadducees, scribal Judaism, Jesus, Paul and so on. It is impossible here to do more than hint at the wealth, variety and scope.

### *Groups in Judaism*

Studies on the Zealots have received no attention in full monographs after the considerable flurry of interest in the preceding generation. Martin Hengel's important book, *Die Zeloten*, has now been translated into English,[9] and perhaps its appearance will spark some fresh interest in the question of Zealot adherence to Israel's Torah. A full-scale study both of Zealots and of Sicarii and their legal understanding is a desideratum. Similarly, Sadducees and Torah continue to receive relatively little attention, despite the great importance of this group. A refreshing social scientific tack is taken in Saldarini's recent book which compares Sadducees, Pharisees and scribes,[10] a wide-ranging work set within a large context, when set alongside Schwankel's narrower exegetical study.[11] Two somewhat earlier works should also be mentioned, those of Le Moyne[12] and Buehler[13] (see further below, p. 137-40). Another group of persons still receiving far too little concentrated attention, but which offers a very provocative case study, are the *'am ha-aretz*.[14]

It is quite otherwise with the Dead Sea scrolls and the question of *torah* within the Qumram community. Pride of place goes to the enormously important issues raised by the Temple Scroll (11QT), at long last published by Yadin both in a critical edition[15] and in a more popular and readily accessible form.[16] The most provocative assessment of the Temple Scroll has come from Wacholder.[17] He claims that "QT is not, as Yadin would have it, a fair summary of the Mosaic law but rather a *torah* that the community held to be superior to the law of Moses. If this is true—and Wacholder has the better of the argument—we have here an indigenous community development which shows a willingness to depart from tradition in ways that are independent and creative. Also significant are the two studies by Schiffmann,[18] the earlier one anticipating some of the insights now more solidly based on complete studies of the Temple Scroll, including his own. Schiffmann's concern for the penal code is also at the centre of the fruitful comparisons investigated by Weinfeld, in which he compares the Qumran sect with other voluntary associations, especially those of Ptolemaic Egypt.[19] Mention should also be made of two Canadian contributions to the understanding of *torah* at Qumran: Newton[20] has, for the first time, looked explicitly at the concept of purity—the importance of which is shown in another context by Neusner—and Garnet[21] has analyzed the attitude of the sect toward atonement—what Sanders has referred to as getting in and staying in. Finally, Beall's study of Josephus[22]—where he compares passages from Josephus with parallels from the scrolls—is important to note as a companion to the important study by Mason of the Pharisees. Beall concludes that Josephus is generally trustworthy, even though he may exaggerate and "hellenize."

It is hardly surprising, in part at least as a result of the provocative studies by Neusner, that Pharisees and Torah continue strongly as a subject of attention. As a preliminary to other works, Mason's extremely important dissertation on Josephus is fundamental from a historiographical point of view.[23] In it he challenges the Smith/Neusner hypothesis, arguing that Josephus is consistent in *War* and *Antiquities* on the role of the Pharisees. Even more important, he challenges the common—almost universal—claim that Josephus was at heart a Pharisee, reinterpreting the basic autobiographical text in *Life* 12 to mean that he chose only to act as if he were a Pharisee. When dealing with the Pharisees the crucial issue is methodological. How does one use the sources at our disposal—intertestamental, New Testament, Josephus, Tannaitic? And in what comparative setting shall we place them—the literate developments of the Mediterranean world, the social-political ferment of Judea, the post-destruction need for stability and continuity?

At one end of the chronological scale is Kampen's study[24] of the origins of the Pharisees, working primarily with the well-known passages of 1 and 2 Maccabees, and arguing that the Hasideans are a scribal group—"leading citizens from Israel"—in disagreement with the historians of the Hasmoneans responsible for 1 and 2 Maccabees. The origins of the later Pharisees may be found in this group. Two important studies on the Pharisees, by Bowker[25] and Finkel,[26] appeared some time ago, but continue to be important because they demonstrate the extent to which many of the concerns about Pharisees arise, directly or indirectly, from the picture painted of them in the records about Jesus. At the other end of the relevant period, Rivkin's analysis, rooted in the Tannaitic sources, has defined one of the main parameters of the problems associated with the Pharisees, the twofold *torah* — oral and written.[27] His debate with Neusner is not resolved, but those differences represent the basic choices that will confront scholars in the next several years (see further below, p. 109-26).

Pharisaic Torah is at one level easily understandable — after all, we have, as Neusner and others have demonstrated, considerable amounts of material explanatory of the oral and written law. But at another level the debate about *torah* for Pharisees still rages because there has been little meeting of minds on the methodology to be used and on the context in which to set the group. The scope of the material is too great and too diffuse to admit of ready solutions.

## Wider Aspects

Several broad-ranging studies bearing on law and religion in the post-Biblical period have also appeared. Segal[28] applies social scientific approaches to the study of both Judaism and Christianity as he argues for them being "twins," each of them relying on root metaphors such as Torah and covenant, each of them accusing the other of abandoning that Torah and covenant. A similarly broad picture in the earlier period is sketched by Schnabel.[29] His analysis of the intertestamental literature under the categories of law and wisdom are very helpful, though his final understanding of Paul — which appears to be the point of the book — is less so. With these can be compared Porton's investigations into *goyim*,[30] and Goodman's analysis of Galilee.[31]

The most useful of these broader studies is a collected work, gathered under the direction of Lindars,[32] as the published version of the Ehrhardt Seminar in Manchester University.

## Jesus and Paul

I have already mentioned Sanders' important study on *Jesus and Judaism* in which matters of *torah* dominate. The most recent study on this topic, somewhat eccentric and rather complex, is by Vouga;[33] it argues that the conflict stories almost all post-date the resurrection and do not come from conflicts between Jesus and the Pharisees but from debates among various groups of early Christians. More traditional are Banks's treatment of the same question[34] — a very theological synthesizing of the various strands — and that of Hübner[35] — likewise theological in its concern but more provocative in its approach. More promising in its scope and its setting of the context is Westerholm's constructive study, which carefully compares and then distinguishes the scribal activities of Jesus and of other makers of *halakah* in a nuanced way.[36] There are also studies based on individual gospels: exploring specifically the Markan controversy stories on authority is Lee's recent dissertation;[37] Segal assesses the whole Matthean tradition of Jesus' *halakah*;[38] and Wilson provides an analysis of Luke and the Law.[39]

There have not been many studies of Jesus and *torah* in the last decade that break out of the usual moulds. One that does so is Marcus Borg's creative investigation that manages to lay alongside each other the political realities of the day, the common quest — albeit in different ways — for holiness, and the conflict stories of the gospels.[40] In the end, his position is somewhat similar to Westerholm's, but the route followed and the starting point are very different. Perhaps there is the beginning of a new axis.

Finally, a few of the outstanding recent contributions on the very vexed and long-debated question of Paul and *torah*. In addition to Sanders, *Paul, the Law, and the Jewish People* (noted above) and Heikki Räisänen,[41] two scholars who have already been mentioned for their studies on Jesus and law require fresh mention. Hübner[42] and Westerholm[43] take very different lines, though both are, to some extent, dominated by their Lutheran framework. Hübner argues vigorously, though in the end not cogently, for a major development in Paul's thought occurring between the writing of Galatians and Romans (on this question Räisänen has in my judgment the best of it); Westerholm extends his investigations on the history of scholarly opinions begun in this present volume, and submits a dozen or so major Pauline scholars to a searching theological assessment. An eirenic Jewish-Christian dialogue is provided by Lapide and Stuhlmacher,[44] the chapter by Lapide being focussed especially on law. Gager's important book on anti-semitism[45] is equally eirenic, and in line with the currents of today's scholarly activity with its use of social-scientific approaches. Also showing the relevance of this social-scientific method is Watson's important investigation of Paul and Judaism.[46]

Of all the recent contributions to the study of Paul, none is more controversial and challenging than Gaston's.[47] He attacks the prevailing consensus on half-a-dozen foundational elements in the usual views of Paul, suggesting that a new and more coherent approach to Paul is possible. Its weakness is that he must argue that Paul has a multi-valent understanding of law, that one must disentangle the various meanings of law; its strength is that his Paul is freed of inherited assumptions about his attitude to *torah*. For Gaston, Paul never speaks against *torah* as it applies to Israel, nor does Paul even imply the rejection of Israel. Paul's sometimes negative comments on law all apply to Gentiles and their experience of law.

---
*Present State*
---

From this brief account of the work of a decade or a bit more, it is clear that scholars are caught between the old and the new. The current consensus on Torah, if there is one, must in many respects be judged to be dominated still by the theological concerns—what effect one's understanding of Torah has upon the believing community to which one belongs. This is true of many Christian scholars as it is also, to a lesser extent, of Jewish scholars. Many studies maintain a strong theological concern, and still have some difficulty appreciating the importance of the various persons or parties, free from long-held convictions about law and religion.

There are however signs of fresh winds blowing, several of which might be savoured as a summary to this section:

(1) Social scientific (especially anthropological and sociological) methods have come to be applied to ancient texts in ways that open up new insights. There is still no agreement or consistency in how these approaches should be used, nor is there yet a "school" of interpretation. But enough has been done, and done well, to show that, especially in the matter of law and religion, more advances wait to be made. The lines sketched out by A. Segal, Watson, Gager, Lightstone—not to mention Theissen, Holmberg, Rubinstein and others—will be followed with increasingly constructive results.

(2) The work on law and religion in the post-Biblical period has been noteworthy also for its eirenic qualities. Some of the most important contributions have been by Jewish scholars working on the Christian developments (Lapide, A. Segal, P. Segal, Finkel) and by Christians working on Jewish developments (Sanders, Gager, Gaston, Saldarini). This is one of the prerequisites for a truly comparative approach, which to a large extent was the main burden of the CSBS seminar.

(3) A growing number of studies are now being produced that are carefully historical in their method of approach. When they are diachronic they are usually avowedly so, seeking an understanding of developments, with continuity across the boundary periods, careful not to make anachronistic jumps or deductions. When they are synchronic, they are concerned for more than mere parallelism and suggestive analogy.

---
## Ethnology and Jurisprudence
---

It was inevitable that historical studies of law should come to focus on this crucial period in the history of Western civilization. In so doing they were unconsciously following a line of enquiry—still overlooked by scholars in religious studies—sketched out in the 19th and early 20th centuries by philosophers, historians, anthropologists and legal scholars. These investigations have laid a theoretical foundation which has more seeped into religious studies than been assimilated deliberately. Yet, even though unknowingly, these intellectual and practical developments have directly influenced us and our predecessors. The remainder of this chapter is devoted to demonstrating that some of these antecedents are quite remote, and that we are the products of those remote predecessors, even when we have remained unconscious of them.

## Religion and Law

Societies at all times and in all places demonstrate an inextricable connection between law and religion. The founding fathers of the USA, the priests of a Mayan city, the elders of a Zulu village, the High Court judges of Britain, the Senate of Rome, the Sanhedrin of post-destruction Judaism, the Kirk session in a Reformation Scottish town—all have wrestled with the connection. Such diverse persons might not all prefer the word "law"; some will want to use "custom," "principle," "interpretation," and so on. And not all might wish to allow an equivalent role to religion and law; yet in whatever precise relationship the two stand, the connection between them and the influence of the one upon the other—the inseparable and powerful attraction between them—can be found in virtually all societies and cultures.

The reasons for this are both simple and complex. On the one hand many societies have had—and some still have—a direct connection between religion and law, where a religious authority, usually but by no means always written (as in Torah or in the Qur'ān), is used as a basis for deriving legal precepts. And the effect can run the other way as well in cases where custom or law circumscribe religious practice, so that almost regardless of the societal pressure for change in religious practice what inhibits religious adaptation is a previous formalizing of a legal statement. One thinks here of the dilemmas facing the modern Roman Catholic Church with respect to celibacy and women priests. Even in so-called secular states the powerful influence of religious convictions shapes the legal provisions of the state through an indirect—sometimes not so direct—system of societal pressure. The pressures being felt today in Canada and the USA, for example, on abortion and women's rights are too evident to need demonstration.

These rather obvious links tying law and religion are commonplaces. At one stage in the intellectual development of Western society, however, such commonplaces gave way to a much more carefully defined set of understandings of this relationship. This very significant turn occurred in early- and mid-19th-century Europe, and developed around the fledgling discipline of ethnology, one of the predecessors of what came to be the discipline of anthropology.[48]

## The Origins of the Modern Understanding

The proximate roots of the modern concern for the relation of law and religion lay in 19th-century reactions to 18th-century fascination with natural law. One of these reactions centred in the Romantic movement, and had as spokesmen Johann Gottfried Herder (1744-1803) and Georg Wilhelm Friedrich Hegel (1770-1831).[49] Herder argued for a view of history less concerned with elite members of a society—the great men—than it was with the life of communities. Each period, each society, had a unique character, rooted in its own history, institutions and customs.[50] Just as there was no absolute standard in literature or art or language, so there was no society that was inherently superior to others. There was no absolute progress. When advocates of natural law imposed uniform principles on very diverse cultures they did great damage to the traditions of those cultures, and when they drew the conclusion that earlier periods were inferior they subverted a proper understanding of history.

For Herder the state was opposed to the natural play of these indigenous qualities of a society. Hegel, who followed him, may have differed on the role of the state, seeing it as a more constructive authority, but he still emphasized that each state possessed independence and self-identity. His emphasis on history and the classics and, perhaps especially, on early Christianity led him to the view—increasingly common as the 19th century moved along—that human history is a story of progress, both moral and spiritual, with a concomitant advance in human self-understanding.[51]

Similar views, when applied specifically to the history of jurisprudence, gave rise to the important claim that law originates in custom; custom in turn arises from the nature of the society—from its *Volksgeist*, as Friedrich Karl von Savigny (1779-1861) put it. His particular contribution to these developments lay in his studies of Roman law, and his concern for its relevance to the reform of Prussian law, with the result that he became the most influential mid-19th-century legal theorist in Germany. The crucial need, he argued, was an appreciation of the genius of particular communities, and following that a recognition that law must accord with that spirit.

The great name in historical and comparative jurisprudence at the beginning of the nineteenth century is F. C. von Savigny in Germany, who
wrote on Roman law in the Middle Ages. Savigny . . . reacted against the
radical rationalism of the French Revolution and the Napoleonic period.
[His] interest in the study of archaic custom, however, was not romantic
but shared with the Romantic movement of that period a conviction that
that which is of the folk is right.[52]

Lloyd and Freeman summarize the basic—and fundamentally
important—truth grasped by this historical school: "law is not an
abstract set of rules imposed on society, but is an integral part of
that society, having deep roots in the social and economic habits
and attitudes of its present members."[53] To that I should only like
to add "and religious," since it is characteristic of most societies that
religious roots are just as deep as, and perhaps less adaptable than,
economic and social roots.

## Ethnology or Comparative Law

In the mid-19th century there is no clear demarcation between ethnologists, lawyers, classicists and other scholars working in comparative fields.[54] In one history of ethnological theory[55] the chapter on
comparative law begins with the great book on the ancient city by
the historian Numa Denis Fustel de Coulanges (1830-1889).[56] He
stresses the great variety of legal institutions, and the fundamental
importance of interpreting these in their context. As the subtitle
already announces, religion and law and institutions must be understood together or they cannot be understood at all.

The history of Greece and Rome is a witness and an example of the inti-
mate relation which always exists between men's ideas and their social
state. Examine the institutions of the ancients without thinking of their
religious notions, and you find them obscure, whimsical, and inexplic-
able. . . . But by the side of these institutions and laws place the religious
ideas of those times, and the facts at once become clear, and their explanation is no longer doubtful. . . . A comparison of beliefs and laws shows
that a primitive religion constituted the Greek and Roman family, established marriage and paternal authority, fixed the order of relationship,
and consecrated the right of property, and the right of inheritance. This
same religion, after having enlarged and extended the family, formed a
still larger association, the city, and reigned in that as it had reigned in
the family. From it came all the institutions, as well as all the private law,
of the ancients. . . .[57]

In this concentration on Greece and Rome Fustel de Coulanges
was at one with those who preceded him, particularly von Savigny
and J. J. Bachofen (1815-87). A Swiss lawyer, Bachofen lived and
breathed classical antiquity. He rejected univocal ways of interpreting civilizations, whether ancient or modern, insisting on the need

to connect religious practice and social structure in a coherent whole. Like many of his generation he was a progressive evolutionist. His importance in the history of ethnological theory is his identification of matrilineal descent and his emphasis on "mother-right" (*Mutterrecht*).[58] He attributes women's authority in household and state to their role as the earthly representatives of female fertility deities.

Starting from Herodotus' account of the Lycians as matrilineal, Bachofen deduces from it a coherent system of law antecedent and antithetical to the patriarchal principle of antiquity. . . . [T]he author interprets mythological references to outstanding women as relics of a one-time gynaecocracy. . . . [S]ecular gynaecocracy merely reflects the primary phenomenon, viz., the cult of a female deity. . . . . Gynaecocracy . . . was not the earliest social condition; it came as a reform superseding promiscuity. . . . Primeval promiscuity [what Bachofen calls "hetairism"] was followed by a revolt of woman, who craved delivery from such humiliation. The result was Amazonian assertiveness. Once in the saddle . . . women devoted themselves more and more to peaceable pursuits, among other things inventing agriculture.[59]

By a curious coincidence, Sir Henry Maine (1822-88) insisted upon a scheme of "father-right" in the same year as Bachofen argued for "mother-right."[60] Like several of the continental scholars just noted, he also maintained a heavy dependence on the legal institutions of Greece and Rome. To these he added a strong interest in law in the Hebrew scriptures and also the ancient law of India.[61] This familiarity with Indian law, based on seven years in India in the 1860s, enabled Maine to broaden the scope of western jurisprudence by comparing Roman law and modern European systems of law with Indian and other eastern systems. Maine broke firmly with all notions of imposing an a priori order upon various human societies of the past. He insisted upon careful study of each past society's development of legal institutions in its historical context; only then could illuminating comparisons be made with contemporary legal institutions. On this basis he made a major contribution through "the empirical, systematic, and historical methods he employed to arrive at his conclusions, and in his striving for generalizations firmly based on the empirical evidence at his disposal. . . ."[62] This judgment is too approving—the emphasis must be on the phrase "at his disposal"—for in fact on quite limited evidence he went on to construct a theory of stages of development that had no basis in observation of primitive society.[63] "Maine summed up the crucial developments of human history in his famous formula of the 'movement of the progressive societies from Status to Contract'"—that is, they moved from a situation where one's destiny is fixed at birth to a more flexible exercise of choice and will. Maine was well aware of the close links between religion and ancient law:

In early law, and amid the rudiments of political thought, symptoms of this belief meet us on all sides. A supernatural presidency is supposed to consecrate and keep together all the cardinal institutions of those times, the State, the Race, and the Family. Men, grouped together in the different relations which those institutions imply, are bound to celebrate periodically common rites and to offer common sacrifices; and every now and then the same duty is even more significantly recognized in the purifications and expiations which they perform. . . . [64]

A slightly younger contemporary of Maine's, John F. McLennan (1827-81), made a more direct contribution to ethnological theory through his insistence — independently of Bachofen — on the importance of matrilineal descent.[65] His claims were bound up with his interest in systematic bride capture, initially focussed on Spartan marriage ceremonies, which he believed he found sufficiently diffused that he could generalize about developments from "primitive" times to the modern period. Though modern scholars have not supported all McLennan's views, some of his contributions have survived: the concepts of "exogamy" and "endogamy" (terms he coined); the widespread importance of exogamy as a legal principle; the fact of archaic polyandry and levirate marriages, the spread and significance of totemism.[66]

The chief American contribution to this wave of ethnological theory came from Lewis H. Morgan (1818-81), whose first publications were on the customs of the Iroquois in up-state New York. Morgan, like others in this period, offered a comprehensive scheme; in his theory history is divided into three main periods: savagery (pre-pottery), barbarian (ceramic age) and civilization (writing). His *Ancient Society* includes more diverse materials and evidence than the writings of any of his contemporaries: American native peoples, Australian aborigines, Greece, Rome.[67] Morgan's legacy lay in "literally creating the study of kinship systems as a branch of comparative sociology," but his renown is actually attributable to the fact that Marx and Engels popularized his ideas.[68] His study of kinship systems, and the terms used for kin relationships across several societies, led him to hypothesize that different terminology reflected differing social relationships. It was in this context that he developed the notions of primitive communism and democracy that were picked up by Marx and prompted him to claim that "capitalistic society violated all that was natural to man. . . ."[69]

Finally, it is instructive to note the significance — especially relevant to this present volume — of W. Robertson Smith (1846-94), whose interest in anthropology stemmed from his contact with McLennan. "The sudden preoccupation of the academic world in research and debate over the evolutionary significance of totemism originated with McLennan. However, it was Smith's determined effort to apply it to the semitic world that supplied the substantive support for the thesis, tenuous though some of the surviving evidence appeared."[70] This interest of Smith's, when coupled with his Biblical criticism,[71] resulted in his being fired from the University of Aberdeen in 1881 as the result of his article "Bible" published in *Encyclopaedia Britannica* in 1875. In one of history's greatest vindications, he was named editor of the Encyclopaedia later the same year as he was fired. Smith stands as a bridge between anthropology and religious studies.

## Conclusion

All of the scholars just described are "functionalists"—that is, they are specially interested in how societies worked, in the mutual inter-relations of culture patterns. They also tended to find patterns of evolution in the data they used as a basis for their theoretical observations, patterns that are now discounted with a good bit of scorn.[72] But they left as a legacy the view that the law is not a self-contained system independent of society with its complex social, cultural and religious dimensions. For law is not simply the private playground of legal professionals; it develops out of other rules of society, especially moral and religious rules. Krader summarizes the postulates of Maine (and some other scholars who followed him) thus: "(1) The law has evolved from implicit and close rules to explicit and fixed rules. (2) The law derives from folk custom and is not the invention of men of the law. (3) The law is embedded in society and is a means to understanding the society in which it is found. (4) The study of society is a means to understanding the law of society."[73]

None of these was a follower of Darwin; indeed it may be that none was even influenced by Darwin, but the same intellectual climate that created Darwin's great book *Origin of Species* in 1859 also nurtured the evolutionary schemes of Bachofen, Maine, McLennan and the others.[74] Marx and Engels interpreted these evolutionary schemes, especially that of Morgan, materialistically. "They used [Morgan's] data and interpretation to chart the erosion of the primitive democratic gentile-based society as a civilization advanced and established itself on a foundation of social, economic, legal and political inequalities."[75] It is perhaps worth asking—even if only rhetorically—whether it is precisely the Marxist dependence upon these early ethnological theories, and the materialist "spin" they gave them, that hindered or even prevented scholars of religion from picking up these very useful insights and applying them directly and deliberately to the study of post-Biblical Judaism and early Christianity?

Certainly the earliest and best records of a society are often the legal records: Sumerian, Babylonian, Hebrew covenant traditions, the Roman Twelve Tables: ". . . a proper understanding of these earliest records can roll back the beginnings of their history for centuries. . . ."[76] This present study grapples with the legal interests of post-Biblical Judaism and early Christianity, a period not used by the earliest ethnologists even though they must have been familiar with it, in some cases deeply immersed in it. This oversight is odd but perhaps understandable; might it have been that the data was too close to their own private beliefs for them to see the period as grist for their ethnological mills?

The final introductory word goes to a modern scholar on the importance of law:

to say, that is to an equal extent organic throughout a community. Law is, within its sphere, the instrument by which a whole community is organized and works; it is also the expression of that working organization. The law and its rules must suit the needs and have the approval of the whole community if it is to be observed; and it is, above all, the needs of the community that determine that approval and shape that law."[77]

## Notes

1 One sign of this growing interest is the creation of the *Journal of Law and Religion* (Hamline School of Law, St. Paul, MN), 1 (1983). See also the series *Nomos* (published in various places for the American Society for Political and Legal Philosophy, 1958ff.). Journals have also been developed in areas of Anthropology of Law and Sociology of Law.

2 E. P. Sanders, *Paul and Palestinian Judaism* (Philadelphia: Fortress, 1977); see also *Paul, the Law and the Jewish People* (Philadelphia: Fortress, 1983) and *Jesus and Judaism* (London: SCM, 1985), and the three earlier collected volumes of papers presented at sessions of the McMaster University research project — directed by Sanders — on *Normative Self-Definition*, 3 vols. (Philadelphia: Fortress, 1980-83).

3 Sanders stands squarely on the shoulders of his mentor W. D. Davies, whose work — especially in *Paul and Rabbinic Judaism* (London: S.P.C.K., 1948 [1970]) — represents another turning point for an earlier generation. And Davies of course stood on the shoulders of his mentor, C. H. Dodd. See further below, p. 75-91.

4 Among other works, see Jacob Neusner, *A History of the Mishnaic Law of Holy Things* (Leiden: Brill, 1978ff.); *Judaism, The Evidence of the Mishnah* (Chicago: University of Chicago Press, 1981); and *The Oral Torah: The Sacred Books of Judaism: An Introduction* (San Francisco: Harper & Row, 1986).

5 Jacob Neusner, *From Politics to Piety: The Emergence of Pharisaic Judaism* (Englewood Cliffs, NJ: Prentice-Hall, 1973); *The Way of Torah: An Introduction to Judaism* (Belmont, CA: Dickenson, 1970); among his students I think particularly of William Scott Green and Jack Lightstone.

6 Jacob Neusner, *Judaism in Society: The Evidence of the Yerushalmi* (Chicago: University of Chicago Press, 1983), and *The Rabbinic Traditions About the Pharisees Before 70* (Leiden: Brill, 1971).

7 Jacob Neusner, *First Century Judaism in Crisis: Yoanan ben Zakkai and the Renais-

*sance of Torah* (New York: KTAV, 1982; augmented from 1975 edition), and *In Search of Talmudic Biography: The Problem of the Attributed Sayings* (Chico, CA: Scholars Press, 1984).

8 Jacob Neusner, *First Principles of Systemic Analysis: The Case of Judaism Within the History of Religions* (Lanham, MD: University Press of America, 1987); *The Systemic Analysis of Judaism* (Atlanta, GA: Scholars Press, 1988); and *The Ecology of Religion: From Writing to Religion in the Study of Judaism* (Nashville: Abingdon, 1989).

9 Martin Hengel, *The Zealots: Investigations into the Jewish Freedom Movement in the Period from Herod I until 70 A.D.* (Edinburgh: T. & T. Clark, 1989).

10 Anthony J. Saldarini, *Pharisees, Scribes and Sadducees in Palestinian Society: A Sociological Approach* (Wilmington, DE: Glazier, 1988).

11 Otto Schwankel, *Die Sadduzäerfrage (Mk 12, 18-27 par): eine exegetisch-theologisch Studie zur Auferstehungserwartung* (Frankfurt am Main: Athenaum, 1987).

12 Jean Le Moyne, *Les sadducéens* (Paris: Lecoffre, 1972).

13 William Wagner Buehler, *The Pre-Herodian Civil War and Social Debate: Jewish Society in the Period 76-40 B.C. and the Social Factor* (Basel: Komm. Friedrich Reinhardt, 1974).

14 Aharon Opennheimer, *The 'Am Ha-Aretz: A Study in the Social History of the Jewish People in the Hellenistic-Roman Period* (Leiden: Brill, 1977).

15 Yigael Yadin, *The Temple Scroll*, 3 vols. in 4 (Jerusalem: Israel Exploration Society, 1977-83).

16 Yigael Yadin, *The Temple Scroll: The Hidden Law of the Dead Sea Sect* (New York: Random House, 1985), and Johan Meier, *The Temple Scroll: An Introduction, Translation and Commentary* (Sheffield: JSOT Press, 1985).

17 Ben Zion Wacholder, *The Dawn of Qumran: The Sectarian Torah and the Teacher of Righteousness* (Cincinnati: Hebrew Union College Press, 1983). See also Wayne McCready, "A Second Torah at Qumran," *Studies in Religion/Sciences Religieuses*, 14, 1 (1985): 5-15, and George J. Brooke in Barnabas Lindars, ed., *Religion and Law* (Cambridge: James Clarke, 1988), p. 34-43.

18 Lawrence Schiffmann, *The Halakah at Qumran* (Leiden: Brill, 1975), and *Sectarian Law in the Dead Sea Scrolls: Court, Testimony, and the Penal Code* (Chico, CA: Scholars Press, 1983). The latter is a functional analysis of various features of the Qumran community (judges, witnesses, property, meals, etc.) within the communal setting.

19 Moshe Weinfeld, *The Organizational Pattern and the Penal Code of the Qumran Sect: A Comparison with Guilds and Religious Associations of the Hellenistic-Roman Period* (Fribourg: Éditions Universitaires/Göttingen: Vandenhoeck & Ruprecht, 1986).

20 Michael Newton, *The Concept of Purity at Qumran and in the Letters of Paul* (Cambridge: Cambridge University Press, 1985).

21 Paul Garnet, *Salvation and Atonement in the Qumran Scrolls* (Tübingen: J. C. B. Mohr, 1977).

22 Todd S. Beall, *Josephus' Description of the Essenes Illustrated by the Dead Sea Scrolls* (Cambridge: Cambridge University Press, 1988).

23 Steven N. Mason, *Josephus on the Pharisees: A Composition-Critical Study* (PhD, Toronto, 1986); forthcoming by Brill.

24 John Kampen, *The Hasideans and the Origin of Pharisaism: A Study in 1 and 2 Maccabees* (Atlanta, GA: Scholars Press, 1988).

25 John Bowker, *Jesus and the Pharisees* (Cambridge: Cambridge University Press, 1973).

26 Asher Finkel, *The Pharisees and the Teacher of Nazareth: A Study of Their Background* (Leiden: Brill, 1974).

27 Ellis Rivkin, *A Hidden Revolution* (Nashville: Abingdon, 1978); see further below, p. 110-14.

28 Alan Segal, *Rebecca's Children: Judaism and Christianity in the Roman World* (Cambridge, MA: Harvard, 1986); see also his *The Other Judaisms of Late Antiquity* (Atlanta, GA: Scholars Press, 1987).

29 Eckhard J. Schnabel, *Law and Wisdom from Ben Sira to Paul*, WUNT 2, Reihe 16 (Tübingen: J. C. B. Mohr, 1985).

30 Gary C. Porton, *Goyim: Gentiles and Israelites in Mishnah/Tosephta* (Atlanta, GA: Scholars Press, 1988).

31 Martin Goodman, *State and Society in Roman Galilee, A.D. 132-212* (Totawa, NJ: Rowman and Allanheld, 1983); see also Sean Freyne, *Galilee from Alexander the Great to Hadrian: A Study of Second Temple Judaism* (Wilmington, DE: Glazier, 1980).

32 Lindars, *Religion and Law*; the essay by Philip S. Alexander, "Jewish Law in the Time of Jesus: Towards a Clarification of the Problem" (p. 44-58), is especially helpful for its examination of law-courts and the law administered by those courts.

33 François Vouga, *Jésus et la loi selon la tradition synoptique* (Geneva: Labor et Fides, 1988).

34 Robert Banks, *Jesus and the Law in the Synoptic Tradition* (Cambridge: Cambridge University Press, 1975).

35 Hans Hübner, *Das Gesetz in der synoptischen Tradition. Studien zur These eine progressiven Qumranisierung und Judaisierung innerhalb der synoptischen Tradition* (Witten: Luther-Verlag, 1973).

36 Stephen Westerholm, *Jesus and Scribal Activity* (Lund: C. W. K. Gleerup, 1978).

37 Marius Young-Heon Lee, *Jesus und die jüdische Autorität: eine exegetische Untersuchung zur Mk 11,27-12,12* (Wurzburg: Echter, 1986).

38 Phillip Segal, *The Halakah of Jesus of Nazareth According to the Gospel of Matthew* (Lanham, MD: University Press of America, 1986). See also Celia Deutsch, *Hidden Wisdom and the Easy Yoke: Wisdom, Torah and Discipleship in Matthew 11:25-30* (Sheffield: JSOT Press, 1976); and John P. Meier, *Law and History in Matthew's Gospel: A Redactional Study of Mt. 5:17-48* (Rome: Biblical Institute Press, 1976).

39 S. G. Wilson, *Luke and the Law* (Cambridge: Cambridge University Press, 1983).

40 Marcus J. Borg, *Conflict, Holiness, and Politics in the Teaching of Jesus* (New York and Toronto: Edwin Mellen, 1984).

41 Heikki Räisänen, *Paul and the Law*, WUNT 29 (Tübingen: J. C. B. Mohr, 1983). See further below, p. 66-72.

42 Hans Hübner, *Law in Paul's Thought: A Contribution to the Development of Pauline Theology* (Edinburgh: T. & T. Clark, 1984; E.T. of German edition of 1978).

43 Stephen Westerholm, *Israel's Law and the Church's Faith: Paul and His Recent Interpreters* (Grand Rapids, MI: Eerdmans, 1988).

44 Pinchas Lapide and Peter Stuhlmacher, *Paulus, Rabbi und Apostel* (Stuttgart: Calwer, 1981).

45 John G. Gager, *The Origins of Anti-Semitism* (New York: Oxford, 1983). See also Peter Richardson, ed., *Anti-Judaism in Early Christianity*, Vol. 1: *Paul and the Gospels*; and S. G. Wilson, ed., *Anti-Judaism in Christianity*, Vol. 2: *Separation and Polemic* (Waterloo, ON: Wilfrid Laurier University Press, 1986).

46 Francis Watson, *Paul, Judaism and the Gentiles: A Sociological Approach* (Cambridge: Cambridge University Press, 1986).

47 Lloyd Gaston, *Paul and Torah* (Vancouver, BC: University of British Columbia Press, 1987).

48 The first courses in ethnology ever given were offered in University College in the University of Toronto by Daniel Wilson, Professor of English and History. He examined his history students on "ethnology" as early as the middle 1850s, and offered explicit courses in ethnology in the 1860s. He is also credited, incidentally, with the English coining of the word "pre-history."

49 On this and what follows see Lord Lloyd of Hampstead and M. D. A. Freeman, *Lloyd's Introduction to Jurisprudence*, 5th ed. (London: Stevens/Toronto: Carswell, 1985), chap. 10, especially p. 865-69.

50 See also Isaiah Berlin, *Vico and Herder: Two Studies in the History of Ideas* (London: Hogarth, 1976) for the influence of Vico on Herder.

51 In the context of this present volume it is deeply ironic to note that Hegel in one of his essays ("The Spirit of Christianity and its Fate") painted Judaism in very dark colours. Humans were not to be the slaves of objective commands as the Jews were slaves to the Mosaic law.

52 Lawrence Krader, ed., *Anthropology and Early Law* (New York/London: Basic Books, 1966), p. 8.

53 Lloyd and Freeman, *Jurisprudence*, p. 870.

54 Clyde Kluckhorn, *Anthropology and the Classics* (Providence, RI: Brown University Press, 1961), p. 4-9, makes a similar point, though in a more limited fashion. See also A. S. Diamond, *The Comparative Study of Primitive Law* (London: Athlone Press, 1965).

55 Robert H. Lowie, *The History of Ethnological Theory* (New York: Holt, Rinehart and Winston, 1937), p. 39.

56 Numa Denis Fustel de Coulanges, *La cité antique* (1864); English translation, *The Ancient City: A Study on the Religion, Laws, and Institutions of Greece and Rome* (Garden City, NY: Doubleday, 1955; originally published 1864).

57 Fustel de Coulanges, *Ancient City*, p. 12-13.

58 Bachofen published *Das Mutterrecht* in 1864.

59 Lowie's summary, in *Ethnological Theory*, p. 41-42. A comparison of these views with those of Riane Eisler, *The Chalice and the Blade* (San Francisco: Harper & Row, 1987), will show that these views are not merely male chauvinism but have been absorbed into modern mainstream feminism. See also I. M. Lewis, *Social Anthropology in Perspective* (Cambridge: Cambridge University Press, 1985 [1976]), p. 40, where he refers to Bachofen's views as a case of woman "queening" it over man, and he describes Bachofen's thesis as a claim that "anarchy eventually gave place to patrician capitalism."

60 Maine published *Ancient Law* in 1861.

61 T. K. Penniman, *A Hundred Years of Anthropology* (New York: William Morrow, 1974 [1935]).

62 Leopold Pospisil, *Anthropology of Law: A Comparative Theory* (New Haven, CT: HRAF Press, 1974), p. 150.

63 Diamond, *Primitive Law*, p. 3-4, and Lewis, *Social Anthropology*, p. 41.

64 Maine, *Ancient Law*, p. 6 (quoted from the edition of 1885).

65 McLennan published *Primitive Marriage* in 1865.

66 Lowie, *Ethnological Theory*, p. 43-49.

67 Lowie, *Ethnological Theory*, chap. 6, especially p. 55-56. He points out a curious omission, that "Morgan, who had himself described fraternities among the Iroquois, found no place in his system for clubs or any other primitive associations based on voluntary affiliation" (p. 58).

68 Lowie, *Ethnological Theory*, p. 62, 54.

69 Fred W. Voget, *A History of Ethnology* (New York: Holt, Rinehart and Winston, 1975), p. 153.

70 Voget, *Ethnology*, p. 153.

71 Smith published *The Prophets of Israel* in 1882, *Kinship and Marriage in Early Arabia* in 1885, and *Lectures on the Religion of Semites* in 1889.

72 Kluckhorn, *Anthropology and the Classics*, p. 11. A harsher judgment is offered by Diamond, *Primitive Law*, p. 3: "taken together ... [the work of Maine, Bachofen, Fustel de Coulanges, McLennan and Tylor] first embodied the idea that primitive societies were a worthy object of study. . . . [T]oday we can see that their materials were scanty and eked out by *a priori* reasoning and conjecture, and though they founded a discipline and left much of permanent value, their general laws of the history of societies were often erroneous and baseless."

73 Krader, *Anthropology and Early Law*, p. 9; see also p. 4-5. He also includes in this assessment late-19th-century scholars such as Paul Vinogradoff, Paul W. Maitland, Frederick Pollock, Rudolf Heubner, Frederic Seebohm and Maxime Kovaletsky.

74 J. O. Brews, ed., *One Hundred Years of Anthropology* (Cambridge, MA: Harvard University Press, 1968), p. 124.

75 Voget, *Ethnology*, p. 161.

76 Diamond, *Primitive Law*, p. 16.

77 Ibid., p. 10.

# Chapter 2

# Whence "*The* Torah" of Second Temple Judaism

## Law in Early Judaism and Christianity: Introductory Comments

To the independent-minded toddler, the proximity of a parent is both wanted and unwanted, a sensed but scarcely to be acknowledged need. Much Christian writing about law is marked by a similar ambivalence.

That, centuries before the beginnings of Christianity, the role and value of law were debated by the Greeks should be acknowledged, but it seems unlikely that the debate influenced at least the earliest Christian discussions. When Greeks deigned to look at barbarian conditions, they might pride themselves in having replaced a tyrant's rule with that of law.[1] On the other hand, the sophistic movement brought expressions of contempt for law as the tool of the weak in restraining the rightful dominance of the strong.[2] And even where law was not opposed, the view was widespread that its need was confined to the masses; the "just" and "wise" achieved virtue without it. To have one's morality imposed by law was for some an offence against nature, for others the sign of the second-best.

Though not all would grant the presumptions, we may venture to think that early Christian attitudes toward law owe rather more to the words and deeds of Jesus. From the debates which arose within the church, we might conclude that Jesus never explicitly renounced the validity of the regnant Mosaic code—otherwise the issue would not have divided his followers—but that there were sufficient indications of a critical attitude toward current praxis to encourage his adherents to depart from it. Such conclusions find

---

Notes to Chapter 2 appear on pages 41-43. This chapter was prepared by Stephen Westerholm.

confirmation in the gospel traditions.[3] Twentieth-century academics are scarcely in a position to pronounce on the legitimacy of the gospel critique; still, it is not without interest to note that the Jesus of the gospels denounces what may be regarded as typical flaws to which any code-oriented ethic is liable: the hypocrisy and self-delusion of those whose outward conduct conforms to prescribed norms while the heart remains unengaged; the lack of perspective evidenced in a failure to distinguish between trivial and weighty matters of the law; the pride which may follow from perceived adherence to the code, and the concomitant temptation to denigrate those who patently fall short. Conversely, the ethical teaching of Jesus, with its lack of specificity, its apparent impractability and "over-demand," is prone to perils which may be overcome by the promulgation of a concrete code. Not surprisingly, then, Christian history bears witness to both the longing for a practicable code and the sense that its adoption would violate something fundamental to the ethos of the Christian faith.

Like the wayward child whose censure is automatic whenever something goes wrong, the apostle Paul has borne the brunt of the blame for Christian misunderstandings of the Jewish Torah and for Christian antipathy toward systems of law in general. To be sure, he has not lacked defenders who would pronounce him innocent on both counts. But there is no denying the passages in which Paul speaks of law as a power from the past, of believers as having left its domain, and of dire consequences which follow a return to its rule. Inevitably Christian proponents of law must domesticate Paul. On the other hand, those who derive from their reading of Paul an opposition to any attempt at codifying Christian ethics must face the problems already put to Paul by his own contemporaries: how, apart from law, is sin to be adequately defined, and how is it adequately discouraged (cf. Rom. 3:8; 6:1, 15; Gal. 5:13)?

But while an ambivalence toward law is a characteristic Christian posture, one would not expect to find it in Judaism. Jews of the homeland gave thanks that they had been entrusted with the commands of the One who spoke and the world came into being; those of the Diaspora boasted that their law-giver was superior to those of the pagans among whom they lived. What the pious never doubted was that the Jews had been blessed with a Torah revealing God's demands to his people. More recent apologetics, however, in attempting to counter the widespread opprobrium for an ethic of law, has adopted the surprising tack of denying that *torah* even means "law." Such a claim, while possessing the grain of truth requisite for plausibility, has introduced considerable confusion into the scholarly literature. A further debate to some extent forced on the study of Judaism by Christian polemics concerns the role of law in Jewish "soteriology," In short, for the study of Judaism and Christianity alike, questions of law have become crucial.

Our task here is to review significant aspects of the recent debate. Of the countless possibilities for discussion, I have been allocated four significant areas for special attention in the next four chapters.

First I explore several accounts of the roots from which grew "*the* Torah" of Second Temple Judaism. A characteristic ideal of the period is the patterning of life and institutions after what is "written in the law of Moses the man of God" (Ezra 3:2). The phrase certainly suggests a measure of continuity with the constitution and ethos of pre-exilic Israel. Yet the question wherein the continuity lies has proven difficult to answer, and the attempt to do so raises profound problems of historical and theological interpretation. Whatever our response, it clearly affects our understanding and assessment of Second Temple Judaism. And, in fact, the answers given by such giants of German Old Testament scholarship as Wellhausen, Noth and von Rad have played a major role in shaping scholarly views of post-exilic Torah-centred piety. I begin, then, with a review of the development of Judaism's Torah.

A second area of concern is whether perceptions of Torah have been skewed by its rendering into Greek as *nomos*, into English as "law." Since the work of Solomon Schechter, such a notion has become a commonplace for many. In chapter three I trace and assess its role in the scholarly debate.

Thirdly, I turn to the common conception, derived from Paul's writings, that Judaism advocates justification by the law (chapter four). Something must be said here of the influence of Luther. Furthermore, the views of Bultmann, which for decades dominated the New Testament debate, will be examined. Then Sanders' full-scale attack on German (Lutheran) understandings of Judaism and Paul will be summarized, and a brief look given to the reaction it has provoked.

The fourth area of concern is scholars' perception of the place of law in earliest Christianity. In this context it will be of interest to by-pass the Germans, who are wont to monopolize the discussion, and focus attention on "the British connection"[4] of Dodd, Daube and Davies. From the writings of the erstwhile Cambridge "triumvirate" there emerges an impressive alternative to the claim that Christian faith is incompatible with law.

No doubt a list of significant scholars and issues omitted from our survey would be many times longer than the modest one proposed for consideration here. It is hoped nonetheless that enough material has been presented to suggest the importance, complexity, and controversial nature of our theme.

I begin, then, with a look at the roots from which "*the* Torah" of Second Temple Judaism developed. The following summary of the

Old Testament debate is of course not meant to be comprehensive. I have chosen to concentrate on the views of a few of the most prominent German scholars. The result is that they become detached from their times: proper credit is not given to their contemporaries with whom they were in dialogue, on whom they were frequently dependent, or whom they stubbornly ignored. This is a serious but inevitable limitation in a survey of this nature. All I can hope to convey is a broad awareness of a few major developments and shifts in emphasis in the course of a century's debate.

## Julius Wellhausen

The name of Julius Wellhausen is usually associated with the so-called "Graf hypothesis." In a discussion of the history of Israelite sanctuaries, sacrifices, feasts, cultic officials and their dues, he attempted to show that the norms set out in the Priestly Code of the Pentateuch were in many cases unknown in the pre-exilic period.[5] Wellhausen concluded that the Priestly Code was a post-exilic creation, the constitution of Ezra's Judaism rather than of pre-exilic Israel.

Wellhausen's reconstruction of Israelite history entailed a reversal of the common understanding of the relation between the Old Testament law and its prophets. The traditional view saw the prophets as "ministers and exponents of the law," whose "business was to enforce the observance of the law on Israel and to recall the people from backsliding to a strict conformity with its precepts."[6] For Wellhausen, the prophets preceded the law.[7] His view of the character of the Torah of Second Temple Judaism may be summed up in a metaphor which occurs several times in his writings: earlier, prophetic insights are represented as the "kernel" which needed the "shell" of Ezra's law book to be preserved (p. 497).

Wellhausen traced the development of Israelite religion into post-exilic Judaism in three stages. In his view, there was nothing unique, nothing even unusual, in Israel's beginnings. "The religious starting-point of the history of Israel was remarkable, not for its novelty, but for its normal character" (p. 437). That history began with Moses, through whom the formula "Jehovah is the God of Israel, and Israel is the people of Jehovah" became the "fundamental basis of the national existence and history" (p. 433). Still, the relation between deity and people was not defined in this period in any strict (i.e., covenantal) way. "The relation between the people and God was a natural one as that of son to father; it did not rest upon observance of the conditions of a pact" (p. 469).

In a sense, Torah did have its beginnings with Moses. Not that a "finished legislative code" existed in his day (p. 438). Moses did, however, exercise judicial functions "in the interest of the whole community and in the name of Jehovah. . . . Thus he laid a firm basis for a consuetudinary law" (p. 434). In this he was followed by the priests. "There is no torah as a ready-made product, as a system existing independently of its originator and accessible to every man: it becomes actual only in various utterances, which naturally form by degrees the basis of a fixed tradition" (p. 395). Though primarily concerned with questions regarding the administration of justice, the priestly torah came to include a ritual tradition as well. "But only those rites were included in the Torah which the priests had to teach others" (p. 395).

Two other aspects to Wellhausen's picture of the pre-prophetic religion of Israel should be noted. First, Israel's cult is said to belong "almost entirely to the inheritance which Israel had received from Canaan" upon settling there (p. 469); it was thus the "heathen element in the Israelite religion" (p. 422). Clearly such worship represented a stage beyond the religion of the desert period; but there is no suggestion that early Yahwism found anything incompatible with its ethos in Canaanite worship and cult. Second, Wellhausen can speak in lyric terms of the "uncommon freshness and naturalness" of the "impulses" of the ancient Israelites. Should anyone be left in doubt as to the contrast implied in such statements, Wellhausen proceeds to make it explicit enough:

The persons who appear always act from the constraining impulse of their nature, the men of God not less than the murderers and adulterers: they are such figures as could only grow up in the open air. Judaism, which realised the Mosaic constitution and carried it out logically, left no free scope for the individual; but in ancient Israel the divine right did not attach to the institution but was in the Creator Spirit, in individuals. Not only did they speak like the prophets, they also acted like the judges and kings, from their own free impulse, not in accordance with an outward norm, and yet, or just because of this, in the Spirit of Jehovah. (p. 412)

Pre-prophetic Israel, then, was not distinct from its neighbours either in its conception of God (bad) or in its preoccupation with cult (bad). But at least its life and worship were spontaneous (very good).

Enter the prophets, who for Wellhausen were "awakened individuals" to whom God spoke in extraordinary ways quite independent of any human institution.

The element in which the prophets live is the storm of the world's history, which sweeps away human institutions. . . . They do not preach on set texts; they speak out of the spirit which judges all things and itself is judged of no man. Where do they ever lean on any other authority than the truth of what they say; where do they rest on any other foundation than their own certainty? It belongs to the notion of prophecy, of true revelation, that Jehovah, overlooking all the media of ordinances and institutions, communicates himself to the *individual*, the called one. (p. 398)

Wellhausen was particularly adamant in denying any dependence of prophets on law. "Their creed is not to be found in any book. It is barbarism, in dealing with such a phenomenon, to distort its physiognomy by introducing the law. . . . The prophets are not the expounders of Moses, but his continuators and equals; the word of God in their mouth is not less weighty than in the mouth of Moses" (p. 399). In fact, of course, Wellhausen was sure that a "code or law in our sense of the word" did not exist in the prophetic period. "Jehovah had not yet made His Testament; He was still living and active in Israel" (p. 468).

What was the message of these exalted individuals? Wellhausen found "the fundamental religious thought of prophecy" to be "that Jehovah asks nothing for Himself, but asks it as a religious duty that man should render to man what is right, that His will lies not in any unknown height, but in the moral sphere which is known and understood by all" (p. 487-88). Note that the prophetic ideal is seen to be universal, not nationalistic; that it is ethical, not cultic; and that it is realized in the heart of the individual, not in the laws of a society.

It is with Elijah that "Israel's conception of Jehovah" seems to enter a new stage (p. 462). He was the first to perceive something amiss in the simultaneous worship of YHWH and Baal. "Jehovah . . . now began in the spiritual sphere to operate against the foreign elements, the infusion of which previously had been permitted to go on almost unchecked" (p. 462). To Elijah first it was disclosed "that there exists over all but one Holy One and one Mighty One, who reveals Himself not in nature but in law and righteousness in the world of man" (p. 462).

When Amos announced that YHWH was about to overthrow Israel through Assyria, his words must have been astounding, even blasphemous to his contemporaries, for whom YHWH was simply the national deity of Israel. But "Amos calls Jehovah the God of Hosts, never the God of Israel" (p. 472). And God's demands, made equally of Israel and of her worst enemies, are of a "purely moral character" (p. 472); he is not concerned with, or influenced by, the cult. Hosea is even more emphatic than Amos in denouncing the cult, "not merely on the ground that it had the absurd notion of forcing Jehovah's favour, but also because it was of heathenish character, nature-worship and idolatry" (p. 475).

With Amos and Hosea, "the limits of mere nationality" were broken through; their mistake lay in "supposing that they could make their way of thinking the basis of a national life" (p. 491). Here we see another of Wellhausen's fundamental convictions—though credit for the insight is given to Jeremiah. "Jeremiah saw through the mistake; the true Israel was narrowed to himself. . . . Instead of the nation, the heart and the individual conviction were to him the subject of religion" (p. 491). Jeremiah, it may be added, was for Wellhausen the last of the prophets worthy of the name. "Ezekiel had swallowed a book (iii.1-3), and gave it out again" (p. 403).

To sum up. The prophets brought an exalted conception of the deity (good), the realization that his demands are exclusively moral, not cultic (very good indeed), while they related to the deity freely, apart from institutions and externally imposed norms (excellent).

The Deuteronomic law represented an attempt to make concrete the ideals of the prophets. Indeed, "nowhere does the fundamental religious thought of prophecy find clearer expression than in Deuteronomy" (p. 487). Prophetic influence can be seen in the insistence that "Jehovah is the only God, whose service demands the whole heart and every energy; He has entered into a covenant with Israel, but upon fundamental conditions that, as contained in the Decalogue, are purely moral and of absolute universality" (p. 487).

Deuteronomy introduces something new, however, in that it was intended "to obtain public authority as a *book*. The idea of making a definite formulated written Torah the law of the land is the important point" (p. 402). The unintended result was the death of prophecy. "With the appearance of the law came to an end the old freedom, not only in the sphere of worship, now restricted to Jerusalem, but in the sphere of the religious spirit as well. There was now in existence an authority as objective as could be; and this was the death of prophecy" (p. 402).

Prophecy died when its precepts attained to the force of laws; the prophetic ideas lost their purity when they became practical. . . . The final outcome of the Deuteronomic reformation was principally that the cultus of Jehovah was limited to Jerusalem and abolished everywhere else, — such was the popular and practical form of prophetic monotheism. (p. 488)

Deuteronomy itself was not greatly concerned with matters of cult. "It took for granted the existence of the cultus, and only corrected it in certain general respects" (p. 404). When, however, the Temple had been destroyed, "the practice of past times had to be written down if it were not to be lost. Thus it came about that in the exile the *conduct of worship* became the subject of Torah" (p. 404). Ezekiel began the process; other exilic priests attached themselves to him, and the Temple cult was reduced to writing and to a system. The ultimate result was the Priestly Code which, with Ezra, became the constitution of Judaism. The process, begun with Deuteronomy, was complete: "the written took the place of the spoken word, and the people of the word became a 'people of the book' " (p. 409).

In his generous moods, Wellhausen can allow the necessity of what happened. At the time of restoration, "the prophetic ideas would not serve as building stones; they were not sufficiently practical. Then appeared the importance of institutions, of traditional forms, for the conservation even of the spiritual side of the religion" (p. 420). "At the restoration of Judaism the old usages were patched together in a new system, which, however, only served as the form to preserve something that was nobler in its nature, but could not have been saved otherwise than in a narrow shell that stoutly resisted all foreign influences" (p. 425).

Nonetheless, in certain respects it is claimed that the "Mosaic theocracy" of post-exilic Judaism represents "an immense retrogression. . . . The cultus is the heathen element in the Israelite religion. . . . If the Priestly Code makes the cultus the principal thing, that appears to amount to a systematic decline into the heathenism which the prophets incessantly combated and yet were unable to eradicate" (p. 422-23). Moreover, the need to conform to the Torah is seen as having a disastrous effect on the freedom, the spontaneity, the naturalness, the joy of religious worship. "The soul was fled; the shell remained, upon the shaping out of which every energy was now concentrated. . . . Technique was the main thing, and strict fidelity to rubric. Once cultus was spontaneous, now it is a thing of statute" (p. 78). When quoted out of context, Wellhausen's depictions of Judaism here and elsewhere strike one as unaccountably extreme, a caricature rather than serious description. They appear less surprising, however, when seen in the context of his understanding of the prophetic ideal as being a matter of universal moral concern addressed to the individual, with nothing of nationalism, cult, institutions or legislated norms. In comparison with *these* ideals, Second Temple Judaism may show its prophetic legacy in its exalted monotheism; but its preoccupation with cult and its legislated morals and worship inevitably appear as an "immense retrogession."

It would be difficult to overstate the influence of Wellhausen. Perhaps no single book in the history of biblical scholarship has matched the impact of his *Prolegomena*. Of course in the decades which immediately followed its publication others introduced variations and refinements on Wellhausen's themes; and there were dissenting voices. Still, the extent to which certain of his basic convictions recur remains astonishing. "When we go back to the most ancient religious conceptions and usages of the Hebrews, we shall find them to be the common property of a group of kindred peoples, and not the exclusive possession of the tribes of Israel."[8] "When we first meet with the Hebrews, their religion, life and belief seem to be hardly distinguishable from those of the nations who were round about them. . . . The great miracle of Judaism is to be found, not in a peculiar origin but in a unique development."[9] Later the prophets "discovered and proclaimed eternal verities." "First and foremost amongst the doctrines of Amos is the truth of the universality of Yahweh," who is the "vindicator of universal moral laws."[10] "The prophetic idea of God is known as 'ethical monotheism,' by which is meant that the emphasis on the moral nature of Yahweh universalized Him beyond all nationalistic limits."[11] "The difference between Jehovah and the gods of the nations is that He does not require sacrifice, but only to do justly, and love mercy, and walk humbly with God."[12] Compared with these ideals, the religion of post-exilic Judaism is "certainly inferior to the religion of the prophets, which is a thing not of form but of spirit."[13] "The restoration of ritual to its old position as the essential element in religion begins with Ezekiel."[14] Malachi most "clearly exhibits the characteristics of the decline. The very forms of religion against which Amos had protested are now elevated to the highest position."[15] The theology of the period was "narrow-minded" and "nationalistic." [16] "Prophecy had run its course, and the religious life of Judaism now diverges along three lines. . . . The first of these is legalism. . . . It presents a strange contrast to the fresh vitality of the Prophets. Yet it had its uses."[17] The patronizing tone of the last remark has many parallels in the literature of the time. When the history of Hebrew religion is presented in these terms, the value of the (post-exilic) law is inevitably that of providing a shell to protect the kernel of moral and spiritual truths discovered and taught by the prophets.

## Sigmund Mowinckel and Albrecht Alt

Before we consider in some detail the work of Martin Noth and Gerhard von Rad, mention must be made of two scholars who applied the form-critical approach of Hermann Gunkel to subjects pertinent to our theme: the Norwegian Sigmund Mowinckel and Albrecht Alt.

The goal of Mowinckel's *Psalmenstudien*[18] was to carry the form-critical study of the Psalms a step beyond the work of Gunkel and define the place of the various psalms in Israel's cult. Not surprisingly, cultic worship was viewed more appreciatively by Mowinckel than by Wellhausen: Mowinckel criticized Wellhausen and his followers (or, more generally, Protestant theology, or modern rationalism) for holding the cultic side of religion in low esteem.[19] Of particular interest here is the place which Mowinckel believed the proclamation of the basic demands of Yahwism occupied in the temple liturgy for the Feast of Tabernacles (which, Mowinckel attempted to show, was also a New Year, enthronement and covenant renewal festival).[20] That liturgy is seen to be reflected in a number of the Psalms; Mowinckel would later suggest that it is reflected in the Sinai narrative of the book of Exodus as well.[21] It included the proclamation of specific "entry requirements" to those in a ritual procession about to enter the Temple gate (cf. Ps. 15:1-5; 24:3-6)[22] as well as a more general appeal to the demands of the covenant in connection with its renewal by the assembled throng in the Temple courtyard (cf. Deut. 31:10-13; Ps. 81:9-11 (8-10); 50:16-21; 95:7-11).[23] We need not concern ourselves here with the details of Mowinckel's understanding of Israelite law and its development.[24] But the suggestion that the basic demands of YHWH were formulated and proclaimed in a cultic setting was to prove most fruitful in subsequent discussions.

In a famous study first published in 1934, Albrecht Alt attempted to apply the techniques of form criticism to the oldest compilation of Israelite law, the Book of the Covenant, in order to arrive at "The Origins of Israelite Law."[25] He distinguished laws in casuistic form from Israel's "apodeictic law." The former laws (the *mishpatim* of Exod. 21:1) spell out in conditional clauses the particular case envisaged by the law, then prescribe in the main clauses the penalties to be imposed. Such laws would have been utilized in the work of the ordinary, secular Israelite courts made up of "elders" from the local community. The evidence suggests that such laws were part of a general legal culture in the ancient Near East. The Israelites would have adopted them from their Canaanite neighbours after the settlement in Palestine, though before the foundation of the Israelite kingdoms.

"Apodeictic law" (in its original form) is found in short series of simple clauses, each of which expresses a categorical prohibition. Such law makes no attempt to deal with cases exhaustively, nor does it "provide a treatment in any way adequate to the practical needs of secular jurisdiction. . . . A context is required in which the whole people, and through them their God, could adopt the imperative tone towards individuals, and impose on them the absolute prohibitions, or threats of a curse or of death, which we find" (p. 124-25). In other words, proclamation of "apodeictic law" must have taken place regularly "and formed part of a fixed rite, which as such could provide the basis for the origin and development of the category" (p. 126). Deuteronomy 31:10-13 suggests that such a rite took place every seventh year at the Feast of Tabernacles as part of a "regular *renewal of the covenant* between Yahweh and Israel" (p. 129).

When was such law introduced? "The creative period in the history of the category would seem in any case to have been the early period of Israel's history, before the founding of the kingdom"

(p. 131). In fact, we can go further.

Since the worship of Yahweh, with which the apodeictic law is inseparably linked, clearly originates from the desert, we can presume the same source for the basis of the apodeictic law, if not for the extant examples in their present form. This would partly explain its severity, and the sharp contrast between it and the Canaanite law. . . . This newly conceived legislative urge in Israel came into violent conflict in Israel with the ancient and highly developed legal system of Canaan; the apodeictic law clashed with the casuistic. (p. 131)

Had the Israelites brought with them "no enduring characteristics" when they encountered "an ancient and alien culture" in Palestine, they

would undoubtedly have been submerged. . . . But this is not what happened. . . . The apodeictic law of Israel displays an unrestrained power of aggression which seeks to subject every aspect of life without exception to the unconditional domination of the will of Yahweh. . . . The struggle between the two forms of law . . . remained a major preoccupation of Israelite law throughout its history. (p. 131-32)

This, it need hardly be said, represents a very different view of the place of law in early Israel from what we found in Wellhausen!

---

## Martin Noth

---

Martin Noth has provided a treatment of our subject both bold and provocative in his study *The Laws in the Pentateuch*.[26] In the discussion which follows, we will supplement the picture which we find in Noth's *Laws* with material from his *History*[27] in order to arrive at a summary of his views. For Noth, "Israel" first appeared in history as an association of 12 tribes linked by their common adherence to a central shrine, the site of the sacred ark.[28] The Israelite "amphictyony" (so called on the basis of parallel associations in ancient Greece) seems not to have functioned as a political or military institution; external affairs were carried on independently by single tribes or, occasionally, by small groups of tribes. The amphictyony was rather a *sacral* league, united by its central shrine with its cultic worship and, above all, by the divine law which was regularly proclaimed at a solemn festival gathering of the tribes. (Here Noth builds on the work of Mowinckel and Alt.) The tribal association was bound to see that the divine law was carried out and that transgressions were punished.

It is, Noth believes, Israel's sacred law which sets her apart from earliest times from her neighbours.[29] Israel's cultic worship—its sacrifices, festivals, and sacred sites—was largely taken over from the Canaanites. Nor was there anything unique about Israel's organization as an amphictyony or even the existence of an amphictyonic law as such: other tribal associations necessarily had their laws outlining the obligations of the member tribes toward the central sanctuary or their relations to each other. Israel's divine law, however, was different: "It was concerned rather with Israel's relationship to its God and was intended to safeguard the inviolability of this relationship in every respect" (*History*, p. 110). That special relationship had its basis in the traditions (preserved among certain clans incorporated in the tribes of Israel) of a covenant entered with YHWH at Sinai. "The twelve-tribe confederacy traced back its relationship with Yahweh, and so its own existence, to the unique experience of a covenant made between Yahweh and Israel" (*Laws*, p. 38).

To the question what part of the Old Testament laws preserves Israel's oldest law, Noth gives no final answer, though he suggests that "the genuinely Israelite part of the Book of the Covenant, the religious and moral prohibitions in Exod. xxii, 17ff. has most right to be considered" a part of "the original divine law of Israel" (*History*, p. 104). In any case, it is the character of that law which must be noted. It is the law of a sacral confederacy, not of a political state. The laws apply, not to all the subjects of a political ruler, nor to all the inhabitants of a geographical area, but to a people marked off by its worship of YHWH, its common historical traditions, its opposition to the "Canaanites" (i.e., those who shared its land without belonging to the association), and its "name of high antiquity — the name 'Israel'" (*Laws*, p. 25).

This distinction Noth holds to be true of all the Old Testament laws dating from pre-exilic times, thus including the Book of the Covenant, the Deuteronomic Law, and probably the Holiness Code. In the latter two cases at least, the legal codes seem to have been drawn up in the period of the divided monarchy; even so, it is still the people of the 12-tribe confederacy, not the subjects of the political state of Israel or Judah, for whom the laws are meant. The confederacy, which grew up before political unity was imposed on the territory inhabited by the Israelites, continued its own life after the monarchy had been established. The Temple of Jerusalem, as the site of the sacred ark, became the central sanctuary for all the Israelite tribes. This alone — not Zion's older history as a Canaanite sacred site nor its adoption by David — explains the attraction which Jerusalem retained for northerners after the split with Judah (1 Kgs. 12:27) and even after the destruction of the Temple (Jer. 41:5).

Once we realize that the pre-exilic laws in the Pentateuch have the sacred confederacy as their background, a number of peculiarities in their content become comprehensible. Some demands seem quite unattainable if conceived as the laws of a state. But no political system was before the law-giver's eyes. . . . So far as the sacral twelve-tribe confederacy bound to Yahweh was concerned, the uncompromisingly strong prohibition against apostasy from Yahweh to "other gods" . . . was not at all impracticable, however unenforceable such a law was for the *states* of Israel or Judah, to which "Canaanites" (who had their own cults) also belonged. But the law was not intended to apply to these "Canaanites." (*Laws*, p. 34-35)

Similarly, the regulations for the waging of "Holy Wars" were not pursued by the Israelite states, for such wars can only be waged by a sacral confederacy.

The situation was, however, reversed by the well-meaning King Josiah, who attempted to make the people of his kingdom "to be the party in covenant with Yahweh—which it could in no wise be" (*Laws*, p. 47). Josiah erred, too, in treating Deuteronomy, which was designed to serve as a covenant between God and his people, as state law, enforcing its measures with the political power at his disposal. Josiah's unfortunate death brought his reform to an end; but the deuteronomic law-code was thereafter treated, quite contrary to its intended sense, as a state law-code, to be implemented by conscientious monarchs.

With the fall of Jerusalem to the Bablyonians, the old 12-tribe association came to its effective end. In one sense this is not self-evident, for, as we have seen, the confederacy was relatively independent of prevailing political conditions. The fact that Israel's cultic centre had been destroyed was, however, "more decisive" (*Laws*, p. 61). Above all, the pre-exilic prophets had spoken of the coming judgment and of the termination of Israel's covenant relationship with God because of Israel's unfaithfulness (Hos. 6:7; 8:1; 1:9; Isa. 2:6; Jer. 11:1-13). When the prophetic message was thus confirmed by the course of events, it clearly followed that the covenant between God and his people was ended. With the cancellation of the covenant, the sacred 12-tribe association which was based upon it could only dissolve; as a result, the laws which pertained to that association no longer had any claim to validity.

Nonetheless, hope for the future remained. Prophets had spoken of a "new" covenant to replace the old—though that particular prophecy was to play little role in the days ahead. More important was the anticipation that the old order would be restored. Those who cherished such a hope naturally preserved what ties they could with the past by observing certain requirements from the old law (such as circumcision and the sabbath), thus "clinging to laws whose validity was really in abeyance" (*Laws*, p. 67). "This certainly meant that the declarations of classical prophecy, interpreting what had happened as a sealing of the end of the covenant between God and people, were not accepted in full earnestness or with complete finality" (*Laws*, p. 67).

Such was the state of affairs in what was believed to be a transitional period before the restoration of the old order. Gradually, however, it became evident that the times were not transitional, and the new circumstances came to take on the character of a new order.

Cyrus's edict commanding the rebuilding of the Temple can hardly be regarded as the fulfillment of the expected restoration. It enabled the catastrophe of the Temple's destruction to be reversed; but this by itself was not a sufficient base for regarding the sacral 12-tribe confederacy as established once more. What the rebuiling of the Temple did mean, however, was the re-establishing of the old cultic observances. Moreover, as we have seen, the non-cultic regulations of the old laws had continued to be observed in what was regarded as a transitional period. As a result, the old laws, still practised, came to be regarded as still in force — a view, however, which lacked any real basis, "because the conditions which had given validity to the laws in ancient Israel had long since disappeared" (*Laws*, p. 79-80).

This brings us to the final stage in the "position and justification" of the Old Testament laws. The various laws came to be regarded as parts of one divine legislation, referred to simply as "the law." And "the law" was regarded as "an *absolute entity*, valid without respect to precedent, time, or history; based on itself, binding simply because it existed as law, because it was of divine origin and authority" (*Laws*, p. 86). It is but one instance of

characteristic and ever-recurring lapses in human history. It is the fate of human institutions which arise out of definite historical situations to decline in the course of history. But the ordinances and statutes, which had had their place in the context of those institutions, obstinately maintain their existence and, after their real basis has disappeared, take on a worth of their own which they had never possessed and which is not their due. Then do men worship dead ordinances and statutes. (*Laws*, p. 106)

Noth develops in some detail what he regards as the distortion and decline involved in the late view of "the law." When the laws were detached from their basis in the sacral association, which was in turn founded on the divine redemption from Egypt and the covenant at Sinai, the decisive emphasis shifted from divine activity to the behaviour of men. "It was now the acknowledgement and observance of the law by the individuals which constituted the community — for whoever undertook to keep the law joined the community" (*Laws*, p. 80). It was now, too, that the concepts of reward and punishment were associated with the law — though properly they have nothing to do with law.

As is customary with other laws, so ancient laws . . . envisaged fixed punishments for particular transgressions. . . . If the individual rendered obedience to these laws it was not a service to be rewarded, but merely an obligation inherent in the situation. The idea of a reward which might be *earned* by the fulfillment of the law's requirements only arose with the dissociation of "the law" from a pre-ordained order, independent of the individual, and basing its authority on the timeless and changeless will of God; so that the theoretical possibility of man's acceptance or rejection was left open. (*Laws*, p. 98-99)

The Pentateuchal source which we call P is a prime witness to the distorted understanding of the divine laws in the post-exilic period. Here the past is depicted "quite consciously from the point of view and attitude of its own time. . . . The regulation of the life of the Israelite tribes as laid down by the proceedings on Sinai" is regarded as "the right and proper arrangement not only for the past, but for always." Moreover, the external, cultic factors of the Sinai legislation are emphasized, "whereas the more important matter of a restoration of the relationship to God is clearly not dealt with, because for the editor of P this relationship did not appear to have been decisively destroyed or interrupted" (*Laws*, p. 84-85).

We may sum up. Unlike Wellhausen, Noth realizes that there was about Israel a uniqueness from earliest times, and that this uniqueness may be traced to the divine law which functioned within the sacred 12-tribe association. Hence the prominence of law is hardly a post-prophetic development. But "the law," understood as a timeless statement of the divine will, and valid without any consideration of its historical origins and setting, does mark a post-exilic development—and distortion. Here there is no patronizing reference to the "inevitability" or "necessity" of the process. It is for Noth a sad but typical instance of the obstinate preservation of old ordinances after their value and validity have ceased.

---

### Gerhard von Rad

---

In the treatment of law in Gerhard von Rad's *Old Testament Theology*,[30] we find again many of the features we have met in Mowinckel, Alt and Noth. Nonetheless, the discussion is carried further along several lines worth noting.

For von Rad, as for Noth, the name "Israel" can first be applied to the sacred alliance of tribes ("amphictyony") in Palestine. The high points in the life of the alliance were the annual pilgrimages—particularly the one which celebrated the harvest festival—to the common sanctuary. Following Mowinckel, von Rad believes that the harvest festival involved the renewal of Israel's covenant with YHWH and the reciting of series of YHWH's commands ("put together by

priests, on the basis of deliberate selection from a very much ampler
store of tradition," 1:191), both in entrance ceremonies at the gates
to the sanctuary and at the climax of the festival when the covenant
was renewed. Against Wellhausen, then, "it is beyond question that
God's will as expressed in law was announced to Israel as early as
the earliest stage of Jahwism" (2:390). Characteristic of Israel even
in the pre-monarchic period was the conviction that "there was
absolutely no meeting-ground with, or participation in, the divine
otherwise than by submitting to these sacred regulations" (1:33).
And uniquely characteristic of Israel was the intolerance towards
other cults expressed in her law: "for Jahwism's exclusive claim certainly repudiated any peaceful co-existence of the cults right from
the beginning. Jahwism without the first commandment is positively inconceivable" (1:26). Such claims, though marking again the
dramatic shift in Old Testament scholarship from the time of
Wellhausen, are by now commonplace.

It is in his discussion of what Israel meant by "law" that von Rad's
treatment takes a distinctive turn. Yahwism, he stresses, was not
what many theologians mean by a "religion of law" (i.e., one in
which human relations with the deity are based on observance of
divine demands). Israel's election by YHWH preceded the giving of
the commandments, "before she had any opportunity of proving
her obedience" (2:391). The commandments were closely tied to the
covenant; yet the covenant relationship was "established only in virtue of a privilege offered by God" (1:130). "In no case were these
commandments prefixed to the covenant in a conditional sense, as if
the covenant would only come into effect once obedience had been
rendered. The situation is rather the reverse. The covenant is
made, and with it Israel receives the revelation of the commandments" (1:194).

How then are the commandments to be understood? In the early
period they were not regarded as the "maximum demands of
Jahweh," "a comprehensive normative law," or "instruction for the
moral life" (1:194-95). The commandments were at first expressed
exclusively in short series of negative demands.

It is only in negatives, that is, from the angle of what is absolutely
displeasing to Jahweh, that the marks of him who belongs to Jahweh are
described. Within the sphere of life thus circumscribed by the commandments there lies a wide field of moral action which remains completely
unregulated (after all, idolatry, murder, and adultery were not constant
occurrences in Israel's everyday life). (1:195)

The commandments, then, merely "demand avowal of Jahweh . . .
in certain marginal situations" (1:195). Obviously there was no
question but that such demands were capable of being fulfilled;
hence, though refusal to accept the commandments would of course

bring a curse, they were not regarded as a burden or a threat. On the contrary, their revelation was "a saving blessing of a very high order. It was a guarantee of her election, for in it Jahweh had shown his people a way and a statute" (1:195). Von Rad finds the situation in early Christianity exactly parallel, for from the beginning the early Christian community "too was conscious of being bound to certain legal norms" (2:392).

Von Rad's emphasis on the flexibility of early Israelite law, and its repeated adaptations to new circumstances, should also be noted. Though Israel of all periods was faced by divine demands, before the publication of Deuteronomy the divine will was not embodied in fixed and recognizable laws. On the contrary, as, in the course of time, the dangers to which Israel's worship was exposed shifted, the first and second commandments were subjected repeatedly to fresh interpretation.

In the last analysis this interpretation of the will of Jahweh, at one time tolerating certain customs and at another sternly rejecting them, was always a charismatic process. For the many detailed decisions which had to be taken in the tangled growth of traditional cultic usage and new religious advances, the summary statements of the old sacral law furnished no more than general guidance. (2:394)

Von Rad stresses in particular how the prophets adapted the old ordinances "to meet conditions and problems that lay far beyond the range of their earlier reference," thus "making them the basis of an entirely new interpretation of Jahweh's current demands upon Israel" (2:400).

In the history of Israel's reinterpretation of YHWH's demands, Deuteronomy occupies a critical position. It represents the result of the preaching activity of Levites who "not only had all of Israel's old traditions at their disposal, but who also believed that they had complete authority to interpret these and apply them to the present day" (1:72). Hence Deuteronomy itself is but a further example of the "actualisation of God's will designed to counter specific dangers which appeared at a definite hour in the already lengthy history of Jahwism" (2:394). But "its fixation in written form almost inevitably had the result that God's revealed will to Israel now began to appear in a new form. One expression of this will, which was to begin with no more than one actualisation among many, from then on became increasingly normative, and the time factor was forgotten" (2:395). Ultimately the result is that the "flexibility of Jahweh's revelation, allowing it to gear itself to the place and time and condition of the Israel at the time addressed, ceases. The law becomes an absolute entity, unconditionally valid irrespective of time or historical situation" (1:91). The latter judgment is, of course, familiar from Noth's discussion of "*the* law" in the post-exilic period.

Von Rad finds Deuteronomy significant in another respect as well. Here the various individual commands are regarded as but parts of a basically indivisible revelation of YHWH's will. At the same time, the concept of YHWH's revelation finally leaves the sphere of the cult.

It was in the cult that older Israel encountered commandments and series of commandments, as well as the priestly *Toroth*. But "the" Torah was a matter for theological instruction, and its *Sitz im Leben* now became more and more the heart of man. . . . Men are to keep these words in their hearts and they are to be present to them in every situation in life. (1:200)

The result is "the picture of a man whose spiritual life is completely filled by God's addressing him." Such Torah-centred piety is of course typical of post-exilic Judaism—witness Psalms 1 and 119! And, von Rad notes, it should not be assumed without further ado that it is necessarily "legal piety" or "Pharisaic comfort" (1:200).

Deuteronomy still regards the commandments as easy to obey. This confidence, however, was shattered by the prophets. The earlier prophets spoke of "Israel's utter and complete failure vis-à-vis Jahweh"; Jeremiah and Ezekiel go further, reaching the "insight that she is inherently utterly unable to obey him" (2:398). It is characteristic of the prophets that they see the "security" given Israel by her "election traditions" as "cancelled out because of her guilt" (2:117). "Theologically speaking, they consigned their audience, and all their contemporaries, to a kingdom of death where they could no longer be reached by the salvation coming from the old saving events" (2:272). As a result, the only thing Israel could "hold on to" was "a new historical act on the part of Jahweh. . . . The prophetic message differs from all previous Israelite theology, which was based on the past saving history, in that the prophets looked for the decisive factor in Israel's whole existence—her life or her death—in some future event" (2:117). Thus, whereas for Deuteronomy, YHWH's commands are given"for life," their fulfillment is not a problem, and what is required is simply a reaffirmation of the old covenant, for Jeremiah and Ezekiel "Jahweh's commandments have turned into a law that judges and destroys" (2:269), Israel is incapable of observing them, yet the future holds out the hope of a *new* covenant brought about by a new saving act on the part of Israel's God.

## Walther Zimmerli

We conclude our summary of authors with Walther Zimmerli, a scholar standing very much in the tradition of those we have already considered. Four points in his discussion of Israel's understanding of law may be noted here.

Mention must first be made of Zimmerli's famous article "I am Yahweh,"[31] for it provides the framework within which Israel's understanding of law must be placed. YHWH's revelation of himself through his name is his free gift to his people, the foundation on which rests their relationship to him and their existence as a people. Zimmerli believes the formula of YHWH's self-introduction was repeated in "a liturgical procedure in which a speaker with the authority of divine commissioning delivers to the community words of the most serious import."[32] He is thinking, of course, of the covenant renewal ceremony as depicted by Mowinckel, when YHWH's commandments were proclaimed to his people. But Zimmerli stresses that YHWH's self-revelation came first (Exod. 20:2); the commands which followed are then, each in its own way, "a bit of explication of the central self-introduction of Yahweh."[33] "The Decalogue itself is already oriented toward the recognition that only in Yahweh's name does one find the legitimate basis not only for his salvation activity, but for his giving of commandments as well."[34]

Second, Zimmerli reaffirms that covenant and law were linked in earliest Israel. Such a claim is by no means new; it takes on current significance, however, in the light of Perlitt's claim that the covenant concept was first associated with the proclamation of commandments at Horeb in the later strata of Deuteronomy.[35] Zimmerli believes that Perlitt has not taken sufficient account of "the explicitly restorative nature of the deuteronomic movement": it was not likely to have created tradition in this way.[36] Moreover, there is predeuteronomic material in Exodus 19:5; 24; and 34, where it is clear that a covenant was thought to be enacted at Sinai which included the imposition of YHWH's commands. This brings us to our third point.

Zimmerli offers an important counter to certain aspects of von Rad's understanding of Old Testament law. For von Rad, as we have seen, "law" in the early period carried no threat; rather, it simply offered the Israelites the opportunity in certain "marginal situations" to express their allegiance to YHWH, whose covenant people they were solely by a gracious act of divine election and salvation. It is first in the prophets that the commandments "turned into a law that judges and destroys." The result (says Zimmerli) is that, for von Rad, "it is the prophets who became the 'Moses' of Paul."[37] But this, he believes, is to distort both the law and the prophets.

Zimmerli first notes the parallel between the Sinaitic "covenant" and the "so-called suzerainty treaties, which the Hittite kings concluded with dependent princes."[38] A well-known study by G. E. Mendenhall had brought these treaties into the forefront of Old Testament discussions of "covenant"[39] and, in the early enthusiasm of their discovery, a number of far-reaching conclusions were based on the analogy. Zimmerli seems to have avoided the pitfalls, noting that the historical relation between the suzerainty treaties and the Old Testament covenants remains "completely obscure,"[40] and contenting himself with a general question which "the consideration of these parallels at least raises." The relationship between suzerain and vassals is described in the historical preamble to the treaties as based on the gracious attitude of the sovereign. This, Zimmerli notes, is similar to the preamble of the Decalogue and the introductory speeches of Deuteronomy. Then the statutes of the treaty are "authoritatively asserted. It is clear that their observance is decisive for the continuing validity of the covenant, and at the conclusion they are guaranteed by words of blessing and curse." Hence, "whilst these treaties are clearly presented as the fruits of a genuine beneficence towards the vassals, there can be no doubt that their validity is dependent on the obedience of the latter." The question then arises

whether the covenant of which Israel spoke, and in which Yahweh's commands were embedded, might not be similar to these treaties. . . . From the divine standpoint are we to say that Yahweh's word, given to Israel in his commandments, is only a word of grace which upholds the people at any cost, or is it not rather a holy fire, by which the unholy could be consumed, and Israel rejected?[41]

Zimmerli then turns to the Old Testament literature on the law with these questions in mind. From a number of passages (Exod. 22:23[24]; 23:21; Deut. 4:24; 6:15; 27:15-26; Josh. 24:19-20; Lev. 26:25) it becomes clear that "disobedience towards Yahweh's commandment will bring death."[42] Even in the decalogue, we meet "Yahweh, who has liberated his people," but who "is also the jealous God who does not tolerate that other gods should receive the love and adoration of his people."[43] Thus, while "it is undoubtedly wrong to characterize the Israel of the Old Testament as a people who, in their faith, stood under a threatening law," it is "equally wrong to present the covenant people of the Old Testament as a people whose faith led them to believe that they were secure in the covenant from any radical threat to life, and who regarded the law solely as a call to show allegiance to Yahweh. . . . The God of Israel . . . remained inexorable in his will."[44] What appears in the prophets is thus nothing new:

it is simply the emergence of a reality which lay dormant in the old law. The zealous God . . . now appears as the guardian of the law which Israel has violated. The curse, with which the Law had already been enjoined at Shechem, and which had been mentioned as a real possibility when the covenant had been established, now turns fully against the transgressor of the divine will and judges him.[45]

Like von Rad, Zimmerli sees in the prophets the declaration that the Mosaic covenant had reached its end through Israel's disobedience, and that "only a new mighty act of God would enable Israel once again, through judgment and privation, to become God's people."[46] For our purposes, however, there is a fourth point of interest in Zimmerli's understanding of the post-exilic Priestly Document.[47] Martin Noth suggested that, with the end of the old Israelite amphictyony and the cancellation of the Sinaitic covenant, "*the* law" on which the post-exilic community was founded lacked any valid base. In a sense, Zimmerli sees the Priestly Document itself as anticipating that very objection.

The Priestly Document in fact contains no account of the establishing of a covenant at Sinai, and no declaration of apodeictic law there. Since Israel is neither constituted as a people at Sinai nor given a law which she must obey if she would continue to exist, P must understand Israel and Israel's relation with YHWH differently.

Now P *does* mention two covenants: one with Noah, and one with Abraham. And part of the covenant made with Abraham in P is the promise, "I will establish my covenant between me and you and your descendants after you throughout their generations for an everlasting covenant, to be God to you and to your descendants after you" (Gen. 17:7). For P, then,

> the whole covenant relationship of Israel becomes anchored in the Abrahamic covenant. Thus it is rooted in a covenant which contains no proclamation of law, but is a complete gift, proclaiming an election of grace. The sword of vengeance no longer has any place here. . . . God's people are wholly founded on his gracious will.[48]

What took place at Sinai, then, is not the establishing of a covenant upon the basis of a law, but the fulfillment of the promise to Abraham, as God ordains "certain permanent institutions" (the tent of meeting and its furnishings, the Aaronic priesthood, the legitimate sacrifices) through which Israel's relation with YHWH is guaranteed. Any danger which Israel's disobedience might pose to her existence is removed by the divine institution of the Day of Atonement. Hence the post-exilic community, according to P, is neither based on nor threatened by law. It owes its existence to the gracious election of YHWH and his faithfulness to the promise made to Abraham. And its primary concern is the careful observance of the cult instituted at Sinai for its own protection.

By way of summary of the current debate, it is fair to say that there is a measure of agreement that Israel from the earliest period saw in YHWH a deity who placed comprehensive demands upon his people. Especially characteristic of Israel's sacred law was the intolerance it displayed toward the worship of deities other than YHWH. It is also widely agreed that in some sense the polemic of the proph-

ets was directed toward violations of Israel's ancient law.[49] Ambiguities remain, of course, and they are legion. What do we mean by
"Israel," now that Noth's "amphictyonic" interpretation has fallen
into disfavour? How much of Israel's earliest law has been preserved, and where is it to be found? What (if any) is the precise relationship between law and covenant before Deuteronomy? Can the
basis on which the prophets applied the ancient laws be more
clearly defined? Answers to these questions have of course been suggested, but there is little that would indicate a growing consensus.
Nonetheless even the broad characterization of earliest Israel given
above represents a major shift from the (once dominant) position of
Wellhausen, and suggests a significant measure of continuity
between earliest Israel and Judaism of Second Temple times.

The prominence of law is thus scarcely a post-exilic development.
Still it is undeniable that certain shifts in the perception of the law
did take place. Several points should be noted.

The first, obvious difference is one of extent. Deuteronomy had
already presented its statement of the divine demands as "the law"
(*torah*); the pre-exilic period saw other compilations of laws as well.
But it is first in post-exilic times that the various codes are combined
into a single, authoritative corpus referred to collectively as "the
Torah." Legal, cultic and social responsibilities were united in a
comprehensive statement of the divine will for Israel.

Of course, the publication of "the Torah" evidences a shift in
form as well as extent. At least before Deuteronomy "the Torah"
had not been associated with a book. And clearly the written form
"fixes" the commandments of God in a way which was previously
not the case. It is questionable how much weight should be placed
upon the change, for obviously the commandments were subject to
formulation long before they took their place in a book; conversely,
Second Temple Judaism did develop tools for adapting even the
written text to current needs. That the change remains significant is,
however, proved by the following consideration.

It is first in the post-exilic period that the divine will is perceived
as requiring compliance with the wording of a fixed corpus of law;
the divine law, we may say, was understood as statute.[50] Whereas
the pre-exilic prophets demanded loyalty to the fundamental principles of Yahwistic religion, YHWH's will was not for them discerned
by the interpretation of texts. That such became the case in the
post-exilic period is, however, abundantly clear: in the rise and
widespread influence of the scribal movement; in the exegetical
debates which determined proper procedure; in the resort to legal
fiction when the terms of scriptural law proved impracticable. Paul
is not unfair in speaking of the Jewish claim to "know [God's] will

and approve what is excellent, because you are instructed in the law" (Rom. 2:18).

Torah was, moreover, perceived as the law of the Jewish *community*. Such a claim should not be taken too strictly, for the very toleration of divergent interpretations of Torah's provisions suggests that conformity could not normally be compelled. Similarly, the numerous statements in the literature in which pagan overlords declare that the Jews are to live according to their ancestral laws should be construed as permission, within certain boundaries, to pursue traditional ways rather than as authorization to enforce them rigidly. Nonetheless Jews and non-Jews alike of the Second Temple period spoke of Moses as the Jewish "law-giver" (*nomothetēs*), of the Pentateuch as the "laws" of the Jews. And Jewish apologetic literature attempted to prove the superiority of Torah's statutes over those by which other people were governed.[51]

None of this means, however, that Jews had forgotten the relation between *Torah* and covenant, divine demand and the divine election. To this important question we return below. Moreover, the word "legalistic," once prominent in discussions of post-exilic Jewish religion, should surely be banned from the literature. The term may indeed be appropriate if taken to mean no more than that Jews were concerned with law, or that they discerned the divine will in conformity with its provisions. But a history of association with charges of hypocrisy, merit-mongering and casuistic pettifoggery mean that "legalistic" is simply not perceived as a term of neutral description. It is better abandoned to the writers of apologetics.

---

## Notes

1  E.g., Herodotus, *The Histories* 7.104; Euripides, *Suppl.* 429-34.

2  See H. E. Remus, "Authority, Consent, Law: *Nomos, Physis,* and the Striving for a 'Given,'" *Studies in Religion/Sciences Religieuses,* 13 (1984): 7-8.

3  For what follows see my *Jesus and Scribal Authority* (Lund: C. W. K. Gleerup, 1978), and "Jesus, the Pharisees, and the Application of Divine Law," *Église et Théologie,* 13 (1982): 191-210.

4  The phrase was suggested by Peter Richardson, who judiciously advised the consideration of these particular scholars.

5  J. Wellhausen, *Prolegomena to the History of Ancient Israel,* first published in English in 1885. I have used the 1973 reprint published by Peter Smith of Gloucester, Massachusetts. With the *Prolegomena* is printed Wellhausen's article on "Israel" in the *Encyclopaedia Britannica* (p. 429-548). Page references in the text are taken from both of these sources.

6  So W. Robertson Smith described the traditional view in his *The Old Testament in the Jewish Church* (New York: Appleton, 1883), p. 215.

7  Broadly speaking, of course. See the qualified statement in *Prolegomena,* p. 366.

8  W. Robertson Smith, *Lectures on the Religion of the Semites* (London: A. & C. Black, 1923 reprint of 1894 edition), p. 3-4.

9  T. H. Robinson, *Prophecy and the Prophets in Ancient Israel* (London: Gerald Duckworth, 1923), p. 6.

10  Ibid., p. 48, 69.

11  H. W. Robinson, *The Old Testament: Its Making and Meaning* (Nashville: Cokesbury, 1937), p. 126-27.

12  Smith, *Jewish Church*, p. 298-99. Whether the prophets condemned the cult as such (as Wellhausen believed) or only its abuse became a subject of much discussion. See the summary and literature in H. H. Rowley, "The Unity of the Old Testament," *Bulletin of the John Rylands Library*, 29 (1945-46): 326-58. The fact that the former position has largely been abandoned today requires in itself a major realignment from Wellhausen's understanding of the relation between the prophetic ideals and the post-exilic reality.

13  Smith, *Jewish Church*, p. 313.

14  T. H. Robinson, *Prophecy*, p. 190.

15  Ibid.

16  Ibid., p. 180-81.

17  Ibid., p. 194-95.

18  S. Mowinckel, *Psalmenstudien* (Kristiania: J. Dybwad, 1921-24).

19  Ibid., Vol. 1, p. v; Vol. 2, p. 16-17. Cf. also Mowinckel, *Religion und Kultus* (Göttingen: Vandenhoeck & Ruprecht, 1953), p. 8. Predictably, Mowinckel's treatment of the relationship between prophets and cult shows considerable differences from Wellhausen as well; cf. *Psalmenstudien*, Vol. 3; and his *The Psalms in Israel's Worship* (Nashville: Abingdon, 1962), Vol. 2, p. 53-73; and, for a general evaluation of the case for "cultic prophecy," H. H. Rowley, *From Moses to Qumran* (London: Lutterworth, 1963), p. 111-38. Note, however, that the religion of Second Temple Judaism still emerges as the loser in the discussion. Whereas it was denigrated by Wellhausen for its preoccupation with cult, Mowinckel suggests that post-exilic Judaism shows a *Gesetzesreligion rather than* a living *Kultreligion*; i.e., cult is observed in obedience to divine commands, not because God is believed to come to the community in the cult and so convey to it his life, power and blessing. See *Psalmenstudien*, Vol. 2, p. 35-36.

20  See *Psalmenstudien*, Vol. 2.

21  S. Mowinckel, *Le décalogue* (Paris: Félix Alcan, 1927), p. 114-62. Mowinckel tried to show that the decalogue as we have it is the product of the school of Isaiah's disciples; but it corresponds in *form* to earlier collections of "entry requirements" to sanctuaries, such as we find in Psalms 15 and 24.

22  *Psalmenstudien*, Vol. 2, p. 118-19; *Décalogue*, p. 141-56.

23  *Psalmenstudien*, Vol. 2, p. 154-56, 178-81; 3:38-40; *Décalogue*, p. 129-33.

24  Cf. *Décalogue*, p. 156-62; and Mowinckel's "Zur Geschichte der Dekaloge," *Zeitschrift für die alttestamentliche Wissenschaft*, 14 (1937): 231-33.

25  Published in English in Alt's *Essays on Old Testament History and Religion* (Oxford: Blackwell, 1966), p. 81-132.

26  M. Noth, *The Laws in the Pentateuch* (Edinburgh/London: Oliver & Boyd, 1966).

27  M. Noth, *The History of Israel*, 2nd ed. (New York: Harper & Row, 1960).

28  Cf. M. Noth, *Das System der zwölf Stämme Israels* (Stuttgart: Kohlhammer, 1930).

29  Interesting in this context is Noth's dismissal of Wellhausen's position: "The view of J. Wellhausen and his school that 'the law' was a late, post-prophetic phenomenon in Israel, is only correct to the extent that the legal sections contained in the Old Testament, which are very disparate, are on the whole fairly late. But as the formulation of the divine law, the 'law' had its roots and its

beginnings in the very earliest constitution of the Israelite association of the twelve tribes" (*History*, p. 104, n. 4).

30  G. von Rad, *Old Testament Theology*, Vols. 1 and 2 (Edinburgh/London: Oliver & Boyd, 1962-65).

31  The article is included in the collection of Zimmerli's essays *I Am Yahweh* (Atlanta: John Knox, 1962), p. 1-28.

32  Ibid., p. 13.

33  Ibid., p. 12.

34  Ibid., p. 25.

35  L. Perlitt, *Bundestheologie im Alten Testament* (Neukirchen-Vluyn: Neukirchener Verlag, 1969).

36  W. Zimmerli, *Old Testament Theology in Outline* (Atlanta, GA: John Knox, 1978), p. 52.

37  W. Zimmerli, *The Law and the Prophets* (Oxford: Blackwell, 1965), p. 51.

38  Ibid., p. 52.

39  G. E. Mendenhall, "Law and Covenant in Israel and the Ancient Near East," *Biblical Archaeologist*, 17 (1954): 26-46, 49-76.

40  Zimmerli, *Law*, p. 52.

41  Ibid., p. 54-55.

42  Ibid., p. 55.

43  Ibid., p. 57.

44  Ibid., p. 60.

45  Ibid., p. 65.

46  Ibid., p. 76.

47  Cf. W. Zimmerli, "Sinaibund und Abrahambund," in his *Gottes Offenbarung. Gesammelte Aufsätze zum Alten Testament* (Munich: Chr. Kaiser Verlag, 1963), p. 205-16.

48  Zimmerli, *Law*, p. 91-92.

49  Cf. the discussion in R. E. Clements, *Prophecy and Tradition* (Atlanta, GA: John Knox, 1975), p. 1-57.

50  Following a lead by B. S. Jackson (see his *Essays in Jewish and Comparative Legal History* [Leiden: Brill, 1975], p. 16), I have developed the point at length in my *Jesus and Scribal Authority*.

51  See my article "Application," p. 193-95.

# Chapter 3

# Torah, *Nomos* and Law

**Solomon Schechter**

In chapter two Torah has been used interchangeably with its tradition rendering "law." Since Solomon Schechter's *Aspects of Rabbinic Theology*,[1] however, it has become common to claim that the English "law" and, indeed, the Greek *nomos* distort the meaning of Torah and, further, that the mistranslation has at least in part been responsible for the common misapprehension of Judaism as "legalistic." The problem is evidently of long standing; *nomos* is, after all, the normal translation for *torah* in the Septuagint. Hence it is sometimes suggested that the distortion begins already in Hellenistic Judaism and that it is reflected, for example (or, as some would have it, above all), in the writings of Paul. The argument has been sufficiently influential to merit attention here.[2]

Schechter's concerns were scarcely with philology. Occasional statements do imply that he is addressing in a general way the question of what the word *torah* means: "It must first be stated that the term *Law* or *Nomos* is not a correct rendering of the Hebrew word *Torah*. ... To the Jew the word *Torah* means a teaching or an instruction of any kind" (p. 117). But the discussion is not developed along the lines of a semantic study. The history of the term is not traced; nor, for that matter, is any attempt made to define *nomos*, or to discover why it was adopted within Hellenistic Judaism as the standard equivalent of *torah*. Schechter's goals, it is apparent, are much broader.

At issue is the claim (made, according to Schechter, by "most modern critics") that legalism constitutes "the whole religion of the Jew" (p. 117). In challenging such a notion, Schechter proceeds by arguing that the contents of "the Torah" are not confined to laws;

---

Notes to Chapter 3 appear on pages 55-56. This chapter was prepared by Stephen Westerholm.

here "the Torah" is used in the developed, technical sense which it has come to acquire as a designation for the Pentateuch, or the whole of the Hebrew scriptures or even "the sum total of the contents of revelation" (p. 127). That "the Pentateuch is no mere legal code" (p. 119) but includes narrative as well is not a difficult argument to sustain; equally clearly the term Torah comes to be used of the prophets and hagiographa as well, and even for revelation in general. Schechter's main point is therefore true, and self-evidently so: there is more to "the Torah" than laws.

The discussion continues with a moving account of what "the Torah" means to the rabbinic Jew. Its identification with the wisdom of God in creation is noted; further, that Torah was perceived as a gift of God's grace and goodness, that "everything wise and good" was believed to be "at least potentially contained in the Torah" (p. 134). The section concludes with a chapter on "The Joy of the Law" (p. 148-69); the sympathetic reader could wish that every scholar for whom rabbinic law appears as an oppressive burden was compelled to peruse, if not to copy a hundred times, Schechter's almost lyrical portrayal. In short, Schechter's treatment of Torah is an artistic and polemical success.

It remains true, however, that Schechter has not proven the remark raised in passing, that the word *torah* does not mean "law." Though often repeated, the argument that *torah* cannot mean "law" because the Torah contains more than laws does not withstand scrutiny. After all, the second "book" of the Pentateuch contains more than the account of the departure of Israel from Egypt—yet it derives its name ("Exodus") from this crucial part of its story. Similarly, the term Torah may have come to designate a collection of disparate material because an integral part of the material is *torah* in the specific sense of divine law. Reminders of the scope of material contained in "the Torah" may still be in order; but it does not follow that *torah* cannot mean "law."

Schechter makes but does not develop the claim that Greek *nomos* mistranslates *torah* as well. The notion has been widely adopted, primarily because it is thought to have been established by C. H. Dodd in a famous chapter in *The Bible and the Greeks*.[3] To Dodd's argument we must now turn.

## C. H. Dodd

Dodd begins with a survey of the semantic field of *nomos*. Broadly speaking it meant "an immanent or underlying principle of life and action" (p. 25), but came to have the force of " 'law,' in the proper sense, i.e., either a single statutory enactment or the legal corpus of a given community" (p. 26). Hebrew *torah* is then said to mean "direction or instruction" (p. 30); though it can be used of instruction given to children by their parents or to students by the wise, it is "most specifically used of guidance or instruction coming from God Himself; and chiefly in two ways, through the oracular utterances or responses of the priests at the sanctuary, and through the prophets" (p. 30). When used of priestly responses, *toroth* (plural) were generally matters of ritual and ceremonial practice, though they seem to have included moral verdicts as well. The singular *torah* could thus be used of a code of ceremonial observances such as we find in the "priestly document of the Pentateuch . . . and also, by an extension of meaning, of the code of commandments, statutes and judgments contained in *Deuteronomy*, since one principal source of these was actually the collection of priestly *toroth* at Jerusalem and perhaps at other sanctuaries" p. 31). Dodd concludes this part of his argument with a statement too little noted in the subsequent discussion: "It is in this sense that *torah* can fairly be regarded as equivalent to *nomos*" (p. 31).

What Dodd objects to is that *nomos* is used in the Septuagint in cases where the Hebrew *torah* is "of a different character," which he refers to as prophetic, and where it amounts to "instruction in the principles of religion" (p. 31). "*Torah* is for the prophets divine revelation in the widest sense, appealing to heart, mind, and will. It may include positive precepts, but it includes much more" (p. 32). To render *this* usage of *torah* by *nomos* is, according to Dodd, "thoroughly misleading" (p. 33). At this point Dodd introduces his famous characterization of Hellenistic Judaism; a lengthy quotation is in order.

While the translation is often misleading as a representation of the original meaning, it is most instructive in its bearing upon Hellenistic Judaism. It is clear that for the Jews of Egypt in the Hellenistic period the developed meaning of *torah* as a code of religious observance, a "law" for a religious community, was the normal and regulative meaning, and they made this meaning cover the whole use of the word in the Old Testament. Thus the prophetic type of religion was obscured, and the Biblical revelation was conceived in a hard legalistic way. In thus rendering the term the translators are no doubt reflecting the sense in which their community read the Hebrew Bible, but their rendering helped to fix and stereotype that sense. (p. 33-34)

By way of contrast, Dodd suggests that Rabbinic Judaism continued to understand *torah* in the broad, prophetic sense of divine revelation.

Three comments seem appropriate here.

(1) Dodd is correct in noting that *torah* in some contexts is adequately rendered by *nomos* "law," and in including in this category those usages in Deuteronomy and the related literature where the Deuteronomic code of "statutes and ordinances" is referred to.

"And what great nation is there, that has statutes and ordinances so righteous as all this law (*torah*) which I set before you this day?" (Deut. 4:8; cf. 32:46; Josh. 1:7; 1 Kgs. 2:3; 2 Kgs. 17:13, etc.). Certainly Israel's law should not be considered in isolation from its covenant. It is also true that the scope of the demands placed upon Israel encompasses areas, such as religious observance and moral behaviour, which fall outside the boundaries of the law in many cultures. Nonetheless, the pattern of commandments issued by a sovereign to be obeyed by his subjects, with sanctions to follow upon their transgression, all but requires the English rendering "law" as an adequate translation; and *nomos* is no distortion here.

(2) There can be little doubt that references to the Pentateuch as "the Torah of Moses" developed out of the usage of the same phrase to refer to the Deuteronomic code;[4] that being the case, Hellenistic Jewry can hardly be faulted for following suit and speaking of the Pentateuch as "the law" (*ho nomos*). It does not follow that Hellenistic Jews were ignorant that the Pentateuch contained stories as well as statutes; and if they did sometimes refer to Genesis as a kind of prologue to the laws[5] the same can certainly be said of the rabbis.[6] Proof positive that Hellenistic Judaism should not be singled out for a charge of legalism because it rendered *torah* with *nomos* is found in Ezra 7. There, in the Aramaic portion of Ezra, Hebrew *torah* becomes Aramaic *dāth* (7:12, 14, 21, 26; cf. 7:6, 10), a term which clearly means "law" (note its use for the "*law* of the Medes and the Persians" in Daniel 6!). We may go further: the evidence from Jewish literature of the Second Temple period *in both Hebrew and Greek* shows that *torah* and *nomos* continued to be used in the Deuteronomistic sense of the divine demands placed upon Israel: the *torah/nomos* is to be "done," not "transgressed"; and the life or death, blessing or cursing of God's people is seen to depend on their response to its statutes.

This [path] is the study of the Law (*torah*) which He commanded by the hand of Moses, that they may do according to all that has been revealed from age to age. (1QS 8.15)[7]

Every man who enters the Council of Holiness . . . and who deliberately or through negligence transgresses one word of the law (*torah*) of Moses. . . . (1QS 8.21-22)

The Lord is faithful . . . to those who live in the righteousness of his commandments, in the Law (*nomos*), which he has commanded for our life. (Ps. Sol. 14:1-2)[8]

He [God] made him [Moses] hear his voice, . . . and gave him the commandments face to face, the law (*nomos*) of life and knowledge. (Sir. 45:5).

She is the book of the commandments of God, and the law (*nomos*) that endures for ever. All who hold her fast will live, and those who forsake her will die. (Bar. 4:1)

You shall rally about you all who observe the law (*nomos*), and avenge the wrong done to your people. Pay back the Gentiles in full, and heed what the law commands. (1 Macc. 2:67-68)

I will not obey the king's command, but I obey the command of the law (*nomos*) that was given to our fathers through Moses. (2 Macc. 7:30)

(3) Dodd is also correct in noting that the Septuagint uses *nomos* for *torah* in cases where the latter cannot mean "law" (e.g., Isa. 1:10; 8:16). Such mistranslations should be attributed, however, to the stereotypical rendering of the term, not to a "legalism" peculiar to Hellenistic Judaism.[9]

We may sum up the scorecard at this stage in the debate. Legitimate points have been made by the claim that (1) "*the* Torah," in its developed sense, contains more than laws, and that (2) the Septuagint rendering of *torah* by *nomos* is *in some cases* misleading. Other claims, however, we have had to disallow: (1) the categorical and simplistic insistence that *torah* does not mean "law"; and (2) the deduction, from the rendering of *torah* by *nomos*, that "legalism" ran rampant in the streets and synagogues of the Diaspora. At this point, though our main treatment of Paul is reserved for another section, we may appropriately consider discussions of the apostle where the notions introduced by Schechter and Dodd play an important part in the argument.

## H.-J. Schoeps

In his well-known monograph on *Paul*,[10] H.-J. Schoeps adopts a catholic view of the impact which the various intellectual forces in the climate of Paul's day had on the thinking of the apostle: none is to be excluded. He finds in Paul's writings evidence both of Hellenistic conceptions and of the influence of Hellenistic Judaism; yet he emphasizes important contributions from the rabbinic school of Gamaliel I as well. On the other hand, Paul's thinking must not be reduced to "the sum of its various component parts" (p. 48). The convictions that Messiah had come and had been crucified and raised to life led Paul to believe that the new age had arrived, and forced him to re-evaluate many traditional notions.

In his discussion of Paul's view of the law Schoeps typically allows for rabbinic, Hellenistic Jewish and Christian influences. That the age of the law has passed was, according to Schoeps, a simple deduction drawn by the apostle from an attested rabbinic view whereby the law is destined to lose its validity at the inauguration of the Messianic kingdom. To be sure, since the latter kingdom, according to Paul's Christian convictions, was established by the death and resurrection of the Messiah, Paul could only conclude that the law had served as a "custodian until Christ came" (Gal. 3:24), and that, far from limiting sin or conveying life, its effects were seen in "rendering sinfulness evident and piling up the measure of sins" (p. 174). Again, like the rabbis, Paul was convinced that no one fully keeps the law; only the Christian apostle, however, used the conviction as a basis for claiming that the law brings death, not life. That angels communicated the law to Moses on Mount Sinai (Gal. 3:19) was Paul's rather reckless transformation of a standard rabbinic view that angels were present at the giving of the law. Even the pessimism of Romans 7, where the human heart is depicted as the scene of a struggle between the desire to do good and the power of indwelling sin, with the latter inevitably prevailing, has close rabbinic parallels: the rabbinic notion of the struggle between the evil and the good "impulses" is well known, and certainly there were rabbis who shared Paul's view that the evil impulse is the dominant one.

When so much rabbinic influence has been allowed, it is somewhat surprising to read Schoeps' claim that Paul took over from Hellenistic Judaism a fundamental distortion of the meaning and role of Torah. Here we find developed Dodd's suggestion that the Septuagint rendering of *torah* by *nomos* is in some cases misleading, yet typical of the perceptions of Hellenistic Judaism. In Schoeps' discussion, the use of *nomos* for Torah in Hellenistic Judaism is seen as indicative of a "shift of emphasis" which accounts for basic Pauline misunderstandings.

Another important tendency of the LXX, which is reflected in a distorted form in Paul, is the following: the tendency to ethicize Judaism, to understand it as a moral law, disconnected and isolated from the controlling reality of the covenant. It is well known that the Old Testament idea of the "Torah" is best explained as instruction embracing both law and doctrine. In the LXX there takes place with the translation *torah – nomos* – a shift of emphasis towards legalism. And the Torah comes to imply a moral way of life prescribed by God. . . . We shall see later (ch. 5) that the source of many Pauline misunderstandings with regard to the evaluation of the law and covenant is to be sought in the legalistic distortion of the perspective for which Hellenistic Judaism was responsible. (p. 29)

Now when Paul speaks of the Jewish *nomos* he implies a twofold curtailment, which was obviously customary in the Diaspora: in the first place he has reduced the Torah, which means for the Jews both law and teaching, to the ethical (and ritual) law; secondly, he has wrested and isolated the law from the controlling context of God's covenant with Israel. (p. 213)

To his heritage in Hellenistic Judaism, then, Paul owed the misconception that Torah amounts to a mere "sum of prescriptions" to be kept (p. 188). Thus reduced to the ethical law, and isolated from the context of the covenant, Torah becomes for Paul a measuring-rod against which human deficiencies can be noted and condemned. Though righteousness and life would follow if Torah (= a sum of prescriptions) was obeyed, humanity is doomed to condemnation and death when it is transgressed. And since the law's demands have not been met Paul concludes that Torah cannot lead to life: only faith in Christ brings salvation.

Yet Torah, Schoeps insists, simply cannot be understood apart from its relation to the covenant. Torah was not given with the demand that all its provisions must be perfectly met if God's favour is to be gained; it was rather God's gracious gift to a people whom he had already made his own, intended to assist them on the path to holiness. Jews need only demonstrate a willingness to obey God's law, a willingness which amounts to their affirmation of the covenant and brings God's aid in overcoming sin. The context of the covenant, Schoeps believes, is missed by Paul, who on this point shared the myopia of Hellenistic Judaism.

Now no one will deny that Paul perceived the role of Torah differently from the rabbis; but Schoeps' account of the origin of the difference is scarcely convincing. Neither Paul nor Hellenistic Judaism in general were ignorant of the doctrine of Israel's election; and, indeed, no rabbi insists more than Paul on the temporal and essential priority of election over law (cf. Gal. 3:15-17). That the law was granted as a privilege to Israel is amply attested in Paul's writings (Rom. 3:2; 9:4); so, too, the view that the law brings knowledge of God's will and the promise of life to its observers (Rom. 2:13, 17-18; 7:10; 10:5). Finally, we must stress again that the use of *nomos* for the "sum of prescriptions" given to God's people is fully in line with, and not a distortion of, Hebrew usage of *torah*.

But Paul also had at his disposal a host of passages from the Hebrew scriptures which insisted that Israel *as God's covenant people* would enjoy blessing only if they obeyed Torah's demands; God's curse and condemnation would inevitably follow transgression.[11]

Behold I set before you this day a blessing and a curse: the blessing, if you obey the commandments of the Lord your God, which I command you this day, and the curse, if you do not obey the commandments of the Lord your God. (Deut. 11:26-28)

See, I have set before you this day life and good, death and evil. If you obey the commandments of the Lord your God which I command you this day . . . you shall live and multiply, and the Lord your God will bless you in the land which you are entering to take possession of it. But if your heart turns away, and you will not hear, but are drawn away to worship other gods and serve them, I declare to you this day, that you shall perish. (Deut. 30:15-18)

To make Israel's blessing or judgment dependent on observance of the law, as Paul does, is not to isolate Torah from the covenant but simply to reiterate the sanctions which, according to scripture, accompanied the giving of Israel's covenantal responsibilities. Paul is not here introducing notions foreign to Torah; the difference from rabbinic views is primarily that, whereas the rabbis believe Torah's sanction of life is the operative one within Israel, Paul believes it is the sanction of death.

Nor need we doubt the main reason for the difference. Given his conviction that God has intervened for humanity's salvation in the crucifixion of Jesus Christ, Paul could only conclude that Torah had not led to the life it promises; hence, its commands must have been broken, leading to condemnation and death. In short, the decisive factor in Paul's reinterpretation of Torah was not Hellenistic Jewish legalism but Christian soteriology. We return to this theme below.

## Samuel Sandmel

Brief, but not without interest, are the remarks of Samuel Sandmel on the *torah-nomos* equation and its effects on the apostle Paul in his popular study *The Genius of Paul*.[12] Like C. G. Montefiore[13] Sandmel argues throughout that Paul was a Hellenistic Jew and insists that, though the "Graeco-Jewish tradition" of Paul's day "overlapped with Palestinian Judaism in many ways . . . it had also come to have facets of its own" (p. 10). Hence, though "Paul's loyalty and allegiance to Judaism" are not in question,

the content of his Judaism, like that of other Greek Jews, had undergone a subtle but radical shift. Not only did he give the terms which he employed meanings different from those of Palestinian Jews, but even beyond such elementary things there was a change in the fabric of religious suppositions and in the goal of the religious quest. (p. 15)

As a Hellenistic Jew Paul was preoccupied "with the same kind of religious problem that any pagan had — the individual predicament" (p. 23). His primary concern, then, was "the salvation of individuals out of the human predicament" (p. 19). It is in this context that his treatment of the "law" must be understood.

Fundamental to Sandmel's discussion is the difference he perceives in the way Torah was understood by Palestinian and Hellenistic Jews. To Palestinian Jews Torah was not restricted to law: "they equated *Torah* with our word 'revelation.' While they would have conceded that the Torah was a revelation which *included* 'law,' they would properly have denied that revelation and 'law' were interchangeable" (p. 47). In support Sandmel cites the now familiar argument that "the Torah" included not only requirements but also "exhortation (as in the pre-exilic prophets), prayer (as in the Psalter), prudential wisdom (as in Proverbs), and the like" (p. 47). On the other hand, Judaism and its Torah were understood by

Greek Jews as "*law* and nothing but *law*" (p. 46). Sandmel remarks
on the "casualness" with which *torah* was translated by *nomos*:
"Greek Jews nowhere raised the question of whether Torah really
means *nomos*, law! And whenever they defended their Jewish convictions, it was always on the premise, startling to modern Jewish students, that *nomos* did adequately translate *Torah*" (p. 47).

Thus reduced to a "legal code," the law of Moses presented Paul
with "a highly personal and intense problem" (p. 25). That problem
was Paul's "inability to live up to the law" (p. 28), an inability
reflected in Romans 7 and the cause of the "unrest in him which
later led to his conversion" (p. 28). For Sandmel, in admitted disagreement with much of modern scholarship, "it is not [Paul's]
Christian convictions which raise the Law as a problem for him, but
rather it is his problem with the Law that brings him ultimately to
his Christian convictions" (p. 28). In his search "for that which was
the ultimate for man in the quest for salvation," Paul came "reluc-
tantly" to conclude "that the Law of Moses was not this ultimate"
(p. 29). Had Paul not experienced "personal difficulty" in observing
the commands, "he would not have been led to a virtual abrogation
of the Law" (p. 32). Paul came to dismiss the law after finding the
"serenity" which the law had not been able to convey in "the aton-
ing death of Christ" (p. 33).

Still, it should be noted that the law to which Paul turned his back
was not Torah, but the *nomos* of Hellenistic Judaism. Unfortunately,
"the Graeco-Jewish equation of Torah and law was picked up and
propagated by church fathers" and "appears in some of the scholarship of our own day." The result is that Judaism has come to be
identified with "legalism" and regarded with condescension (p. 48).

We cannot enter here into a broader discussion of Sandmel's
reading of Paul. Note, however, that to the extent that the rendering of *torah* by *nomos* is taken to have perverted the perceptions of
Paul and of Hellenistic Jews in general, the argument is ill founded.
Paul may or may not have found himself unable to fulfill Torah's
demands. Such an inability may or may not have been a significant
factor in his Christian understanding of the law. The point here is
that such questions should be discussed without reference to
Torah's supposed distortion in the Diaspora, and without the
absurd implication that Paul as a Hellenistic Jew was unaware that
Judaism and its Torah had a place for exhortation, prayer and prudential wisdom as well as for divine demands! That the demands of
Torah require doing is not an innovation of the Septuagint version.
And the problem of whether or not such demands can be met could
arise for a Palestinian as well as a Hellenistic Jew.

## W. D. Davies

This chapter can be concluded with a brief look at an author to whose views we will return in more detail later. Reflecting on "pitfalls" in the interpretation of Paul and the law,[14] W. D. Davies insists that *torah* was for Paul a "very comprehensive" term (p. 92). Four aspects to its usage are listed.

First, it includes commandments (*mitzwoth*) which are to be obeyed: it is doubtful whether the term *torah* at any time is completely free of the element of demand, either explicitly or implicitly. Second, it encompasses much that is not legal in the sense of commandment: in particular . . . it includes the history of the people of Israel as variously interpreted at different stages, the messages of the significant prophets of Israel, and an impressive tradition of wisdom. Third, . . . the Torah in its totality had come to be regarded as the wisdom after the pattern of which and by means of which God created the world. . . . It is therefore the means of expressing the divine activity both in creation and in morality and knowledge. . . . Fourth, in sum, the term the Torah (the Law) connoted for Paul as a Jew the whole of the revealed will of God in the universe, in nature, and in human society. (p. 92-93)

It will be noted at once that Davies' Paul perceived in Torah the full wealth of meaning which the term had for rabbinic Jews; indeed, the notion that the apostle laboured under misconceptions peculiar to Hellenistic Jewry is hardly to be expected from the author of *Paul and Rabbinic Judaism*.[15] In Davies' view the misunderstanding to be exorcized is not Pauline but that of "Protestant theologians generally," and particularly "those in Germany" who "have often understood *torah* as commandment and interpreted the Jewish tradition as one requiring obedience to the commandments as the ground of salvation" (p. 93). It is this "tendency to treat *torah* as if it simply meant *mitzwah*, commandment," which constitutes the first "pitfall" to be avoided in the interpretation of the apostle's work (p. 93).

Davies' Paul shares the insight of "religious Jews" in general that the Torah was not confined to the divine demands and traditions of their interpretation. Paul was certainly aware that Torah includes "the history that was the background of the commandment" (p. 94), a history which "pointed always to a grace of God which preceded his demand. . . . The precedence of grace over law in Israelite religion persisted, despite its frequent neglect, in Judaism. . . . And the gift of the law itself for Jews, because it was not solely commandment, was regarded as an act of grace and a means to grace" (p. 95). Hence "it follows that the opposition of law to grace which has marked so much of Protestantism . . . is a distortion of Paul" (p. 95). "There is little doubt that for him the Torah was an expression of divine grace" (p. 118).

But this, it seems to me, is not the whole story; nor is a contrast between law and grace the invention of Paul's interpreters. Paul wrote to readers who, in his terms, were once "under law" but now found themselves "under grace" (Rom. 6:14-15). A return to law signals for Paul a fall from grace (Gal. 5:4). The Abrahamic promise, for Paul, was conditioned on faith, not law, in order that it might "rest on grace" (Rom. 4:13, 16). To Paul's mind, where deeds are required, human desert enters the picture, so that God's grace no longer operates in sovereign, splendid isolation (Rom. 4:4-5; 11:6); but fundamental to law is precisely its demand for deeds (Rom. 2:13; 10:5; Gal. 3:12). Judaism may not contrast law and grace; demonstrably, Paul does.

His reasons for doing so will be explored below. Here we must simply note that, once again, the reminder that *the* Torah is not confined to law has been misused, this time to blunt the force of the Pauline contrast between law and grace. Deuteronomy had long since legitimized the use of *torah* in the restricted sense of the sum of "statutes and ordinances" imposed on Israel at Sinai. Of course Paul believed that the giving of the law was itself an act of divine favour and love for Israel; nonetheless, it clearly suits his purpose — as we shall see — to contrast the obedience which Torah on any reading requires with the grace revealed in Jesus Christ.

To conclude. *Torah* may well mean "law," and, frequently, *nomos* involves no mistranslation. Jewish sources of the Second Temple period routinely use the terms for the divine and sanction-sealed obligations given to Israel. Judaism does not contrast this divine *torah* with divine grace. It does not follow, however, that Paul does not do so (against Davies), nor does it follow from his so doing that he misunderstood what Palestinian Jews meant by the term *torah* (against Schoeps and Sandmel). Christian convictions provide an adequate explanation for the change in perspective.

---

## Notes

1 Solomon Schechter, *Aspects of Rabbinic Theology* (New York: Schocken Books, 1961 [originally published in 1909]).

2 For a wider sampling of opinions to the effect that *torah* does not mean "law," with a more detailed refutation, see my article, "Torah, *Nomos*, and Law: A Question of 'Meaning,'" in *Studies in Religion/Sciences Religieuses*, 15 (1986): 327-36.

3 C. H. Dodd, *The Bible and the Greeks* (London: Hodder & Stoughton, 1935), p. 25-41.

4 Cf. R. E. Clements, *Old Testament Theology* (Atlanta, GA: John Knox, 1978), p. 110-20.

5 Cf. Samuel Sandmel, *The Genius of Paul*, 3rd ed. (Philadelphia: Fortress, 1979), p. 47.

6 E. Urbach, *The Sages: Their Concepts and Beliefs* (Jerusalem: Magnes, 1975), Vol. 1, p. 315-17.

7 For the Qumran texts, I have used the translation of G. Vermes, *The Dead Sea Scrolls in English* (Harmondsworth: Penguin, 1962).

8 The translation is that of R. B. Wright, in J. H. Charlesworth, ed., *The Old Testament Pseudepigrapha*, Vol. 2 (Garden City: Doubleday, 1985).

9 Cf. E. Tov, *The Text-Critical Use of the Septuagint in Biblical Research* (Jerusalem: Simor, 1981), p. 55.

10 H. J. Schoeps, *Paul* (Philadelphia: Westminster, 1961).

11 Here we may recall Zimmerli's corrective to von Rad's depiction of law, summarized in Chapter 2 above.

12 See n. 5 above.

13 C. G. Montefiore, *Judaism and St. Paul* (London: Max Goschen, 1914).

14 W. D. Davies, "Paul and the Law: Reflections on Pitfalls in Interpretation," in his *Jewish and Pauline Studies* (Philadelphia: Fortress, 1984), p. 91-122.

15 W. D. Davies, *Paul and Rabbinic Judaism*, 4th ed. (Philadelphia: Fortress, 1980).

# Chapter 4

# Law, Grace and the "Soteriology" of Judaism

Since the Dead Sea Scrolls began to be published, the revolutionary discovery that Judaism of the Second Temple period was diverse has been announced in several scores of scholarly works. Not to be overlooked, however, are a number of factors which contributed to an underlying cohesion. Most significantly for our purposes, religious Jews of the period appear united in the conviction that God's will for his people was enshrined in the statutes of Torah. Admittedly, competing views were held as to who was competent to interpret and apply the divine law. The statutes themselves were variously construed. Even the extent of the authoritative code was a matter of debate, since the Pharisees supplemented the written law with traditions handed down from "the fathers" (Josephus, *Ant.* 13.297), while the people of Qumran may well have accorded other documents such as the so-called *Temple Scroll* comparable status. Divergence there was, but at the same time a common commitment to the principle that God had entrusted his people with his law.

Law was central; but the definition of its role in Jewish "soteriology"[1] of the time remains problematic. Recently controversy has been sparked by the question whether Jews believed they "earned" their "salvation" by the "works" they did in observing the law. The question thus put has an undeniably Protestant ring to it, and the charge has been raised that German Lutheran scholars have first read into Paul's polemics against the Jews and Judaizing Christians of his day the concerns of the 16th-century Reformation, then treated their distorted view of Paul's polemics as an accurate base for depicting early Judaism. The discussion merits a closer look. We begin with a brief look at Luther himself, proceed with a survey of

Notes to Chapter 4 appear on pages 72-74. This chapter was prepared by Stephen Westerholm.

the position of Rudolf Bultmann, then turn to E. P. Sanders' critique and to the reaction it has provoked.

## Martin Luther

For Luther, humanity may be divided into those who adhere to the doctrine of justification by faith and those who do not. The former recognize that "we are redeemed from sin, death and the devil and endowed with eternal life, not through ourselves and certainly not through our works . . . but through the help of Another, the only Son of God, Jesus Christ."[2] To this doctrine the rest of the world is opposed, everyone going "his own way, in the hope of placating a god or a goddess or gods or goddesses by his own works, in other words, of redeeming himself from evil and sin by means of his own work, without the help of Christ."[3] The attempt to gain God's favour by one's own righteousness is for Luther "the fundamental principle of the devil and of the world";[4] to it the heathen, the Jew and the Christian heretic, despite insignificant variations in creed and practice, give united allegiance.

There is no difference at all between a papist, a Jew, a Turk, or a sectarian. Their persons, locations, rituals, religions, works, and forms of worship are, of course, diverse; but they all have the same reason, the same heart, the same opinion and idea. . . . "If I do this or that, I have a God who is favorably disposed toward me; if I do not, I have a God who is wrathful." There is no middle ground between human working and the knowledge of Christ.[5]

In commenting on Galatians, Luther does in fact allow the Jews who opposed Paul one significant distinction: the laws with which they attempted to conform were commanded by God himself. Nonetheless even the very law of God is "weak and useless for justification."[6] To imagine that salvation may be gained by human works of any kind is to suggest that human effort can bridge the immense chasm between Creator and creature, or that deeds of men and women can so impress the devil as to oblige him to grant them release from his grasp.[7] Luther goes still further: to rely on human works for salvation is to transgress the first commandment, which demands that God alone be acknowledged as the source of every good.[8] It is to rob God of glory which belongs exclusively to him. And since Christ died for human sins, none should imagine that his or her iniquity is so "trivial" that "some little work or merit . . . will remove it."[9] It is "an intolerable and horrible blasphemy to think up some work by which you presume to placate God, when you see that He cannot be placated except by this immense, infinite price, the death and the blood of the Son of God, one drop of which is more precious than all creation."[10]

Indeed, it is not simply blatant sin for which atonement is needed; in Luther's view, even so-called "good works," apart from faith, are sinful in God's eyes. A man does not become a bishop by performing the offices of a bishop; on the contrary, unless he already has been made a bishop, his acting in a bishop's role is a mere farce. Similarly, deeds done by those who do not give God glory by acknowledging that all goodness comes from him remain wicked and damnable sins.[11] An evil tree can only bear evil fruit. Where there is confidence in God's grace a deed as simple as picking up straw will meet with God's approval. Where such confidence is lacking, where deeds are done in a dubious attempt to gain God's favour, then "the work is not good, even if the work were to raise all the dead and if the man were to give his body to be burned."[12] "For the works are acceptable not for their own sake but because of faith."[13]

But do not the sacred scriptures themselves contain laws prescribing human deeds? The objection leaves Luther unperturbed, for law remains important in his scheme though it must not be conceived as the path to justification; in Luther's own terms it must not be confused with "gospel." Here "law" is by no means restricted to the Mosaic code but is found wherever scripture makes a demand. The Old Testament is, primarily, "a book of laws, which teaches what men are to do and not to do—and in addition gives examples and stories of how these laws are kept or broken."[14] But the New Testament too contains commandments, given as "expositions of the Law and appendices to the Gospel."[15] By way of contrast, "the gospel teaches exclusively what has been given us by God, and not—as in the case of the law—what we are to do and give to God."[16]

Therefore the Law and the Gospel are two altogether contrary doctrines. . . . For the Law is a taskmaster; it demands that we work and that we give. In short, it wants to have something from us. The Gospel, on the contrary, does not demand; it grants freely; it commands us to hold out our hands and to receive what is being offered. Now demanding and granting, receiving and offering, are exact opposites and cannot exist together.[17]

Why was law given? Here we may confine our attention to Luther's understanding of its primary function. Luther's God suffers from no illusion about the human capacity to obey his law; on the other hand, his intention was certainly not to mock humanity by imposing commands impossible to fulfil. What "the law does, according to Paul, is to make sin known."[18]

Scripture . . . represents man as one who is not only bound, wretched, captive, sick, and dead, but in addition to his other miseries is afflicted, through the agency of Satan his prince, with this misery of blindness, so that he believes himself to be free, happy, unfettered, able, well, and alive. . . . It is Satan's work to prevent men from recognizing their plight and to keep them presuming that they can do every thing they are told. But the work of Moses or a lawgiver is the opposite of this, namely, to make man's plight plain to him by means of the law and thus to break and confound him by self-knowledge, so as to prepare him for grace and send him to Christ that he may be saved. They are therefore not absurd but emphatically serious and necessary things that are done by the law.[19]

By their very nature, the commandments of scripture declare what needs to be done but impart no power to do it. "They are intended to teach man to know himself, that through them he may recognize his inability to do good and may despair of his own ability."[20] Once one has despaired of one's own righteousness solace can be found in the Saviour.

In short, for Luther, Jews share in the fundamental flaw of all human religion: they attempt to gain God's favour by their own deeds. Admittedly, the commands which they strive to obey were given by God himself. Yet God's purpose in giving his law was not to provide a path to justification but to awaken in men and women an awareness of their sin and need for salvation. Such salvation can only be found in reliance on the divine grace offered in Jesus Christ.

## Rudolf Bultmann

No reader of Luther will be surprised at what no student of the subsequent debate can ignore: the influence of the reformer has been profound. For our purposes, a review of the work of Rudolf Bultmann, undoubtedly the dominant New Testament scholar of this century, must suffice.

"Justification by faith" is as central for Bultmann as it is for Luther, and it again serves to divide humankind into two classes. While humanity as a whole is marked by the "striving . . . to gain recognition of one's achievement,"[21] the Christian message of "justification by faith alone" rejects "all self-glorying based on one's achievements,"[22] requires the surrender of all self-reliance, and insists on the utter dependence of humanity on divine grace. The themes are recognizable from Luther; so too is much of the detail.

Since humans owe their being to God and live out their lives before him, their relationship to God ultimately determines whether they are good or evil. Specifically, the "possibility of being good or evil" confronts men and women in "the choice of either acknowledging the Creator and obeying Him, or of refusing Him obedience"[23] and thus "[failing] to acknowledge one's own creatureliness."[24] But to refuse to acknowledge God or find one's good in him is to pursue life in the created sphere at one's disposal — where, however, life is not to be found. Thus is committed "the ultimate sin": "the false assumption of receiving life not as the gift of the Creator but procuring it by one's own power, of living from one's self rather than from God."[25]

The preceding description has been taken from Bultmann's account of Pauline anthropology in his New Testament *Theology*. In his "New Testament Mythology" Bultmann attempted to penetrate beneath the mythological imagery of the New Testament to the "understanding of existence which it enshrines."[26] The result is a more detailed and sophisticated but essentially similar portrayal of the human condition. Again Pauline anthropology is the starting-point. Human existence is lived in the "flesh"; that is, in "the sphere of visible, concrete, tangible, and measurable reality, which as such is also the sphere of corruption and death."[27] No real security can be found in this transitory sphere, and those who seek life and security in the realm of the "flesh" mistake their condition and lose their very life in the process. Attempting to find life in what is corruptible they become prisoners of corruption. Such living "according to the flesh" may take any one of a number of different forms: the realm of the flesh includes not only sensual pleasure "but all human creation and achievement pursued for the sake of some tangible reward. . . . It includes every passive quality, and every advantage a man can have, in the sphere of visible, tangible reality (Phil. 3.4ff.)."[28] Wherever life is oriented toward, and pride is taken in, what belongs to the created, corruptible world, authentic life has been forfeited. True life is only to be found in abandoning "all self-contrived security" and opening oneself to the "unseen, intangible reality" of the grace of God.[29] This is the life of faith, "giving up every attempt to carve out a niche in life for ourselves, surrendering all our self-confidence, and resolving to trust in God alone. . . . It means radical self-commitment to God in the expectation that everything will come from him and nothing from ourselves."[30]

Now to the existentialist philosopher the choice between authentic and inauthentic living is always open; the New Testament, however, disagrees. "For the latter affirms the total incapacity of man to release himself from his fallen state."[31] "The New Testament addresses man as one who is through and through a self-assertive rebel who knows from bitter experience that the life he actually lives is not his authentic life, and that he is totally incapable of achieving that life by his own efforts."[32] Deliverance must come from an act of God, from the revelation of God's love in the person of Jesus Christ. In the cross of Christ humanity must recognize its own judgment, the condemnation of every human accomplishment and boast, the call to abandon the quest for security in oneself and to find security in the love of God. "The event of Jesus Christ . . . makes a man free from himself and free to be himself, free to live a life of self-commitment in faith and love."[33]

For Bultmann, then, as for Luther, faith involves an acknowledgment of one's dependence on God, whereas the fatal flaw of humanity apart from faith is its self-reliance. But Bultmann, too, must account for the law of God and explain why Jews, in adhering to divine law, share in the human dilemma. His answer Bultmann derives from the writings of Paul; the legitimacy of the derivation will concern us below.

For Bultmann, God's demand is encountered in the Old Testament law. Properly understood, the law is a radical demand for true obedience; that is, for an obedience which springs from an acknowledgement of the Creator and a refusal to seek one's life and security anywhere but in him. The commandment is thus designed "to snatch man out of his self-reliant pursuit of life, his will to rule over himself,"[34] and to provide men and women with an opportunity to submit their very selves in obedience to God; in this way the law would lead to life. At the same time, however, the law is liable to a subtle perversion, for in promising life to those who do its commands it presents self-reliant men and women with an occasion to imagine that they can secure their *own* salvation by performing the prescribed tasks. An apparent conformity with the law's terms may thus conceal a fundamental distortion of the law's purpose. God's law may be transformed into a tool for human self-assertion. This, according to (Bultmann's) Paul, is what has taken place in Judaism: the universal human striving for recognition of one's accomplishment has "taken on its culturally . . . distinct form"[35] in Jewish attempts to gain God's favour by keeping his commands. Thus Jews, too, share in the "ultimate sin" of humanity.

The inadequacy of Judaism is, in fact, apparent on two counts. In the first place, Jews "do not fulfil the *whole* law which it was their business to fulfil (cf. Gal. 3:10)."[36] But it is the second consideration which is crucial. "It is not evil works or transgressions of the law that first make the Jews objectionable to God; rather the intention to become righteous before him by fulfilling the law is their real sin, which is merely manifested by transgressions."[37] It follows that "the person who fulfils the law needs grace as much as the one who trespasses against it—indeed it is he most of all who needs it! For in seeking to establish his own righteousness, he is acting *fundamentally* against God."[38]

Thus Jewish zeal in observing the law, no less than Gentile sensuality, is an instance of life "according to the flesh." Furthermore, the sinful self-reliance of the Jew, like that of the Gentile, finds its extreme expression in human boasting. "It is characteristic both of the Jew, who boasts of God and the Torah (Rom. 2:17, 23), and of the Greek, who boasts of his wisdom (1 Cor. 1:19-31)."[39]

In "boasting" is revealed a misconstruing of the human situation, a forgetting of the fact implied by the question, "What do you have that you have not been given? And if it has been given you, why do you boast as if it had not been given you?" (1 Cor. 4:7 tr.). And God insists upon this: All standards of human greatness must be shattered "so that no human being may boast before God". (1 Cor. 1:29 tr.)[40]

The language of 20th-century philosophy and the hermeneutic of demythologization must both be recognized in Bultmann. For our purposes, however, it is more significant to note what he derives from Luther: justification by faith alone is the central Christian doctrine; the fundamental human sin is reliance on self rather than on God's grace; and Jewish observance of Torah is but an illustration of this basic human propensity.

---

### E. P. Sanders

---

In theory, at least, there appear to be two possible paths by which the preceding assessment of Judaism might be challenged: either one might reject Luther's contrast between law and gospel (or between law and grace) on which it is based; or, allowing it to stand, one might claim that, contrary to popular opinion, the Jews were (in effect) good Protestants and champions of grace centuries before the Reformation. Both approaches have been taken, not infrequently by one and the same author. The former approach may perhaps be seen in claims that law is itself a gift of divine grace, designed to provide God's people with a path to life and happiness.[41] Perfect obedience to the law's commands (it is then pointed out) was never expected, and God stood always ready to forgive his people's sins.[42] On the other hand, Judaism (it may be insisted) does not share Christian (or Pauline) pessimism about human nature: there is observance of the law in the world as well as its transgression;[43] and though God's help is essential, it is "not supposed that human efforts count for nothing."[44] In short, since God gave the law as Israel's path to life, assists in its observance and forgives the transgressions of all who repent, a rigid distinction between law and grace inevitably misrepresents Judaism.[45] Law is not found without grace in Judaism, nor is observance of the commandments an expression of self-reliance or self-righteousness.[46] On the other hand, observance of the law is insisted upon, and it may be pointed out that failure to recognize human goodness and exclusive reliance on divine grace serve to undermine the very foundations of human morality.[47]

A defence along these lines has become almost classical in Jewish apologetics; yet its impact on New Testament scholarship (and particularly on German Lutherans) has been minimal. A lively debate has, however, been sparked by the monumental work of E. P. Sanders (*Paul and Palestinian Judaism*),[48] which, despite elements of the approach summarized above, perhaps comes closer to representing the second line of attack:[49] Jews have been on the side of grace all along; indeed, the relation between grace and works in Judaism is no different from that which we encounter in Pauline Christianity. To Sanders' provocative study we now turn.

After a detailed study of early rabbinic materials, the Dead Sea Scrolls, and the (Old Testament) Apocrypha and Pseudepigrapha, Sanders concludes that nearly the whole of the literature is characterized by what he calls "covenantal nomism": the notion that Israel's standing before God is based on the divine election of Israel as his covenant people, and that obedience to the law, while necessary if the Israelite's position in the covenant is to be maintained, is rather a response to God's grace than the means by which salvation is earned. Since rabbinic literature is usually cited in depictions of Judaism as a religion of works-salvation, we will concentrate here on Sanders' interpretation of the early rabbinic evidence.

(1) God's covenant with Israel was universally understood to provide the framework for Israel's relations with God. As a divine institution the covenant was viewed as irrevocable. Disobedience to its terms would certainly be punished, and *individual* Israelites, by deliberately repudiating its demands, might forfeit their part in its blessings. In this sense obedience to God's law was a *condition* for life and "salvation," but it was not its *cause*. God's gracious commitment to Israel was regarded as unconditional, firm and foundational.

(2) No single answer was given to the question why God chose Israel as his covenant people. At times the gratuitous nature of the election was stressed. Elsewhere human merit was mentioned as a factor: Israel may be said to have been chosen because of some merit of the patriarchs, or of the wilderness generation, or with a view to the obedience which Israel would render to God's law in the future. Homiletic needs of the moment determined the emphasis; hence no one answer should be isolated and granted status as *the* position of the rabbis. We may only conclude that, on the one hand, all rabbis believed in the election of Israel and the imposition of God's law on his people, and that, on the other hand, divine grace and human merit were not perceived as mutually exclusive categories.

(3) While it is readily apparent that much rabbinic literature is concerned to spell out the correct interpretation and application of the divine law, it does not follow that the rabbis believed salvation was earned by compliance with its commands. A sufficient motive for devotion to Torah is surely found in the conviction that obedi-

ence to its terms represents Israel's covenantal privilege and responsibility.

(4) The rabbis were certainly convinced of the justice of God's judgments, and believed that he both rewarded obedience and punished transgressions. But, in the case of God's people, retribution was always worked out within the context of the covenant; Israel's standing before God remained fundamentally the result of God's election. Moreover, even when God did reward or punish the deeds of his people his dealings were not determined by strict measurement and justice. His mercy was thought to prevail and to be granted to all Israelites whose basic intent was to obey. Forgiveness was available "for every transgression, except the intention to reject God and his covenant" (p. 157). "What counts is being in the covenant and intending to be obedient to the God who gave the covenant. Rejection of even one commandment with the intent to deny the God who gave it excludes one from the covenant, while acceptance of a fundamental commandment . . . may show one's intent to be obedient" (p. 135).

(5) Rabbinic soteriology, then, most emphatically did not involve a conviction that God weighs fulfillments of the law against transgressions, and grants salvation to those who merit it by the preponderance of their acts of obedience. On the contrary, the fundamental statement of rabbinic soteriology is the claim that "all Israelites have a share in the world to come" (*m. Sanh.* 10.1), with only "the worst individual sinners" and the "most unregenerate generations" serving as exceptions to prove the rule (p. 149). Hence, not perfect or even 51 percent fulfillment of the law's commands is the basis of a Jew's standing before God, but rather membership in Israel, the covenant people of God.

In effect, Sanders has argued on the basis of the rabbinic evidence that Judaism, no less than Pauline Christianity, believed in salvation by divine grace: decisive for Israel's status as God's people were the election and gift of the covenant. Since, however, the Pauline evidence about the Judaism of his day is usually interpreted as depicting Jews who seek salvation by their "works," Sanders proceeds with a re-examination of the epistles.

(1) Whereas Sanders grants that Paul insists, in opposition to Judaism, that righteousness is by faith, not works, he believes that the formula "misstates the fundamental point of disagreement" (p. 551). For Paul, gaining "righteousness" means gaining a standing before God — and his Jewish contemporaries would have agreed that this was by grace. On the other hand, when Palestinian Jews talked about being "righteous" by observing the law, they meant that such deeds are necessary if one's standing, granted initially by divine grace, is to be maintained; and Paul too, Sanders claims,

required "works" for that purpose. Hence the essential *agreement* is concealed by the different senses given to "righteousness."

(2) Sanders is emphatic in denying that Paul rejected the law because its observance leads to self-righteousness and boasting, and that he depicted the Jews as guilty of boasting of their "own" (self-) righteousness. "The supposed objection to Jewish self-righteousness is as absent from Paul's letters as self-righteousness itself is from Jewish literature."[50] The "boasting" rejected in Rom. 3:27 springs from Jewish pride, not in the achievement of keeping the law, but in the special privileges granted to Jews (cf. Rom 2:17, 23). And when Paul condemns Jews for seeking to establish their "own" righteousness (Rom. 10:3; cf. Phil. 3:9), he refers not to their personal achievements in law observance but to their pursuit of a kind of righteousness available only to themselves ("their own," i.e., that which follows from observing the *Jewish* law and is therefore not accessible to Gentiles). Not Jewish self-righteousness, but the equality of Jews and Gentiles is the point of his argument.

(3) In fact, Sanders believes, Paul is wrongly interpreted when we think to find in his arguments against the righteousness of the law the root of his opposition to Judaism. Paul's thinking proceeded from solution to plight, from his Christian conviction that salvation is available only in Christ to the conclusion that all must need salvation and that the law cannot provide it. "If salvation comes only in Christ, no one may follow any other way whatsoever" (p. 519). The "logic" which dominates Paul's view of the law is "that God's action in Christ alone provides salvation and makes everything else seem, in fact actually *be* worthless" (p. 485).

For Sanders, then, Judaism, like Paul, advocates "salvation" by grace. Paul's rejection of Judaism proceeds not from his assigning priority to grace over works (Judaism did the same) nor from a conviction that Jewish law observance is marked by self-reliance, self-righteousness and boasting, but from his exclusivist soteriology: since salvation is by faith in Christ it cannot be by law. Galatians 2:21 provides Paul's real reason for finding the law inadequate: "if justification were through the law, then Christ died to no purpose."

---

## Heikki Räisänen and Other Responses

---

Sanders' portrayal of Judaism has met with widespread, though not universal, acceptance. The most persistent doubts centre on the suspicion that Sanders has imposed upon the Jewish sources a pattern scarcely supported by the documents themselves. Saldarini notes that "the term covenant is not frequently used in rabbinic literature" and that though the rabbis certainly "read Scripture and accepted the covenant . . . neither their practice nor their self-consciousness centred on it." Sanders' picture, he claims, "derives from Christian theological interests rather than from second and third century Jewish religion."[51] G. Brooke suggests that, while the pattern defined by Sanders may indeed be found in Jubilees and the Qumran literature, it is hardly apparent in Ben Sirach or 1 Enoch.[52] John J. Collins contends that, while "covenantal nomism" is certainly attested in the Jewish Diaspora, "it was not the only, or even the dominant, factor in the religion of Hellenistic Judaism";[53] nor is it the dominant pattern in Jewish apocalyptic or wisdom literature.[54] In short, Sanders' "search for an almost supra-historical consistency" has, in the view of some scholars, led to unwarranted "generalizations"[55] — and the generalizations themselves are determined by a debate extraneous to Judaism.

On the other hand, it should be noted that Sanders' argument is more subtle than an isolated reading of the criticisms cited above might suggest. His claim, after all, is not that covenantal language dominates the literature but that the notion of the covenant is the underlying conviction, too self-evident to require constant reiteration, on which it is based.[56] That, in discussing the role of "grace" and "works" in Judaism, Sanders has allowed the Christian theological discussion to determine the agenda is no doubt true; yet such a procedure is perhaps inevitable when the task at hand is to counter common misrepresentations of Judaism. Nor need Judaism be falsified in the process provided, as Sanders claims, a distinction can be fairly consistently observed in Jewish writings between electing grace as foundational and obedience as the condition for remaining in the elect state.

What is abundantly clear is that the self-understanding of Jews of any period is misrepresented when human works and divine grace are posited as alternative paths to salvation and Judaism is said to have opted for the former. That human compliance with the law, or at least the intention so to comply, was a necessary condition is not to be denied; given the dozens of biblical texts which insist on obedience if life and blessing are to be enjoyed such a requirement remains an inevitable part of Jewish "soteriology." But reliance on divine grace is also apparent where election and the law itself are perceived as gifts of God's favour, divine help in obeying Torah is both entreated and acknowledged, and divine mercy and forgiveness for transgressions, however great, are held open to those who repent.

The question remains what we are to make of Paul. In the wake of Sanders' study attempts have been made to interpret the apostle in terms other than "the thin, tired and anachronistic ones of Lutheran polemic."[57] Paul is then said to oppose not reliance on "works" in general but insistence on, and dependence upon, such "works of the law" as set Jews apart from other nations (e.g., cir-

cumcision, food laws, sabbath observance). Jewish exclusivism, not
human self-reliance, is seen as the target of Paul's polemics.[58] But
here, I believe, Heikki Räisänen is correct: *in Paul's view* obedience
to Torah's demands is the path Jews pursue for salvation. And Paul
does indeed contrast the "works" required by the Jewish law with
reliance on divine grace.[59]

According to Galatians 5:4-5, God's approval on the day of judgment is sought by some on the basis of law, by others (i.e., by true
Christians) on the basis of faith; the former, in Paul's terms, are cut
off from grace. In Romans 9:30-31, Israel is said to pursue "the
righteousness which is based on law," and such righteousness is
again contrasted with that "through faith." In the context, "righteousness" can only mean "righteous status in God's eyes."[60] A similar distinction between the two "righteousnesses" is drawn elsewhere (cf. Rom. 4:13; 10:5-6; Phil. 3:9), and its basis seems clear
enough: in Paul's eyes, the fundamental principle of the "righteousness which is based on the law" is that life is granted to those who
obey its commands (Rom. 10:5; Gal. 3:12); the law, in other words,
demands deeds (Rom. 2:13; 3:20; and note the parallel between the
exclusion of the law, Rom. 3:21, and that of works, 4:6, with "apart
from works of law," 3:28, providing the link: where "works" are
excluded, 4:6, law cannot be a factor, 3:21). It is this requirement
for human deeds which means that a righteousness based on law is
for Paul incompatible with one based on God's promise (Gal. 3:18),
grace (Rom. 4:16, in the context of 4:13-14; also see 4:4), or faith
(Gal. 3:12; Rom. 4:4-5, 13, etc.). In Räisänen's terms, "grace, faith,
promise, and Spirit are, according to [Paul], something diametri-
cally opposed to the law. The entirety of Paul's argument is, indeed, little more than a constant reiteration of this axiom."[61]

Räisänen concludes that Paul was wrong, that, since Judaism did
not in fact understand the law to be the means of salvation, Paul's
view of Jewish religion is distorted. In explaining the origin of
Paul's notion, he suggests that Paul may have misinterpreted the
insistence of conservative Jewish Christians that uncircumcised Gentile believers be excluded from their table fellowship. Paul may have
mistakenly inferred that the uncircumcised were thought to be
excluded from salvation as well, and thus that the law was viewed by
his opponents as the means of salvation.[62]

But such cannot have been the course of Paul's thinking. Had
Paul believed that his opponents were *wrong* in imagining that the
law demands deeds for salvation the error might well have lain in
his perception of their position. But, to Paul's mind, Moses himself
announced the requirement of "the righteousness which is based on
the law" that deeds must be done if life is to be gained (Rom. 10:5).
If, then, Paul first encountered the notion in a (mistaken) percep-

tion of his opponents' position we would have to assume that he thereupon searched for scripture to support *their* cause and came to concede that they had Moses on their side! But few will suspect the Paul of the epistles of pursuing the matter so. Rather we must recognize that what he says about the "righteousness of the law" is based on his own Christian theologizing and meditating on the sacred scriptures. He has derived from texts such as Leviticus 18:5 the conviction that the age of the Law required deeds of those who would be counted righteous in God's sight. What he perceives as his opponents' error is their clinging to this path which, though indeed announced by Moses, has proven unable to lead to righteousness because of human sin (Rom. 3:20; 8:3); a path which, moreover, has now and forever been set aside (Rom. 10:4) by the manifestation of righteousness "apart from law" through faith in Jesus Christ (Rom. 3:21-22; cf. Gal. 3:23-26); an "old" covenant which, though divinely instituted and glorious, led to condemnation and death, but which has now been superseded by a "new" covenant of righteousness and life (2 Cor. 3:6-17).

That Jews pursue a righteousness based on law and requiring human deeds is thus Paul's Christian perception of what their conduct amounts to, in the light of the gospel; it is not an attempt to portray, accurately and objectively, the self-understanding of contemporary Jews. Distortion enters the picture when the character of his writing as Christian theology is forgotten, and the conclusion is drawn that Judaism itself distinguishes law from grace and opts for the former.

The question remains: why did Paul, the Christian theologian, ignore the aspect of grace in the election of Israel and the giving of Torah when he characterized the old age as one of law? Any attempt at reconstructing his thought is bound to be speculative; the following factors should at least be borne in mind.

(1) Axiomatic and fundamental to Paul's thought was the conviction that Messiah had come — and been crucified. C. G. Montefiore attributed to Paul's pre-Christian thinking a pessimism about human nature which is simply not found among the rabbis and which, he believed, must have resulted from Paul's upbringing as a Hellenistic Jew; had Paul's training been rabbinic, he would have seen no need for a redemption involving such "an amazing expedient and a terrific catastrophe"[63] as the death of a "sinless divine being."[64] But Montefiore's reasoning is patently backwards. Paul did not devise the scheme of a crucified Messiah as the solution to his own pessimistic perception of the human plight; it was rather Paul's encounter with the crucified but risen Lord which convinced him that Messiah had died, and that his death must have been necessary for humanity's redemption. In the light of this conviction he

then reinterpreted the human plight in the drastic terms which such a redemption requires. The same consideration applies to Paul's understanding of Judaism and its covenant: if God deemed the death of his son necessary for the salvation of humanity then the old salvific institutions cannot have been adequate. Paul's thinking thus inevitably begins with a premise which, to the rabbinic mind, is simply inconceivable: that the election of Israel and granting of Torah, though undeniably gifts of divine grace, cannot by themselves lead to life.

(2) We should not be surprised, then, if Paul, forced to account for the inadequacies of the old institutions, understands their essence differently than do those who find them adequate. When Israel's institutions are deemed a sure and sufficient pathway to life the divine grace at their roots is not likely to be lost to view. On the other hand, Paul's view appears all but inevitable once the premise is granted that the Sinaitic covenant *cannot* lead to the life it promises. The failure can hardly be attributed to unfaithfulness on God's part; necessarily, then, *the law's demand for deeds becomes its operative feature* (Rom. 2:13, 25; 10:5; Gal. 3:10, 12; 5:3, etc.), and the conclusion drawn that a human failure to meet those demands accounts for the inadequacy of the old salvific institutions (Rom. 3:20).

(3) But did not the Sinaitic covenant provide its own means of atonement for human transgressions? Paul does not address the issue directly; but Romans 3:25 implies what would in any case be the natural conviction for a believer in a crucified Messiah to hold: that Christ Jesus is the *true* propitiatory provided by God, of which the Mosaic cult can at best have been meant to serve as a foreshadowing.[65]

(4) In any case, it must be remembered that Paul was not the first to believe that the Sinaitic covenant had failed to provide a lasting basis for God's dealings with his people, nor was he the first to attribute the failure to Israel's transgressions of the law. Jeremiah 31:31-32 enunciates precisely that position, and it is implied in other prophetic texts as well.[66] And that God's favour in choosing Israel as his people and granting them his law could be presumed upon as assuring his blessing apart from deeds of obedience was a position attacked by the prophets of the "old" covenant as well as by the "forerunner" and "mediator" of the new (e.g., Amos 3:2; Mic. 3:11; Matt. 3:8-10; 8:10-12). Thus Paul merely adapts for his purposes the traditional motifs that God's covenant with Israel requires deeds and that Israel has failed to produce them.

(5) But if it follows from the inadequacy of the "old" covenant that its operative feature was its demand for human works, it is equally natural to conclude from the conviction that the new covenant is adequate that it operates on divine grace. To this we may

add that the redemption under the new covenant was not accompanied by a signal imposing of divine demands as that of the old so spectacularly was; whereas the giving of the law is on any reading central to the covenant instituted at Mount Sinai, the covenant established on Golgotha features solely an act of incomprehensible divine grace. Furthermore, Paul's own overwhelming sense that the new age is one of grace would have been enhanced by his gratuitous acceptance into the service of the Lord whose church he had sought to destroy (1 Cor. 15:9-10; Gal. 1:13, 23).

(6) But does not Pauline Christianity place a demand for works on believers as surely as the Mosaic covenant did on Israel? And is it not true that, essentially, the same pattern of salvation granted by grace but maintained by works applies to both? And does not the common pattern prove the falsehood of the characterization of the Mosaic dispensation as law, the Christian as grace?

Here we must be content with a few suggestions why Paul does not perceive the matter so. For Paul (and the early Christians in general) the period before Christ was one of unfulfilled anticipation; it is with Christ that the day of salvation had dawned (2 Cor. 6:2), full access into God's grace has been granted (Rom. 5:2), and justification is so assured in hope that it can be spoken of as a present reality (Rom. 5:1; 8:30; cf. 8:1). Since, to Paul's thinking, none of this was possible under the old dispensation, it cannot be said that Israel had already been granted salvation by divine grace and that the prescribed works provided only the means for maintaining what had been granted. On the contrary, in an age of anticipation the prescribed works take on the character of preconditions for entering a salvation yet to be revealed. Thus Paul not unnaturally depicts Israel pursuing a path which requires deeds for justification, while Christians are thought to enjoy already the salvation of the new age, a gift of divine grace received by faith.

Are human "works" then necessary to maintain the Christian's status as "justified"? Certainly Paul believes that obedience is incumbent upon believers. Yet fundamental to Pauline ethics is the conviction that the age of the law and its demands has been replaced by the age when the Spirit has been given to guide and empower ethical living (Rom. 7:6; 2 Cor. 3:6; Gal. 5:18).[67] Consequently the "fruit" which is indeed expected of Christians is repeatedly construed as rather the product of the divine Spirit than the accomplishment of believers themselves (Gal. 5:16-25; Rom. 8:4-14), and God's grace remains the operative factor in Christian living in a sense which (to Paul's mind) was not possible when "the Spirit was not yet given" (Rom. 15:15-16; 1 Cor. 15:10; 2 Cor. 12:9-10, etc.).

All of this is—patently—Christian theology. Paul's writings are misused when their theological nature is overlooked and he is thought to be depicting, rightly or wrongly, soteriology as understood by contemporary Jews themselves. Judaism is not ignorant of divine grace, nor is "salvation" thought to be "earned" by human "works." Since, however, Judaism does not as a rule distinguish law from grace, nor exclude human obedience as a precondition for life, the possibility was open to Paul to allow that the Sinaitic covenant was divinely instituted while explaining its failure to convey life: "all have sinned," and hence "no human being will be justified by works of the law." Now, however, the "righteousness of God has been manifested apart from law . . . through faith in Jesus Christ" (Rom. 3:20-23).[68]

## Notes

1  That the term itself is somewhat misleading when applied to Judaism is pointed out by E. P. Sanders, *Paul and Palestinian Judaism* (Philadelphia: Fortress, 1977), p. 17-18.

2  All quotations from Luther are taken from the American Edition of *Luther's Works*, edited by H. Pelikan and H. T. Lehmann, and published by Concordia Publishing House of Saint Louis and Muhlenberg Press of Philadelphia. The quotation here is from the "Lectures on Galatians," Vol. 27, p. 145.

3  Ibid., p. 146.

4  Ibid.

5  Ibid., Vol. 26, p. 396.

6  Ibid., p. 407.

7  Ibid., p. 41.

8  Ibid., p. 227-29, 253-54.

9  Ibid., p. 33.

10  Ibid., p. 176.

11  "The Freedom of a Christian," Vol. 31, p. 360-61.

12  "Treatise on Good Works," Vol. 44, p. 25.

13  Ibid., p. 26.

14  "Preface to the Old Testament," Vol. 35, p. 236.

15  "Lectures on Galatians," Vol. 26, p. 150.

16  "How Christians Should Regard Moses," Vol. 35, p. 162.

17  "Lectures on Galatians," Vol. 26, p. 208.

18  "The Bondage of the Will," Vol. 33, p. 127.

19  Ibid., p. 130-31.

20  "The Freedom of a Christian," Vol. 31, p. 348.

21  R. Bultmann, "Christ the End of the Law," in his *Essays: Philosophical and Theological* (London: SCM, 1955), p. 43.

22  Ibid., p. 45.

23  R. Bultmann, *Theology of the New Testament* (London: SCM, 1952), Vol. 1, p. 228.

24  Ibid., p. 232.

25  Ibid.

26  R. Bultmann, "New Testament and Mythology," in H. W. Bartsch, ed., *Kerygma and Myth* (London: S.P.C.K., 1953), p. 11.

27  Ibid., p. 18.

28  Ibid.

29  Ibid., p. 19.

30 Ibid., p. 19-20.
31 Ibid., p. 27.
32 Ibid., p. 30.
33 Ibid., p. 32.
34 Bultmann, *Theology*, p. 250.
35 Bultmann, "End," p. 43.
36 Ibid., p. 50.
37 R. Bultmann, "Romans 7 and the Anthropology of Paul," in his *Existence and Faith: Shorter Writings of Rudolf Bultmann* (Cleveland: World Publishing, 1960), p. 149.
38 Bultmann, "End," p. 46.
39 Bultmann, *Theology*, p. 242.
40 Ibid.
41 Cf. C. G. Montefiore, *Judaism and St. Paul* (London: Max Goschen, 1914), p. 30-31; J. Z. Lauterbach, *Rabbinic Essays* (Cincinnati: Hebrew Union College Press, 1951), p. 268-69; and G. F. Moore, *Judaism in the First Centuries of the Christian Era* (Cambridge, MA: Harvard University Press, 1927), Vol. 1, p. 491.
42 Ibid., Vol. 1, p. 494-95, and Vol. 2, p. 94.
43 Montefiore, *Judaism*, p. 72; Moore, *Judaism*, Vol. 1, p. 454; and M. Buber, *Two Types of Faith* (London: Routledge & Kegan Paul, 1951), p. 79-80.
44 Montefiore, *Judaism*, p. 78, and R. T. Herford, *The Pharisees* (New York: Macmillan, 1924), p. 127, 131.
45 H.-J. Schoeps, *The Jewish-Christian Argument* (London: Faber and Faber, 1965), p. 40-52.
46 Ibid., p. 43.
47 Herford, *Pharisees*, p. 126-27, 133; Lauterbach, *Essays*, p. 265-66; and J. Klausner, *Jesus of Nazareth* (New York: Menorah, 1979 [originally published in 1925]), p. 379-80.
48 See n. 1 above.
49 Note the assessment of P. S. Alexander, who, as a clear representative of the first approach, is critical of Sanders: "Perhaps Sanders has not identified the point at issue here with total accuracy. His answer to the charge of 'legalism' seems, in effect, to be that Rabbinic Judaism, despite appearances, is really a religion of 'grace'. But does this not involve a tacit acceptance of a major element in his opponents' position—the assumption that 'grace' is superior to 'law'? The correct response to the charge must surely be: And what is wrong with 'legalism', once we have got rid of abusive language about 'hypocrisy' and 'mere externalism'? . . . If we fail to take a firm stand on this point we run the risk of seriously misdescribing Pharisaic and Rabbinic Judaism, and of trying to make it over into a pale reflection of Protestant Christianity." (See his review of Sanders' *Jesus and Judaism* in *Journal of Jewish Studies*, 37 [1986]: 105.)
50 E. P. Sanders, *Paul, the Law, and the Jewish People* (Philadelphia: Fortress, 1983), p. 156.
51 A. J. Saldarini, review of Sanders' *Paul and Palestinian Judaism*, *Journal of Biblical Literature*, 98 (1979): 300.
52 G. Brooke, review of Sanders' *Paul and Palestinian Judaism*, *Journal of Jewish Studies*, 30 (1979): 248-49.
53 J. J. Collins, *Between Athens and Jerusalem* (New York: Crossroad, 1983), p. 244.
54 Ibid., p. 13-15.
55 Brooke, Review, p. 248.
56 Cf. E. P. Sanders, "Puzzling out Rabbinic Judaism," in W. S. Green, ed., *Approaches to Ancient Judaism* (Chico, CA: Scholars Press, 1980), Vol. 2, p. 65-79.

57  N. T. Wright, "The Paul of History and the Apostle of Faith," *Tyndale Bulletin*, 29 (1978): 87.

58  Ibid., p. 62-88, and J. D. G. Dunn, "The New Perspective on Paul," in *Bulletin of the John Rylands Library*, 65 (1983): 95-122.

59  H. Räisänen, *Paul and the Law* (Philadelphia: Fortress, 1986), p. 162-64.

60  C. E. B. Cranfield, *A Critical and Exegetical Commentary on the Epistle to the Romans* (Edinburgh: T. & T. Clark, 1975-79), Vol. 2, p. 506.

61  H. Räisänen, "Legalism and Salvation by the Law," in S. Pedersen, ed., *Die paulinische Literatur und Theologie* (Aarhus: Forlaget Aros, 1980), p. 72.

62  Ibid., p. 78-82.

63  Montefiore, *Judaism*, p. 70.

64  Ibid., p. 78.

65  Cf. B. F. Meyer, "The Pre-Pauline Formula in Rom. 3:25-26a," *New Testament Studies*, 29 (1983): 198-208.

66  See the summary of the work of M. Noth and G. von Rad in Chapter 2 above.

67  See my article "Letter and Spirit: The Foundation of Pauline Ethics," *New Testament Studies*, 30 (1984): 229-48.

68  The position on Paul summarized here is developed at length in my monograph, *Israel's Law and the Church's Faith: Paul and His Recent Interpreters* (Grand Rapids: Eerdmans, 1988).

# Chapter 5

# Law and Christian Ethics

Does law have a place in Christian ethics? The long history and complexity of the discussion resist facile summation. Here a look at the work of three significant British scholars must suffice to indicate some of the issues involved.

The links between the scholars of our study are strong ones indeed. Dodd and Daube were at one time colleagues at Cambridge University. Davies studied under them both. The three of them were among the participants in Dodd's famous New Testament seminar, where they formed, in the words of Dodd's biographer, "a kind of triumvirate."[1] Daube and Davies were co-editors of a *Festschrift* for Dodd,[2] Davies was a co-editor in a *Festschrift* volume of New Testament studies for Daube[3] and Daube has contributed to the Davies *Festschrift*.[4] The works of all three scholars provide abundant testimony, in prefaces and footnotes, to their mutual indebtedness and esteem. Strong personal ties as well as a common approach to our theme make the combination of these three scholars a suitable subject for review.

## C. H. Dodd

We begin with Dodd and, specifically, with a series of lectures he delivered at Columbia University and published under the title *Gospel and Law*.[5] Dodd is of course aware that

many Christian theologians, in almost all periods of the Church, and certainly at the present time, have protested against any construction of the Christian religion which, by introducing legal conceptions, seems to blur the splendor of the Gospel as the affirmation of the free and unconditioned grace of God to sinful men or to question the complete adequacy

Notes to Chapter 5 appear on pages 89-91. This chapter was prepared by Stephen Westerholm.

of a life directed inwardly by the Spirit in independence of external authority of any kind. (p. 65)

Yet Dodd finds such a position at odds with the evidence of the New Testament itself. We may summarize his argument under the following points.

(1) The New Testament writers understood the Christian faith as a "new covenant" which (like the old) "rests upon a divine initiative," but (again, like the old covenant) also "lays consequential obligations upon the Church" (p. 67). The early Christian documents leave no room for imagining that Christian "freedom" implies the autonomy of the individual, or that Christians have no moral guide but their own "inner light" (p. 70). After all, the "basic postulate" of New Testament Christianity is "the Kingdom of God; and a kingdom implies authority" (p. 70).

(2) Furthermore, the New Testament provides abundant substantiation of the conviction that Christian ethics may be communicated in the form of precepts requiring obedience. It seems apparent that there was at an early date a "traditional body of ethical teaching given to converts from paganism to Christianity" (p. 15). Paul's own ethical teaching features a "downright peremptory tone" as he "gives 'orders'" which are "severely practical and commonsense" (p. 13-14). In the New Testament epistles we encounter "perfectly straightforward general maxims which you could transfer directly to the field of conduct," taking them "quite literally as they stand" (p. 52). The same cannot be said of the precepts of the gospels: few are "capable of being made into direct regulations for behavior, enforceable, if necessary, by judicial or disciplinary measures" (p. 73). Indeed, much of Jesus' ethical teaching is "simply not suitable . . . for use as a plain guide to conduct, it you take [it] literally" (p. 53). Rather, in poetic, imaginative forms with dramatic power we are shown the "*quality* and *direction* of action which shall conform to the standard set by the divine *agapē*" (p. 73). But while we are not given "exact rules of behavior in particular situations" it remains true that an ethical task is set forth which is understood as obligatory (p. 62).

(3) "The basic statement of the obligation which the new covenant entails" may be expressed as "an obligation to reproduce in human action the *quality* and the *direction* of the act of God by which we are saved" (p. 71; cf. John 13:15, 34). Thus early Christian teachers drew up schemes of ethical instruction to which they gave "force and vitality" by supplying references "to the fundamental quality and direction of the divine act by which we are saved, as it is declared in the Gospel" (p. 72). And, as noted above, the teaching of Jesus, though poetic in form, is not less authoritative in its proclamation of the required "quality and direction" of behaviour.

(4) Particularly as expressed in the teaching of Jesus, the moral demands of the New Testament are nonetheless distinct from "all systems of ethics which present a code of rules and regulations to be carried out 'to the letter'" (p. 69). A code of concrete regulations can be observed; transgressions of what it commands are readily apparent. The problem is that "exact rules" may be scrupulously followed in a way which has "little to do with fundamental morals, with justice, mercy, and the love of God" (p. 76). On the other hand, when a "quality" and "direction" of action are demanded as in Jesus' teaching, "vistas" are opened up "towards an unattainable and even inconceivable perfection" (p. 76). No room is left for complacency; yet "positive moral guidance for action" has been provided (p. 64).

(5) Since God does not change, the "law of the new covenant" is "aboriginal. It is the law of our creation, and its field of application is as wide as the creation itself" (p. 79).

From this astute but general discussion of the problem we turn to a significant article on a peculiar phrase in Paul's first letter to the Corinthians. Here[6] Dodd describes the thought process behind Paul's writing of 1 Corinthians 9:19-22 as follows. To convert Jews Paul "voluntarily submits to the precepts and prohibitions of the Torah, although as a Christian he holds himself to be free from them" (p. 135). Paul is thus *anomos* in the sense that he is "as free from the obligations of the Torah as any Gentile" (p. 135). But the term *anomos* could be misunderstood to refer to one who leads "an unregulated and irresponsible life" (p. 135). To avoid giving this impression, Paul adds that he is not *anomos theou*, "without law toward God." Here "Torah is not conceived as being identical, or equivalent, or at any rate co-extensive, with the law of God, which is either a different, or a more inclusive, law than the law of Moses" (p. 135-36). Paul is thus claiming that he is "not subject to Torah," but he *is* subject to the "ultimate law of God" (p. 137). The latter should perhaps be regarded as the equivalent of the "law of Christ" in verse 21: "the law of God which at one stage and on one level finds expression in the Torah, may at another stage and on a different level find expression in the 'law of Christ'" (p. 137).

What, more concretely, is the "law of Christ"? It would seem (Dodd argues) from its usage in Galatians 6:2 at the conclusion of a section of injunctions that "it can be stated in the form of a code of precepts to which a Christian man is obliged to conform" (p. 138). Its connection with the Mosaic code may perhaps be described by saying that the "ultimate law of God can be discerned in the Torah when it is interpreted by Christ" (p. 139).[7] Paul's use (explicit in some passages and to be inferred in others) of commands of (the earthly) Jesus must mean that such concrete precepts would be a part of the "law of Christ" ("the solid, historical and creative nucleus of the whole," p. 148).[8]

It appears therefore that to "fulfil the law of Christ" means a good deal more than simply to act "in a Christian spirit" (as we say). It connotes the intention to carry out—in a different setting and in altered circumstances, it is true—the precepts which Jesus Christ was believed to have given to his disciples, and which they handed down in the Church. This is to be *ennomos Christou*. (p. 147)

For Dodd, then, the writings of early Christianity including those of the apostle Paul provide ample justification for speaking of law as a part of Christian ethics. David Daube supports the same conclusion, though from different considerations.

---

### David Daube

---

The published works of David Daube defy classification. His contributions to biblical studies (not his primary field of competence, though the phrase has little meaning in this case) include important lexicographical, form-critical, and more traditional exegetical studies as well as illuminating discussions in the history and nature of biblical law. Yet in spite of the broad range of topics which Daube addresses, his work is always that of an informed scholar, never that of a dilettante. Moreover, though much of what he has written is startling in its originality, one never suspects that novelty is being pursued for its own sake. Careful marshalling of the evidence and balanced argumentation mark everything he has written.

When all this has been said, however, it remains true that Daube has written little that is directly pertinent to our subject.[9] We may confine our attention here to two significant studies.

(1) Daube has noted similarities between the form of the antitheses in Matthew 5 and rabbinic formulas.[10] "In Rabbinic discussion, *shome'a 'ani*, 'I hear,' 'I understand,' or rather, 'I might understand,' introduces an interpretation of Scripture which, though conceivable, yet must be rejected" (p. 55). Often it involves a "primitive, narrow, literal" understanding of the text (p. 55). The correct understanding is then usually introduced by the verb *'amar*, "to say." The "setting in life is academic, dialectic exegesis" (p. 57). In Matthew 5, we see as well the introduction of a conceivable but unacceptable interpretation of scripture with the verb "to hear"; the approved understanding follows the verb "to say." Here, however, the "tone is not academic but final, prophetic, maybe somewhat defiant" (p. 58). Jesus is the "supreme authority," and the setting in life is the "proclamation of true law" (p. 58). The distinction should not, however, be too rigidly drawn, since rabbinic exegesis might be "tantamount to legislation" as well (p. 59). And Jesus, though "leg-

islating," is also portrayed as interpreting Torah, revealing its "fuller meaning for a new age" (p. 60). Daube does not explore the wider implications of his study; nonetheless it forms an important background for Davies' work on the Sermon on the Mount.

(2) In an impressive "appended note" to E. G. Selwyn's commentary on First Peter,[11] Daube developed the thesis that the usage of the participle as an imperative in the New Testament *Haustafeln* is inadequately explained as a Hellenistic development and is better seen as reflecting the usage of the participle in Tannaitic Hebrew, where it is common in rules of conduct.[12] In Section IV of Part II of his *The New Testament and Rabbinic Judaism* Daube makes some interesting comments about the nature of *halakah* and (by implication, at least) early Christian paraenesis on the basis of the "participle of the correct practice."

The usage of the participle in an imperatival sense, Daube notes, is not found in the Old Testament, that is, in the "age of authoritative revelation" (p. 91). It is common, however, in the later period when "all further legislation bore the character of interpretation and stabilization of custom." The suggestion is made that "the form reflects the Rabbinic view of the secondary, derivative, less absolute nature of post-Biblical rules" (ibid.). It expresses

the course to be taken in accordance with proper interpretation and custom. . . . There was a wide gulf between the Bible, the direct word of God, and Rabbinic elaboration and systematization; and the Rabbis, conscious of it, evolved their own form, significantly different from the forceful imperatives and imperfects of the Old Testament. (p. 92)

Since the participle in itself is not a direct command, it represents rather a statement of correct practice than an order, and must have been employed (originally) among an "élite" where the "right thing, provided only it is known, is done" (p. 94). The form "appeals to the self-respect of a superior group. . . . Clearly it would accord with the attitude of the early Pharisees: they were the *perushim*, 'those who kept apart'" (p. 94).

Similar considerations determined the rabbis' use of the term *halakah* for "a binding rule" as it was defined in early Tannaitic times. The term is not used in the Old Testament, where "judgments," "statutes" or "commandments" were enjoined. These the rabbis

did not feel entitled to lay down. . . . Their main task was a subordinate one: to interpret, elaborate, protect by a "fence" and order the traditional material. . . . In other words, they had carefully to work out the proper course to take in any set of circumstances, the *halakhah*, the walking expected of a man who desired to do the right thing. (p. 97)

Finally, Daube suggests that the same principles were operative in early Christianity, where the "participles of the correct practice" were adopted, as among the early rabbis. The participles appear in directions as to the proper behaviour of members of the new Christian society: they appeal to the pride of those addressed—"that ye walk worthy of the vocation wherewith ye are called"; they are meant for a small group only, for the elect. . . . Everything points to the existence of early Christian codes of duties in Hebrew, from which the participles of the correct practice crept into the Greek of the epistles. Freedom in the spirit did not relieve the Church of the necessity of insisting on a definite moral order. (p. 102-103)

The final two statements, which we may take as the critical ones, do not of course depend on the rather more subjective judgments that precede them.[13] And the concluding remark—that Christian "freedom" did not do away with the need for "insisting on a definite moral order"—may be allowed to serve as a transition to our study of W. D. Davies, for whom it is fundamental.

## W. D. Davies

Even a brief summary of each of the many works of W. D. Davies related to our topic is here out of the question. We will confine our remarks to his views on the Messianic Torah as it was understood in Judaism, Paul and the gospel of Matthew. In the process, most of what is distinctive and significant about his approach will, I believe, at least be touched upon.

### The Messianic Torah in Judaism[14]

Since the early Christians believed that Messiah had come, Davies proposes that a study of the views held in Judaism about the status of Torah in the Messianic age might illuminate the attitudes adopted in the early church toward the law. He concedes that the overwhelmingly predominant view in the sources is that the (Mosaic) Torah is immutable and eternal, and that it will remain in full force in Messianic times. Yet he is obviously concerned to discover whether there might nevertheless be traces of an expectation that Torah's status would undergo some change or that a Messianic Torah would be forthcoming.

A peril immediately apparent lurks in the simple fact that no one who searches the enormous body of literature (Old Testament, Apocrypha, Pseudepigrapha and rabbinic texts) for support for a given theory is likely to come away empty-handed. Still, anyone familiar with the painstaking care which Davies shows in presenting a balanced view on every issue will not be overly concerned on that account. And rightly so, for Davies' conclusions are qualified by prudent reminders that the dominant view differs from those he has detected, that the sources are in many cases late and their interpretation uncertain.

Davies arrives at the following conclusions: (1) "There are a few passages which suggest the cessation in the messianic age of certain enactments concerning sacrifices and the festivals." Other texts "suggest changes in the laws concerning things clean and unclean."[15] These modifications, however, were understood within the context of the existing Torah, which continues to be valid. (2) In the Messianic age, there would be a clearer understanding of the (already existing, Mosaic) law; its difficulties and incomprehensibilities would be explained. (3) Some rabbis believed that Gentiles would submit to the yoke of Torah in the Messianic age. (4) There is some evidence (late, but earlier views along these lines may have been suppressed) for the expectation of a new law in the Messianic age. Other texts suggest the abrogation of the Mosaic Torah at that time.[16] Thus "we can at least affirm that there were elements inchoate in the Messianic hope of Judaism, which could make it possible for some to regard the Messianic Age as marked by a New Torah."[17] And in fact, Davies claims, Matthew and Paul did see in the words of Jesus the "basis of a new halakah."[18]

## The Messianic Torah in Paul[19]

Before focussing attention on the particular subject under discussion, we may note briefly several aspects of Davies' picture of Paul. The main thrust of his *Paul and Rabbinic Judaism* is that "Paul belonged to the main stream of first-century Judaism, and that elements in his thought often labelled as Hellenistic, might well be derived from Judaism" (p. 1). "Paul is grounded in an essentially Rabbinic world of thought"; he was, "in short, a Rabbi become Christian and was therefore primarily governed both in life and thought by Pharisaic concepts, which he had baptized 'into Christ'" (p. 16). In fact, Paul remained a Pharisee, and "observed the Law, and that in the pharisaic manner, throughout his life" (p. 70). "Paul throughout his life might be described as a Pharisee who had accepted Jesus as the Messiah, i.e., he was living in the Messianic Age which preceded the Age to Come" (p. 71-72). Here, and not in Paul's attack on the old Torah or even in his doctrine of justification by faith, lies the centre of Paul's thought.

With this background in mind, we turn to Davies' well-known view that for Paul, Jesus himself represents a "New Torah."

1. What Davies means by this equation includes (though it is not exhausted by) the statement that Jesus had come to occupy the place in Paul's life once taken by Torah. "In a real sense conformity to Christ, His teaching and His life, has taken the place for Paul of conformity to the Jewish Torah" (p. 148). "For St. Paul the person

and teaching of Jesus had replaced the Torah as the centre of his religious life, and had assumed for him, therefore, the character of a New Torah" (p. 172). Such statements could be multiplied, but it would be pointless to do so. Had Davies meant no more by his celebrated equation than that Paul's life, once centred around Torah, was now centred around Christ, his terminology might have been questioned, but scarcely the sentiment.

2. But Davies means more. For one thing, Paul must have thought of Christ as a "New Torah" since he ascribes to Christ attributes which Judaism ascribed to Torah (p. 147-76). Here Davies is thinking of the attributes of "pre-existence and participation in the creation of the universe as well as the moral discipline or redemption of mankind" (p. 172). For the description of Christ in these terms, the crucial text is of course Colossians 1:15-20, and Davies has been criticized for assuming the authenticity of Colossians and hence the admissibility of its evidence.[20] In any case, his suggestions as to the background for the Christology of Colossians 1 represent a credible view of the matter. Still, when Davies speaks of Christ as the "new Torah" he means more than that attributes once applied to the Mosaic code are now used of Jesus.

3. Paul "recognized in the words of Christ a *nomos tou Christou* which formed for him the basis for a kind of Christian Halakah. When he used the phrase *nomos tou Christou* he meant that the actual words of Jesus were for him a New Torah" (p. 144). Elsewhere Davies sees in the "law of the Messiah" a "comprehensive expression for the totality of the ethical teaching of Jesus that had come down to Paul as authoritative."[21] Clearly, for Davies, gospel and law are not to be pitted against each other.[22] On the contrary, Paul's understanding of the Christian life is "patterned after that of Judaism" (p. xxx) as seen in the Exodus tradition: here not only redemption, but also the subsequent giving of commands to God's redeemed people play a part. Hence, when Davies speaks of Christ as being the "New Torah" for Paul he means that Christians, like God's people under the Mosaic dispensation, are subject to "law" as defined by and in the person of Christ.[23]

Several points call for clarification.

First of all, what more particularly is the content of this "New Torah" which is binding on Christians? The equation between Jesus' *words* and the law of Christ perhaps suggested by the first quotation under (3) above is in fact too narrow. Davies makes it clear that it was "the totality of [Christ's] life, death, and resurrection, the Living Person," that constituted the New Torah (p. xxxiii).[24] "When Paul refers to himself as an imitator of Christ he is doubtless thinking of Jesus as the Torah he has to copy—both in his words and deeds."[25]

Second, what is the relation between the "New" and the Mosaic
Torah? Christ is the New Torah, Davies tells us, "not in the sense
that he contravened the old but that he revealed its true character,
or put it in a new light" (p. xxxiv). Paul "was no antinomian." On
the other hand, he did sit "lightly to certain specific commandments, and while he elsewhere retains others they do not play an
important, and certainly not an independent, part in his thinking.
He brings the legal tradition of his fathers before the judgment seat
of the *agapē* of Christ and thereby achieves an immense and
penetrating simplification of it."[26]

Third, in spite of the "New Torah" terminology he employs
Davies is fully aware that Paul "did not formulate a 'Christian-
rabbinic' casuistry on the basis of the words of Jesus that he had
received."[27]

---

### The Messianic Torah in Matthew

---

Here we begin with a summary of an important article dealing with
Matthew 5:17-18.[28] How Matthew understood the statement in 5:17
is clear in the light of the whole passage (5:17-48) to which it serves
as an introduction. Jesus is seen in a "legislative cloak," "fulfilling"
the law by inaugurating a "New Torah which included specific commandments which He Himself promulgated" (p. 34).[29] What is particularly interesting here, however, is Davies' suggestion that it is
possible to find a setting for these verses in the ministry of Jesus.
Matthew's view of Jesus as lawgiver is said to have been his own;
Jesus did not regard himself as "having legislative functions"
(p. 44). Jesus' essential attitude to the law is revealed in those
antitheses where the law's demands are deepened "to the $n$th degree," and brought to their "eschatological or ultimate fulfilment"
(p. 44). In this sense, 5:17 is possible on the lips of Jesus. What was
the basis of Jesus' proclamation of God's demands? Davies finds a
claim to be Messiah implicit in Jesus' words (the "I" of 5:22, etc., is
said to be "Messianic" and Jesus' interpretation of divorce is taken
to imply the inauguration of a new creation, i.e., the Messianic age)
and suggests that Jesus' proclamation of the will of God is the expression of his "intuitive awareness" of what it is (p. 46).[30]

But Matthew 5:18 is also possible on the lips of Jesus, spoken ("in
a spirit, no doubt, of hyperbole") perhaps to counter "irresponsible
iconoclastic elements among the crowds who followed Him" (p. 52),
and perhaps even to conciliate and enlist the support of Pharisees at
some early stage in his ministry. That the law is said to stand "while
heaven and earth last" is perhaps to be interpreted in line with the
Pauline teaching that the dispensation of the law ended with the
death of Christ: the old law remains in force while the present order

endures. Davies thinks it beyond dispute that "at some point in the Ministry Jesus became convinced of the necessity of His death," and that he came to regard himself as the suffering servant of Deutero-Isaiah (p. 55). As the servant, Jesus would expect to bring his own Torah (cf. Isa. 42:4). Yet "only through death could He justify Himself as Servant and thus bring into being a New Torah to transcend the old" (p. 56).

> Before His death He could, by word and deed, give signs that there was now a deeper Torah to be obeyed than the old, and in private, among His disciples, He could explicitly annul parts of the old Torah, but He would not explicitly state this in public: although the sheer pressure of human need sometimes led Him to break the Law openly. But after His death the principle of freedom from the Old Law would ultimately be established. (p. 59)

We turn now, briefly, to the understanding of Jesus revealed in the gospel of Matthew as a whole.[31] We may (Davies argues) quite rightly use the designation "law" to describe Jesus' ethic as presented in the first gospel: the Christian life is one of discipleship (a term drawn from the religion of law, though, to be sure, the category is transcended in the relationship between Christ as *Lord* and his followers); Christ's "yoke" is to be carried (which, for Davies, implies the existence of a law of Christ). In fact, the Sermon on the Mount is seen as the "'law' of Jesus, the Messiah and Lord," a Messianic Torah given on a mountain—though Matthew avoids the *express* concept of a New Torah and a New Sinai (p. 108). This Messianic Torah is not new in the sense that it is *different* from the Mosaic law; it is rather a new interpretation of the old. "Not antithesis but completion expresses the relationship between the Law of Moses and the teaching of Jesus" (p. 107). Yet Jesus' words are certainly regarded as binding law. "In some rabbinic circles the Messiah had a didactic function. And it is this emphasis that Matthew found congenial. His is, in this sense, a rabbinic Christ, whose words were for him *halakah* and the ground for *halakah* both for Israel and for the Gentile world" (p. 189).

Davies' famous explanation of the sermon's *Sitz im Leben* may here be noted briefly. While the original *Sitz im Leben* of elements in the Sermon on the Mount involved Jesus' encounter with sectarian Judaism, its present form and purpose are dictated rather by the Pharisaic-Christian encounter after 70 C.E. With characteristic reserve Davies only claims that

> one fruitful way of dealing with the Sermon on the Mount is to regard it as the Christian answer to Jamnia. . . . It was the desire and necessity to present a formulation of the way of the New Israel at a time when the rabbis were engaged in a parallel task for the Old Israel that provided the outside stimulus for the Evangelist to shape the Sermon on the Mount. (p. 315)

Finally, we must note Davies' discussion of what "happened" to the words of Jesus when they were used in a regulatory manner, as in the Matthean material. "The demands of Jesus were initially preserved . . . because they constituted an indispensable part of the Gospel itself without which it could not be adequately comprehended in its moral seriousness. In other words, they were essential as revelatory of the nature of the Gospel" (p. 413). The ethical teaching of Jesus as preserved in Q remained radical and uncompromising—and largely unadapted to catechetical needs. Yet in the Matthean special material there is repeated evidence of how Jesus' words have been made "practicable" and "regulatory." Davies finds a "tendency to present Jesus as a practical legislator, who has his feet on the ground. The radicalism of his absolute ethic, as revealed in Q, is softened" (p. 396). The M material shows the attempt to make Jesus' teaching "applicable . . . to the problems of daily living. . . . In the process it took what was radical, modified it, and made it regulatory. The process wherein this happened is contained and continued in the Christian-rabbinism of Matthew, where we see slowly emerging a neo-legalistic society" (p. 401).

Does this represent a serious distortion of Jesus' intention? Davies thinks not. For one thing, we must not too readily assume that Jesus himself was "always merely concerned with proclaiming the eschatological demand and not also, sometimes, with the contingencies of existence" (p. 434). Perhaps Jesus did give "directions for the actualities of life as well as words of crisis" (p. 398). In any case, Matthew is right in showing "that there is a demand, as well as succour, at the heart of the Gospel" (p. 433). For "nowhere in the New Testament is the Gospel set forth without moral demand" (p. 435).

## Conclusion

This is a suitable note on which to conclude the chapter. It is a great merit in the writings of all three scholars that they have emphasized the element of moral demand which is both inherent in the concept of a new covenant and expressed in all parts of the New Testament. Whether the presence of moral demand entitles us to speak of "law" in Christian ethics depends largely, no doubt, on what we mean by "law." It may be worthwhile, by way of summation, to remind ourselves once again of some of the reasons why the introduction of the term is widely viewed with misgivings.

(1) The normal (though admittedly not the exclusive) use of "law" in the New Testament is with reference to the Mosaic code; and a crucial issue there raised is the question of its validity and applicability to members of the new faith. Opinions on the matter differed

sharply in the earliest church; still it is noteworthy that none of the writings of the New Testament canon enjoins in any straightforward way the observance of the Mosaic law. Matthew preserves evidence of the most conservative position (assuming that Matt. 5:19 refers to the commandments of Torah); but the same gospel records Jesus' radical reinterpretation of Torah's statutes, including the claim that certain of its provisions, while necessitated by human evil, fall short of God's will (5:31-32, 33-37; 19:3-9); furthermore, Matthew suggests that some matters of the law are "weightier" than others (23:23), that the love commandments are the essential demands (22:34-40), and that those who rigidly adhere to the letter of the Mosaic code are frequently found to oppose God's purposes (Matt. 12:7; cf. 9:13).

The Johannine writings[32] provide another witness to the way in which parts of the early church distanced themselves from the Mosaic law. "The law was given through Moses" (John 1:17); it is consistently spoken of as the law of the Jews ("*your* law," in the disputes of the Johannine Jesus with "the Jews," 8:17; 10:34; cf. 7:19; and, even more tellingly, "their law" in words spoken to his disciples, 15:25). But with Jesus Christ has come a new age marked by "grace and truth" (1:17); its ethic is summed up in the "new commandment" which Christ left for his church: "that you love one another" (13:34). The Mosaic law is not used as the basis of obligations placed upon Christians. And though this may in part be due to shifts in time and milieu which have made the Jewish law seem irrelevant, it should also be noted that any dependence on the law for moral guidance would contradict Johannine principles.[33] Those who come to Jesus are said to be taught by God (6:45), to have an "anointing" which obviates the need of teaching from without (1 John 2:20, 27). Here, then, there is no trace of any sense that believers are subject to the Mosaic law.

The epistle to the Hebrews also expresses the conviction that the old dispensation is passing away, that a new has taken its place (8:13) — and that the change affects the law as well: "For when there is a change in the priesthood, there is necessarily a change in the law as well" (7:12). The message once declared by angels had its validity, "and every transgression or disobedience received a just retribution"; but a new revelation and a great salvation now obtain, and it is these which must be heeded (2:1-4). To be sure, the specific ordinances mentioned as obsolete are of a ritual rather than moral nature. But the writer to the Hebrews clearly shared the conviction that the binding force of all parts of a code of law stood or fell together (cf. 7:12; Jas. 2:10; Gal. 5:3); and it may be noted again that the Christian's obligation is never stated in terms of fulfilling the Mosaic law.

And then there are the letters of Paul! While it may be true that for Matthew the Christian is subject to the Old Testament law *as interpreted by Christ*, the same can scarcely be said of Paul. In his writings we find the categorical insistence that Christians have been set free from that law (Rom. 6:14; 7:4-6; Gal. 4:5, etc.), which was intended (to bring "knowledge of sin," Rom. 3:20; and even to make sin worse, Rom. 5:20; cf. 7:7-11; Gal. 3:19) only for the period before God's "children" came of age (Gal. 3:19, 23-25; 4:1-6). The ethical portions of Paul's letter do not comprise Christian reinterpretations of Old Testament statutes (though the latter are very occasionally cited as corroboration). Rather Paul is concerned to work out the implications of the new life "in Christ," of "walking in the Spirit"; and the Spirit is introduced in an explicit contrast with the written Mosaic code as determining Christian moral behaviour (Rom. 7:6; 2 Cor. 3:6; Gal. 5:18; cf. Phil. 3:3).[34]

Finally, we should note that there are roots in the life and teaching of Jesus himself to these early Christian attitudes toward the Mosaic code. Jesus did not explicitly speak of its abrogation;[35] nonetheless there is a perceptible difference between the Torah-centred piety of the Pharisees of his day, where life in all its aspects was to be governed by the interpretation and application of Torah's statutes, and that commended by Jesus. On the one hand, Jesus consistently downplayed the importance of certain areas of Torah's legislation (e.g., regulations concerning ritual purity, tithing and the sabbath); he proclaimed the good news of God's salvation to "sinners" who did not comply with such laws without suggesting that they need observe them. On the other hand, the demands he made on his followers focussed on the attitude of the heart. The latter must, of course, find expression in deeds (a good tree bears good fruit!), but only the general character of such deeds is outlined. There is no attempt to make of Torah an exhaustive code of behaviour.

Since the New Testament uses "law" primarily of the Mosaic code and both explicitly and frequently distinguishes the ethos of the new age from the "law" which expressed the essence of the old, it is, to say the least, misleading when scholars such as Dodd and Davies insist that "law" plays an identical role under the new covenant to that which it played in the old.

(2) But if the status of the Mosaic law is problematic does there not remain the "law of Christ"? Does not Jesus himself make demands on his followers, while the New Testament epistles address commands to their readers?

The answer to these questions is, of course, yes. Christian "freedom" is not construed as autonomy; moral demands are a regular feature of the New Testament writings; believers are clearly to do the will of God, and that will, in certain circumstances at least, is found sufficiently concrete to permit formulation in precise prescriptions. Still, to speak of an ethic of law would seem to imply not simply the recognition of certain moral obligations but also the existence of a code whose provisions represent an authoritative and (more or less) comprehensive statement of that obligation, to be interpreted and applied as the need arises. It is here that questions multiply.

The early Christians did recognize figures of authority whose judgment was consulted and given in matters of doubt. But, in New Testament times at least, nothing like a comprehensive code emerges. References to a "law of Christ" (Gal. 6:2; cf. 1 Cor. 9:21) are apparently *ad hoc* and somewhat polemical formulations, suggesting that the authority recognized by Christians is not Mosaic but that of Christ; there is really no evidence that anything like a particular code of prescriptions was in mind.[36] That the paraenetic sections of the epistles employ common patterns and motifs is certainly of interest; but the differences which remain are themselves indicative of the fact that no single authoritative code was being promulgated. Furthermore, there are indications that the absence of a code is no mere accidental oversight but consistent with the peculiar genius of early Christian faith.

(3) "The law," for the early Christians was the Mosaic code. Divinely given, its commands were acknowledged to be "holy and just and good" (Rom. 7:12). The various critical postures adopted toward Torah are scarcely based on a sense that its provisions can be improved upon and a more adequate code devised. At stake are, on the one hand, a sensitivity toward the weaknesses inherent in any ethic based upon law and, on the other, a sense that the age of the law belongs to the past.

As noted earlier the Jesus of the gospel tradition faults contemporary piety on precisely those counts to which a code-oriented ethic is liable: a merely external observance of statutes, the failure to distinguish between matters of greater and lesser importance, pride in one's achievements in observing the code. Moreover, Jesus himself did not identify the will of God in any direct way with observance of the prescriptions of Torah: large areas of Torah's demands are downplayed or ignored in Jesus' proclamation while certain provisions of Torah are found positively inadequate as statements of God's will. Finally, we should recall Dodd's comments about the impossibility of reducing Jesus' own demands to a prescriptive code, given their open-ended as well as poetic character. The gospel tradition thus presents a formidable obstacle to the understanding of Christian ethics as "law."

Paul's writings prove still more obstinate. Law served a purpose during the "minority" of God's appointed heirs; but that era has now passed (Gal. 3:23-4:7). The mark of the new age is hardly a revised or updated edition of the law but rather, and in explicit contrast with the Mosaic code, "freedom" and the life in the Spirit (Rom. 7:1-6; 2 Cor. 3:6, 17; Gal. 5:1-4, 18, etc.). In principle at least, all foods are declared "clean" (Rom. 14:14; 1 Cor. 10:25-26), the observance of any day is indifferent (Rom. 14:5), "all things are yours" (1 Cor. 3:21-22), "all things are lawful" (1 Cor. 6:12; 10:23). Such statements admit qualifications, to be sure: not everything is profitable, consideration is to be taken for the needs of others, and so on. But the fundamental declarations of freedom remain, and they seem scarcely compatible with the existence of a code prescribing and proscribing certain kinds of behaviour.

The confidence of the New Testament writers that no comprehensive code is needed rests not in their perception of the moral sensitivity and maturity of their converts but in their assurance that the new age has begun, that the Spirit of God has been given. There is no doubt that authoritative figures felt entitled to interpret God's will for others; but there are also indications that at times they felt reticent to do so, hesitating either at the need or even the propriety of issuing directives to believers who themselves possessed God's spirit (cf. Rom. 15:14-15; 1 Cor. 10:15; 2 Cor. 1:24; Phil. 3:15; 1 Thess. 4:9; 1 John 2:27). Thus fundamental Christian convictions are at stake whenever the attempt is made to draw up and impose a code of Christian behaviour.

Yet for some the "antinomian" danger is paramount. Two thousand years of untransformed history have taken their toll on the early Christian sense of belonging to the "new creation" with moral resources unknown to Adamic humanity. Hence Christian writers often evidence the dilemma of the independent-minded toddler: the call to freedom is fearful, yet it refuses to be suppressed.

## Notes

1  F. W. Dillistone, *C. H. Dodd: Interpreter of the New Testament* (Grand Rapids: Eerdmans, 1977), p. 149.

2  *The Background of the New Testament and its Eschatology: In Honour of Charles Harold Dodd* (Cambridge: Cambridge University Press, 1956).

3  *Donum Gentilicium: New Testament Studies in Honour of David Daube* (Oxford: Clarendon, 1978).

4  *Jews, Greeks and Christians: Religious Cultures in Late Antiquity. Essays in Honor of William David Davies* (Leiden: Brill, 1976).

5  C. H. Dodd, *Gospel and Law* (New York: Columbia University Press, 1951).

6  C. D. Dodd, "*Ennomos Christou*," in his *More New Testament Studies* (Manchester: University Press, 1968), p. 134-48.

7  Cf. C. H. Dodd, "Natural Law in the New Testament," in C. H. Dodd, *New Testament Studies* (Manchester: University Press, 1953), p. 142.

8  By way of anticipation of our discussion of W. D. Davies, the following quotation is of interest: "Maxims which formed part of the tradition of the sayings of Jesus are treated as if they were in some sort elements of a new Torah" (*"Ennomos Christou,"* p. 145).

9  One suspects that his greatest contribution here has been in guiding and subjecting to rigorous cross-examination the thinking of his colleagues!

10  Page references throughout the section on Daube are to his *The New Testament and Rabbinic Judaism* (London: Athlone Press, 1956).

11  E. G. Selwyn, *The First Epistle of St. Peter*, 2nd ed. (London: Macmillan, 1947), p. 467-88.

12  Daube's explanation has won widespread acceptance. Note however the critical remarks of V. P. Furnish, *Theology and Ethics in Paul* (Nashville: Abingdon, 1968), p. 39.

13  See ibid., p. 41-42, for a criticism of the characterization of early Christianity involved.

14  See especially W. D. Davies, *Torah in the Messianic Age and/or the Age to Come* (Philadelphia: Society of Biblical Literature, 1952), and also his *The Setting of the Sermon on the Mount* (Cambridge: Cambridge University Press, 1964), p. 109-90.

15  W. D. Davies, "Law in First-Century Judaism," *The Interpreter's Dictionary of the Bible* (Nashville: Abingdon, 1962), Vol. 3, p. 95.

16  For this latter interpretation Davies has been especially criticized. Cf. E. P. Sanders, *Paul and Palestinian Judaism* (Philadelphia: Fortress, 1977), p. 479 and the literature there cited.

17  Davies, *Torah*, p. 85.

18  Ibid., p. 92.

19  Page references in the following section are from Davies' *Paul and Rabbinic Judaism*.

20  Ibid., p. xxxii-xxxiii, where Davies replies that the authenticity of Colossians is at least an open question, and that there are clear anticipations of Wisdom Christology elsewhere in Paul.

21  Davies, *Setting*, p. 353.

22  Cf. Davies, *Paul*, p. xxvii-xxxviii.

23  Cf. Davies, *Setting*, p. 352.

24  Cf. Davies, "The Moral Teaching of the Early Church," *Jewish and Pauline Studies* (Philadelphia: Fortress, 1984), p. 278-88.

25  Davies, *Setting*, p. 364.

26  W. D. Davies, "Paul and the Law," in Morna Hooker and S. G. Wilson, eds., *Paul and Paulinism*, C. K. Barrett Festschrift (London: S.P.C.K., 1982), p. 12.

27  Davies, *Setting*, p. 366.

28  W. D. Davies, "Matthew 5:17, 18," in *Christian Origins and Judaism* (Philadelphia: Westminster, 1962), p. 31-66.

29  Cf. the discussion in *Setting* as to whether Matthew intended to present Jesus as the "new Moses." There is, Davies concludes, some slight evidence that Jesus is presented "after the manner of Moses, albeit a Moses whom he supersedes as 'the unique and definitive teacher of mankind'" (p. 56). Jesus is seen not as Moses come as Messiah so much as Messiah who has absorbed the Mosaic function (p. 93).

30  Ibid., p. 432.

31  Page references are from *Setting*.

32 The following two paragraphs are taken from my article "The Law and the 'Just Man' (1 Tim 1:3-11)," *Studia Theologica*, 36 (1982): 87.

33 Cf. B. Gerhardsson, *The Ethos of the Bible* (Philadelphia: Fortress, 1981), p. 108-109.

34 Cf. my article "Letter and Spirit." That the results of Christian moral behaviour in the Spirit are not opposed by Law (Gal. 5:23) but in fact fulfil the requirement of righteousness set forth in Torah (Rom. 8:4; 13:8-10; Gal. 5:14) does not mean that Christians find in Torah binding prescriptions for their conduct; cf. my article "On Fulfilling the Whole Law (Gal. 5:14)," *Svensk Exegetisk Årsbok*, 51-52 (1986-87): 229-37.

35 What follows is again taken from my "The Law and the 'Just Man,'" p. 86-87.

36 Cf. H. Räisänen, *Paul and the Law* (Philadelphia: Fortress, 1986), p. 77-82.

# Chapter 6

# *Torah* and Early Christian Groups

### F. C. Baur

The range of attitudes toward the Jewish law which may have been present in early Christianity has been explored in great detail as a focus of 19th- and 20th-century research into the development of the church in the New Testament period. Evidence for diverse attitudes has been culled from the full range of early Christian sources, but amongst these the Pauline corpus and the book of Acts have played the leading role. The key conflicts over Jewish law attested in the earliest literature concern the applicability to the Christian church of circumcision and purity laws, particularly purity laws having to do with eating. Since F. C. Baur's epoch-making dialectic theory of the evolution of the early church, different positions on these key issues have generally been seen as reflecting different tendencies or groups within early Christianity. The theories which have arisen since Baur's work combine tendencies or groups in various ways to explain the rise of the early catholic church. This chapter outlines the attitude toward the Jewish law of the tendencies or groups postulated by each of five of the most influential of the theories of early church development.

While the research reviewed in this chapter often discusses Jewish law as a general concept, when the discussion becomes more specific its subject is almost always those aspects which reflect Jewish particularism, or at least Jewish particularism as understood in the 19th and 20th century. Even within this area, discussion is further generally restricted to what has often been called "ritual purity law." Other aspects of Torah-observance are not considered to any major extent until about the time of Jean Daniélou. All the authors surveyed here assume that the groups or parties they set out would

---

Notes for Chapter 6 appear on pages 106-107. This chapter was prepared by Michael Pettem.

have demanded observance of a high standard of ethical or moral conduct. The theoretical basis for this, of course, would have varied from group to group. The aspect of law explicitly discussed by the authors reviewed here does correspond to a major point of friction in the early Christian community as recorded by our earliest sources.

F. C. Baur's goal in tracing the early history of Christianity is to understand the development of mankind's religious consciousness.[1] The motor which moves the process of development forward is the dialectical clash of thesis and antithesis giving rise to a synthesis. In the early history of Christianity the thesis is a particularistic Jewish Christianity; it is oriented toward one nation and expresses itself in the forms of Jewish cult. These forms characteristically include circumcision, obedience to the Mosaic Law and certain regulations respecting relations with gentiles. The antithesis might be called Hellenistic Christianity, Paulinism or (due to the element which quickly predominated) gentile Christianity. This Christianity is universalizing, tending to include all nations and expressing itself in forms not limited by Jewish tradition. It would not see any further need for circumcision or obedience to the Mosaic Law, nor would it countenance any discrimination in relations between Jewish and gentile Christians. The synthesis, early catholic Christianity, maintains the universalizing aspect of gentile Christianity and the historical roots and ecclesiastical structure of Jewish Christianity while tempering the stress on faith versus works of the former and rejecting the Jewish exclusiveness of the latter.

Baur is able to trace an outline of the development of the early church consistent with his theory, following the account of the book of Acts. The earliest Christian community in Jerusalem was made up of both Hebrew and Hellenist Jews. The Hebrews continued, as Christians, to identify with the Jewish nation and culture and to observe the Jewish law. The Hellenists had a more universalist view of religion. Their new perspective was first clearly expressed by Stephen, whose challenge to Judaism necessitated the flight of the Hellenists from Jerusalem. In their new surroundings the Hellenists' universalizing principle found expression in their preaching of the gospel to gentiles. Their movement came to flower in the thought and career of Paul, who preached Christianity as a universal religion, not bound by the particularism of the Mosaic Law.

The two views of the shape of the Christian religion in general, and particularly its relation to the Jewish law, clashed in Antioch. This confrontation and the subsequent meeting in Jerusalem led to the recognition and theoretical acceptance of each group by the other. The Jewish Christian party, led by James, Peter and John, was to preach to Jews a gospel including full observance of Torah, while the gentile Christian party, spearheaded by Paul, was to preach to the gentiles a gospel not including observance of Torah. Paul travelled west preaching this gentile Christianity. Jewish, law-observant Christianity spread throughout the Empire, and most especially to Rome, by the natural medium of the Jewish Diaspora. Although the two parties in theory accepted each other, in practice they came into very sharp conflict. This was particularly the case when, as in Galatia, members of the Jewish Christian party were at least partly successful in convincing gentiles that they must obey the whole Jewish law.

The synthesis of these two approaches to Christianity was worked out in the period following Paul's death. It was brought about by the realization that the two parties really belonged together. The Jewish Christian party had originally insisted on the absolute necessity of circumcision for salvation. As the number of gentiles entering the church became overwhelming, Jewish Christians abandoned this position, and in a move toward Christian universalism replaced circumcision with baptism (this is even the case in the pseudo-Clementine literature). Only a small group of Jewish Christians rejected this accommodation. The next step in this process was marked by the Apostolic Decree, which is dated quite late by Baur. With the promulgation of this decree (a sort of minimum of law) and the substitution of baptism for circumcision, free association between Jewish and gentile Christians became possible. The fellowship thus created brought together the two parties, leaving out only certain backwater movements such as Ebionism. The final, early synthesis included elements from Jewish Christianity, such as the formal ecclesiastical structure including the office of bishop. In this synthesis, however, the principle of universalism had won the day. Ritual purity laws, and any other aspects of *torah* which were not part of the developing human religious consciousness but were rather only part of Judaism, were progressively eliminated.

## Albrecht Ritschl

Baur studied the early history of Christianity to understand the development of mankind's religious consciousness. Ritschl's orientation was very different: at the heart of his study of the history of the early Christian Church is the question of its understanding of mankind's reconciliation to God.[2] This being the case, it is not surprising that the problem of how Christianity related to *torah* is of great importance for Ritschl.

In sharp contrast to Baur, Ritschl does not see the early catholic church as a synthesis of Jewish Christianity and gentile Christianity, but rather as a development of gentile Christianity which had finally separated itself from its Jewish roots. This separation was brought about both by external factors such as culture and politics and by internal factors such as the inordinate demands made by the Jewish Christians on gentile Christians in the Apostolic Decree. Catholic Christianity was not a triumph of "Paulinism" either, since Ritschl by no means ascribes as much significance to Paul as Baur does. The catholic church misunderstood Paul as much as it did Peter, and neither had an overwhelming influence on it.

The divorce of the catholic church from its Jewish roots meant that it lost its context for interpreting the Old Testament presuppositions on which it was built. This led to a drift into a new type of legalism, a legalism which was distinctly Christian and not Pauline or Jewish Christian. From Ritschl's Protestant point of view this loss was by no means religiously neutral but was a real disaster for mankind, a disaster only to be reversed in the Reformation.

We begin with the history of early Christian church, and especially its struggles about the Mosaic Law, as viewed by Ritschl.

The apostles at first followed Jesus' example in going only to Israel, believing perhaps that all Israel must be saved before the entry of the gentiles. Peter's conversion of the Roman centurion Cornelius does not really represent an exception because Cornelius was added to the church as a proselyte. The initial attitude of the Christian church toward the law was set by Jesus himself. He distinguished between two types of laws: those laws which pertain to man's highest end and are therefore permanently and universally binding; and those laws which exist for the sake of men and are therefore *adiaphora*. As long as Christendom was contained within Israel the apostles could not distinguish between the national and the religious facets of the law.

The mission to the gentiles started in Antioch independently of the apostles. In this city gentiles were baptized without being asked to observe the Mosaic Law, but some time thereafter former Pharisees from Jerusalem demanded that they be circumcised and obey the whole law. This demand, Ritschl notes, is an indication of true Jewish Christianity. The original apostles did not support this demand and found themselves in the position of having to oppose and yet conciliate this group. At the meeting held in Jerusalem, attended by Paul and Barnabas as delegates from Antioch, the solution adopted was the Apostolic Decree. The decree is pivotal for Ritschl's understanding of this period. In effect it gave proselyte status to the new converts, thus preserving the priority of the Jews, while still allowing for full recognition of the gentiles as brothers and sisters. Gentile Christians, however, still remained ritually unclean, and thus full table fellowship was not established within the church itself. Ritschl is highly critical of this attempt at a solution:

In dem Dekrete ist eine Norm des mosaischen Gestzes direkt auf die Verhältnisse der christlichen Gemeinde angewendet. Muss man dies nicht so verstehen, dass eigentlich das ganze mosaische Gesetz im Christenthume gilt, jedoch aus äusseren Gründen nur ein Minimum davon bei den Heidenchristen durchgesetzt wird?[3]

The fact is, even James and Peter saw the converted Jews as the true people of the old covenant, and as the core of the new covenant—as we can see even from their letters (which Ritschl accepts as genuine).

The Apostolic Decree made sense in Palestine where most Christians were Jewish. In the Diaspora, however, where most Christians were gentile, full communion locally between Jewish and gentile Christians was more important than full communion between Jewish Christians in the Diaspora and their co-religionists in Palestine. It quickly followed that this full communion was established in the Diaspora on gentile terms, that is to say, without observance of Torah. This practice represents Paul's position. While this was not a formal breach of the Decree it was certainly less than full observance of the law by all Jews, which is of course what James had wanted.

Peter was sympathetic to Paul's position, and when he came down to Antioch he ate with the gentile Christians without concerning himself about their ritual uncleanness. When representatives came from Jerusalem to recall Peter to James's understanding of the Decree, Peter withdrew from such fellowship. Ritschl cannot find indisputable evidence that Peter returned to his position of ignoring questions of ritual purity and to full communion with gentile Christians, but he clearly suspects that Peter did eventually return to that Pauline position. This question is secondary. What is central is that Paul, Peter and even James were in complete agreement that faith in Christ is the condition for admission to the new covenant.

At this point there were essentially two groups within Christianity. The first group recognized faith in Christ as the only condition for full Christianity: within this group we find the Pauline tendency which, while accepting the Apostolic Decree, did not require any further observance of the Mosaic ritual law from anyone; and also the tendency of James, which expected the gentiles to observe the Apostolic Decree and ethnic Jews to observe the whole law. The second major group within Christianity at this time comprised the Jewish Christians in the strict sense of the term, which Ritschl often calls the "*strenge* (as opposed to *milde*) *Judenchristen*." They did not recognize any form of Christianity except that which was based on the Jewish people. Gentiles might therefore become Christians only through circumcision and obedience to the whole Law of Moses. This group of course did not recognize the apostleship of Paul and includes the people to whom Paul refers as demanding the circumcision of Titus and those responsible for the opposition to Paul's work in Galatia. With the passage of time those who held James's position became the Nazarenes, while the extreme Jewish Christians became the Pharisaic and Essene Ebionites.

The reason for the split between what became mainstream Christianity and the "strict" Jewish Christianity is self-evident. "Moderate" Jewish Christianity (the position represented by James), despite the general observance of the Apostolic Decree, still could not accept full communion with gentile Christians. Its influence on gentile Christianity disappeared no later than the Bar-Kochba revolt, when Jewish Christians (with all Jews) were banished from Jerusalem and gentile Christians replaced them there. The positions of Paul and Peter did influence general Christianity, but not to a great extent. The true development of Christianity moved with the current of the increasing gentile majority. It grew in response to factors in the gentile world (such as Gnosticism and Montanism) toward a new type of legalism, a "Christian nomism" as Ritschl calls it, with no relation to Jewish Christianity, and no real appreciation of the Jewish law.

---

## H.-J. Schoeps

---

In the latter part of the 19th and early 20th century, most researchers rallied to a schema which is an amalgam of the two we have been examining. They adopted an analysis similar to Ritschl's of the early groups in Christianity: a strict Jewish Christian group, demanding full observance of the Jewish law by all, which was fairly quickly marginalized; a moderate Jewish Christian group, usually seen as demanding full observance by Jews of the law but observance by gentiles only as outlined in the Apostolic Decree; and a gentile group usually seen as recognizing no Jewish law, or only the Apostolic Decree. Most, however, did not accept Ritschl's conclusion that the catholic church developed almost entirely on a gentile basis; they reintroduced Baur's analysis and applied it to Ritschl's groups. After the strict Jewish Christian group left the mainstream church the moderate Jewish Christian group was made the thesis in this new schema, the gentile Christian group the antithesis, and the early catholic church the synthesis of these two remaining groups. The only major author who consistently maintained Ritschl's position was Adolf Harnack.

The work of H.-J. Schoeps moves within the framework of this early consensus position, yet develops helpful new ideas on early Christian attitudes toward the Jewish law.[4] His analysis of early church development leads him to accept the three positions on Torah outlined above, although he holds that before the time of the flight of the Jerusalem community to Pella these positions were only tendencies and not separate parties. The strict Jewish Christian tendency gained the upper hand in the community after its flight to Pella, and that group eventually developed into the Ebionites.

The position of the middle and late second-century Ebionites on the Jewish law is worked out in detail by Schoeps as a part of his more general research into the theology and history of this group. The Ebionites were all zealots for the law, but after their own peculiar fashion. They intensified the law in several ways. Their practice of vegetarianism overcame imperfections in the ritual slaughter of animals for food. They obeyed a commandment of poverty (their name comes from *'ebyon*, "poor") and communal sharing of goods. Their purification regimen consisted of ritual washings culminating in baptism (distinct from initiatory baptism, which they also practised). On the other hand, they rejected several parts of the Torah, including all animal sacrifice, the Temple and the Israelite monarchy. The rejection of these institutions was squared with their strict law observance by a theory of false pericopae. According to this theory the law and its interpretation were passed from Moses to the seventy, who in turn passed them on (which equals the "oral law," comments Schoeps), but false pericopae were allowed to creep in to test the believers—those whom God loved being led to see the error of these. They finally came to the position that the law was to be judged on the basis of the life and teachings of Jesus. All of Jesus' critique of the law was to bring out again the unity between the law and the will of God.

The position on the Jewish law as outlined by Schoeps is that of the descendants of the strict Jewish Christians in the mid- to late-second century. However, as has already been pointed out, he holds that there were no true parties but only tendencies in the Jerusalem church before the flight to Pella. It follows then that the second-century Ebionite view of the law is descended not just from a party but from the early Jerusalem community. While Schoeps certainly does not suggest that Ebionite views were identical to those of the early Jerusalem community, he does assert that the Ebionite group was as legitimate a successor of the early Jerusalem community as the early catholic church was of Pauline Christianity. Since his area of specialization is Ebionism, he does not work this idea out in detail. It would have been interesting to see what he thought this idea implied for the early Jerusalem community's view of the law.

## Jean Daniélou

It has been a widely held view that Christian theology in the narrow sense of the term first came about when the tenets of Christianity were expressed in the categories of Greek thought. In active rejection of this view Schoeps set himself the task of recording the theology of the Ebionites, who were a Semitic group less open to Greek thought than the gentile Christian church. Daniélou[5] does not agree that the Ebionite group was a legitimate descendant of the Jerusalem community, but he does agree that Semitic thought could produce a Christian theology using only its own genius, without recourse to Greek thought forms. In his view, long before the highly cultured Greek mind reflected on the Christian message and gave us what we now think of as Christian theology the earliest Christian community had produced a theology conceived entirely within the bounds of Semitic thought patterns. The major formal factor in this theology was apocalyptic. It was not until the late second century that a Christian theology worked out in Greek categories began to dominate Christianity. Daniélou's goal is to enrich modern Christianity by recovering and setting out this early, Semitic, Jewish Christian theology.[6]

Daniélou divides the problem of early Christian attitudes toward the Jewish law into two distinct issues, and holds that these two were dealt with in very different ways. The first issue was a religious one and was quickly resolved. According to Daniélou, at the religious level the church developed in one great stream, under the guidance of God and an authoritative leadership. Groups which did not follow the decisions of apostolic councils effectively removed themselves from the main, legitimate stream of the Christian church. Questions concerning the basis of the admission of gentiles and the fundamental significance of the Jewish law for the Christian church would fall into this category. The second issue might best be termed sociological: how was the church to relate to the nation of Israel? This question was resolved over a longer period of time by the fact that as inclusion of gentiles became overwhelming and gentiles took over the leadership, the church naturally moved away from any identification with the nation Israel.

The two aspects of the problem may be illuminated by examining Daniélou's analysis of how the early church dealt with circumcision and table fellowship. The religious question of the circumcision of gentile Christians was resolved in a definitive manner in a few clear steps. The God-fearing gentile Cornelius and the members of his household were filled with the Holy Spirit, and this fact Peter took as authorization to baptize them without any other conditions being imposed (Acts 10:1-11:18). Gentiles in Antioch and in the cities of Paul's first missionary journey were converted to Christianity without being told to keep the Jewish law. When objections were raised, the leaders of the Antioch church sent Paul and Barnabas to Jerusalem to submit the question to the apostles and elders. The meeting in Jerusalem was a fully authoritative apostolic council presided over by Peter, and recounted in Acts 15:1-12 and Galatians 2:1-10. There it was definitively affirmed that salvation is based only on faith in Christ, and the mission to gentiles without the Jewish law was fully vindicated. Though battles may yet have been fought over this question, it was fully resolved for Paul, Peter, James and the whole orthodox church.

The question of circumcision had a second part which belongs to the second aspect of the legal question, the sociological issue. It had been agreed that faith in Christ was the sole basis for membership in the church. It was further generally agreed that this implied that circumcision was unnecessary for gentiles. But what did it imply for Jews? The conclusion for Paul clearly was that circumcision was not necessary for Jewish Christians. The scandal of this position for most Jewish Christians was not at the theoretical but at the sociological level. Not to circumcise their sons, to abandon the Jewish law, would inevitably lead to a break with the Jewish nation. Betrayal of Judaism would have been particularly grave at that time when Jewish nationalism was especially strong and building toward the revolt against Rome. Most Jewish Christians therefore continued to practise Torah. The true question was, then, one of solidarity with the Jewish nation.

In his mission Paul was concerned with presenting the gospel to the gentiles, and with liberating Christianity from Judaism. Peter, on the other hand, was concerned with showing Jewish nationalists that being a Christian was not inconsistent with commitment to the Jewish law and nation. Paul's work brought him into continued and growing conflict with Jewish nationalist Christians; his position was ultimately victorious but only at the terrible price of complete rupture with Judaism.

The incident between Paul and Peter concerning table fellowship took place after the apostolic council's decision on the religious question of circumcision, and in no way called that decision into question. The clash led to another delegation being sent to Jerusalem, but this time the representative of Antioch was Symeon. This meeting in Jerusalem was only a meeting of the local Jewish Christian church presided over by James, and not an apostolic council. The occasion of this meeting is described in Galatians 2:11-14 and the account of it is to be found in Acts 15:13-34. The Symeon mentioned in Acts 15:14 is Symeon the representative of Antioch mentioned in Acts 13:1, and not Simon Peter. The decision, the so-called Apostolic Decree, in effect maintained the idea of food regulations, while reducing them to a minimum.[7] Gentiles converted by Jewish Christians subject to James's authority were instructed to observe this decree. (They also observed the Sabbath, Pentecost, other Jewish feasts and followed Jewish liturgies in their services.)

The Apostolic Decree was, however, merely a disciplinary compromise and proved in the long run to be unworkable.

The position of James and the Jewish Christian church in Jerusalem with regard to table fellowship was not shared by Paul or by the author of the book of Acts. For Paul there was no fundamental reason for any sort of food regulations. The fusion of the two meetings in Jerusalem into one account in the book of Acts (Acts 15:1-35) and the omission of the incident in Antioch make Peter's role in Acts almost that of a precursor and supporter of Paul.

During the whole period of Paul's missions Jewish Christians were still the majority in the church, and thus most Christians would have been law-observant. But the fall of Jerusalem and the consequent blow to Jewish nationalism changed the sociological situation in such a way that Christianity could go its way separate from Judaism. The balance of the church changed from majority Jewish to majority gentile, and by the late second century church leadership was gentile, assuring total rupture with any Jewish legal observances which might have been maintained out of solidarity with Judaism. Certain aspects of Torah-observance, such as the keeping of festivals and some laws not sanctioned by the Christian hierarchy, were maintained at popular levels and in some fringe movements. Some of these observances were re-introduced into the church in the fourth century.

## R. E. Brown

Raymond Brown's view of the development of the early church focusses on the various early Christian communities he identifies on the basis of the New Testament writings.[8] Like Daniélou, Brown does not believe that gentiles made important contributions to the thought of the early church. Drawing the logical conclusion from this he vigorously rejects the idea that there were theological or legal positions in New Testament times which could be called "Jewish Christian" and "gentile Christian." He holds that early Christian theological and legal diversity is to be traced to the varying points of view of the apostles and of the early, ethnically Jewish, Christian evangelists, as well as to differences in the development of the various communities they founded. Each early, ethnically Jewish, Christian community made gentile converts, thus creating various Jewish/gentile communities. Every one had its own distinctive history, including internal debates and occasionally schisms. A given community was usually held together by a moderating centre which reconciled the opposing views as far as possible. In the same way the early catholic church developed from these communities by means of compromise and consensus around a moderate, middle position.

Brown claims the following four types of "Jewish/gentile Christianity" can be clearly identified, each with its own attitude toward the Jewish law: (1) those who believed that circumcision and obedience to the whole Mosaic Law were necessary for full participation in salvation brought by Jesus the Christ; (2) those who did not require circumcision of gentile Christians but did require the observance of some purity law; (3) those who required neither circumcision nor observance of food regulations by gentile Christians (but were not necessarily opposed to such observances by Jewish Christians); (4) those who did not require circumcision or observance of food regulations and had fundamentally broken with all Jewish practices, seeing no lasting significance in the Jewish cult or feasts.

These groups and their legal views in some ways represent an extended and a more nuanced version of the groups set forth in the tradition from Baur and Ritschl to the early consensus. They are, however, in many ways quite different because they are part of a very different schema; that is, they are conceived of as having arisen and interacted in a very different way. Unlike Baur and the early consensus schema Brown does not suppose a three-stage dialectical relationship. Unlike Ritschl he most assuredly does not think that a gentile theological stream quickly predominated, losing all real understanding of its Jewish roots. Brown is closer to Daniélou in that the attitude toward the Jewish law of each of his groups is a critique developed from within Judaism by Jews. It is in the true diversity of traditions where Brown differs most greatly from Daniélou. In Daniélou's schema there was always one orthodox, authoritative, developing stream of Christianity. According to Brown, from the very earliest times there were several traditions in Christianity which were different from each other in significant ways. His groups' attitudes toward the Jewish law may best be understood by briefly tracing some of their history.

The views described as type 1 were held by Christians from the Pharisaic party mentioned in the book of Acts, as well as by Paul's opponents in Galatians. Their arguments won over at least some gentile Christians. This group was never reconciled to Paul, and would also have considered Peter a traitor. It was represented in Rome, and it may have been some of its members who betrayed Peter and Paul to their deaths.

Type 3 Jewish/gentile Christianity in its classic form was advocated by Paul early in his career. In Antioch, this type 3 Christianity clashed with type 1. Peter, who had originally also held a type 3 position, adopted a mediating position, that is type 2 Jewish/gentile Christianity. Paul's sharp reaction to Peter's adoption of this type 2 position may have been due more to his own loss of face in Antioch than to opposition in principle to Peter's argument. Paul's position

changed with his experiences. Even as late as his letter to the Galatians he had held a fully apocalyptic view of Christianity, which
made Christianity something totally new and left no place for
Torah. But his troubles in Corinth led him to see some of the
weaknesses of his position and the strengths of Peter's mediating
position. By the time he wrote to the Romans he had worked out a
greater place in his thought for salvation history and thus was able
to give a more positive evaluation of Judaism and of the Jewish law.

The Christian community at Rome is the outstanding example of
a Jewish/gentile Christian group of the type 2. It had been evangel-
ized before the fifties by Jerusalem Christians of type 2. Even
though by the time Paul wrote to them gentiles may have formed
the majority, they continued in the type 2 beliefs they had
received — holding the Jewish heritage in high regard and maintaining a mediating view on the law (although some of its members
adhered to a type 1 position). This position of Rome goes far in
explaining why Paul was at such pains in his letter to the Romans to
deny the accusation that he held the views of group 4. Because of
his moderated position Paul was well accepted at Rome, but the
more moderate Peter was always given the first place of honour.
After the fall of Jerusalem Rome took over much of the oversight of
the missionary work of Jerusalem, and also of Paul's churches.

The vanguard of Brown's type 4 Christianity was the Jerusalem
Hellenists whose sharp critique of Judaism is recorded in Stephen's
speech in the book of Acts. While type 4 is also represented in the
New Testament by the letter to the Hebrews, Brown has developed
his understanding of them largely from analysis of the Johannine
literature. They began as a group of Christian Jews with little to distinguish them from other such groups. The entry of Jews opposed
to the Temple and also of Samaritans into their group led them to
adopt the "high Christology" so characteristic of the Gospel of John.
Adoption of this Christology resulted in their expulsion from the
synagogue. This sharp and traumatic break from the Jewish community set the stage for the fundamental rejection of Jewish law
characteristic of type 4 Jewish/gentile Christianity. In the second
century the type 4 Johannine Christians who produced 1 John
merged with the catholic church. They accepted its very foreign
authoritative teaching structure while the catholic church adopted
the Johannine community's high Christology. Thus ended this
community's separate trajectory with its radical rejection of the Jewish heritage.

## Conclusion

What is the correct attitude for the Christian church to hold concerning the Jewish law? This question lies near the heart of the ideas which in Baur's dialectic schema leads the Pauline antithesis to rise up against the Jewish Christian thesis. Ritschl's understanding of the development of early Christianity is in general very different; nevertheless, disputes about Torah are central in separating what becomes the mainstream of the church, first from the strict Jewish Christians and then from the moderate Jewish Christians. The church thus lost contact with its roots. The question loses some of its sharpness in Daniélou's work. An authoritative decision having been made by the apostolic council, there is no place in Daniélou's schema for the question of Torah to cause basic, religious division within the orthodox church. Brown also gives the legal question fundamental importance. He replaces Daniélou's one authoritative decision on the place of the Jewish law in Christianity with a fuller spectrum of attitudes. The result is that in a century and a half the scholarly debate has moved from postulating two antithetical early Christian attitudes toward Torah to a continuum of closely related positions successively coming together by compromise.

Brown founds his four types of Christianity on careful study of the New Testament; nevertheless, there are serious inconsistencies between his categories and the evidence of the texts themselves. By eliminating any position which might be unequivocally labelled "gentile Christian" and by having Paul move toward a type 2 Christianity it becomes difficult to account for some of the statements in Paul's letters and for the tensions between those letters and Acts. The question whether the gentiles were to be subject to Torah remained quite sharp as far as Paul was concerned. He does not hesitate to make his answer to this question quite clear to the Galatians and to the Philippians. Even in Romans, where Brown stresses Paul's movement toward Peter's position, Paul can still claim that in principle "all things are clean" (Rom. 14:20). Later in the Pauline tradition the writer of Ephesians still feels the question important. This writer is not speaking from a mediating position when he claims Jesus has made Jew and gentile one, having abolished the law (Eph. 2:15). It is true that Acts, a secondary source with respect to Paul, presents an early resolution of these Pauline problems. Unfortunately for Brown's argument, our primary source with respect to Paul (the letters of Paul) creates notorious difficulties for the Acts' account.

The correspondence between Brown's categories and the textual evidence is no better in the gospels. The Gospel according to Mark has traditionally been connected with Rome (Brown is hesitant about this), the very city which represents the quintessential moder-rating, type 2 Christianity in Brown's system. Yet, on the issue of food laws—one of the crucial issues we have been highlighting—Mark comments that by one particular saying Jesus "renders all foods clean" (Mark 7:19). This is not a type 2 or even a type 3 posi-tion: since it represents a fundamental break with the Old Testa-ment and Second Temple Judaism it is closer to a type 4 position! In like manner Matthew, which for Brown comes out of the moder-ate type 2 Antiochene consensus, can also say "It is not that which goes into the mouth which renders a person unclean" (Matt. 15:11). There has been no shortage of careful special pleading to explain how this does not fundamentally question Leviticus, or the Apostolic Decree, or a moderate central position. Nevertheless, Brown's schema in its present form cannot fully account for the sharp polemical statements on ritual purity here or in the Pauline corpus.

There is no question that study of the evolution of the New Testa-ment church has advanced greatly since the work of F. C. Baur. The revaluation of Christianity's Jewish roots and the feeling for its diversity must not be lost. The question of early Christian attitudes toward the Jewish law, however, raised on the basis of specific texts by Baur and extensively discussed for over a century, is still not ade-quately treated in the work of Raymond Brown. What is called for in New Testament studies is to pose the sharp question "what atti-tude concerning the Jewish law is implied here?" to each pertinent early Christian text. It is likely that Brown's categories will not stand the test without significant modification, and that such research will show that the attitudes toward Torah reflected in most if not all New Testament writings can reasonably be called gentile Christian.

## Notes

1 The principal works of F. C. Baur consulted in the preparation of this section are "Die Christuspartei in der korinthischen Gemeinde, der Gegensatz des petrinischen und paulinischen Christenthums in der ältesten Kirche, der Apostel Petrus in Rom," *Tübinger Zeitschrift für Theologie*, 4 (1831): 61-206, re-printed in *Ferdinand Christian Baur, Ausgewählte Werke in Einzelausgeben*, edited by K. Scholder (Stuttgart-Bad Cannstatt: Friedrich Frommann, 1963), Vol. 1, p. 1-146; *Kritische Untersuchungen über die Kanonischen Evangelien* (Tübingen: L. F. Fues, 1847); and *The Church History of the First Three Centuries*, translated by A. Menzies, 2 vols. (London: Williams & Norgate, 1879; first German edition, 1853). A complete bibliography of F. C. Baur may be found in P. C. Hodgson, *The Formation of Historical Theology* (New York: Harper & Row, 1966), p. 285-94.

2 For the general orientation of Ritschl's work, I am following the extremely helpful article by Philip Hefner, "Baur Versus Ritschl on Early Christianity," *Church History*, 31 (1962): 259-78. The outline of early Christianity's develop-ment is as found in A. Ritschl, *Die Entstehung der altkatholischen Kirche*, 2nd ed.

(Bonn: Adolph Marcus, 1857). There is a major change in Ritschl's thinking between the first and second editions of this work.

3 Ritschl, *Entstehung*, p. 131.

4 The principal works of H.-J. Schoeps consulted in the preparation of this section are *Theologie und Geschichte des Judenchristentums* (Tübingen: J. C. B. Mohr, 1949); *Urgemeinde Judenchristentum Gnosis* (Tübingen: J. C. B. Mohr, 1956); *Paul: The Theology of the Apostle in the Light of Jewish Religious History*, translated by H. Knight (London: Lutterworth, 1961); *Jewish Christianity*, translated by D. R. A. Hare (Philadelphia: Fortress, 1969). Inspired by F. C. Baur, Schoeps' main literary sources are recovered by careful historical criticism of the pseudo-Clementine literature. He also makes use of Symmachus's Old Testament translation, of what he can reconstruct of the Gospel of the Nazoreans and the Gospel of the Ebionites, and of reports in the Christian patristic and rabbinic literature. It is a great weakness of his work that he does not have direct access to any Ebionite sources but must rely on reconstructions from later works and reports by hostile outsiders.

5 The works of Daniélou consulted for this section are Jean Daniélou and Henri Marrou, *Nouvelle histoire de l'Église*, Vol. 1. *Des origines à saint Gregoire le Grand* (Paris: Éditions du Seuil, 1963); Jean Daniélou, *The Theology of Jewish Christianity*, translated and edited by John A. Baker (Philadelphia: Westminster Press, 1964); and *L'Église des Apôtres* (Paris: Éditions du Seuil, 1970). In 1946, Daniélou took over the column "Bulletin d'Histoire des Origines Chrétiennes" in *Recherches de Science Religieuse*. In 1947 he introduced a section called "Judaïsme et Christianisme," which he continued to write until 1973. This column consists of detailed reviews of current literature on Christian beginnings, and is a mine of information both on the literature itself and on Daniélou's views.

6 His main sources for reconstructing the theology of early Jewish Christianity are certain Old Testament pseudepigrapha, some non-canonical Gospels, the *Didache*, the *Shepherd of Hermas*, the *Letter* of Barnabas, the *Letters* of Ignatius, *1 Clement* and traditions surviving in the Fathers.

7 This division of traditions in Acts 15 (and a related division in Acts 10) is outlined in *L'Église des Apôtres*. His division of Acts 15 follows Stanilas Giet, "L'assemblée apostolique et le décret de Jérusalem," *Recherches de Science Religieuse*, 39 (1951): 203-20. An interesting argument on separate Jewish and gentile eucharists at the basis of the Antioch incident is set forth in *Nouvelle histoire de l'Église*, at which time he did not yet seem to divide Acts 15 into two traditions.

8 The works of Raymond E. Brown consulted for this section are *The Gospel According to John*, 2 vols. (Garden City, NY: Doubleday, Vol. 1, 1966; Vol. 2, 1970); *The Community of the Beloved Disciple* (Toronto: Paulist, 1979); *The Epistles of John* (Garden City, NY: Doubleday, 1982); R. E. Brown and John P. Meier, *Antioch and Rome* (New York: Paulist, 1983); and *The Churches the Apostles Left Behind* (London: Chapman, 1984).

# Chapter 7

# Rivkin and Neusner
# on the Pharisees

If the First Temple period can be characterized as an era in which Israelites debated whether or not to worship the God of the Bible alone, that question was eventually answered for most as a result of the Babylonian exile: only that God was to be acknowledged. The Jews of the Second Temple period therefore were preoccupied with what can be readily understood as the next question in logical order. Once a commitment to the God of the Bible alone and to his Torah is made, the crucial matter becomes what interpretation of the Torah should prevail. This issue is particularly important because the nature of the Torah is such that one virtually cannot live by it alone without some sort of interpretation. During the years of the Second Temple groups will coalesce around these interpretations, with the legal foundations of each group being paramount in the way they understood themselves.[1] All will acknowledge the authority of the written law, but each group will propose its own "supplement" to that law and will try to connect its supplement to the ultimate source of authority. Effectively, therefore, study of the Torah in the Second Temple period is largely synonymous with study of the different parties and sects. This last observation is particularly true of research on the Pharisees. That group provided the family which ultimately was to lead rabbinic Judaism for several hundred years after the destruction of the Temple. While its place in pre-destruction days is subject to debate (see further below), it certainly saw itself as the embodiment of the theoretical and practical significance of the Torah.[2] Survey and analysis of recent research on the Pharisees is therefore one of the best means at our disposal for determining scholarly understanding of what was a crucial manifestation of Torah, in all its senses, in antiquity.

---

Notes to Chapter 7 appear on pages 121-26. This chapter was prepared by Albert I. Baumgarten.

Nearly 40 years have passed since the appearance of Ralph Marcus's review of scholarship on the Pharisees,[3] and almost 20 since Jacob Neusner's bibliographical reflections on the subject.[4] Since Marcus wrote, two significant contributions have appeared: one by Neusner himself and the other by Ellis Rivkin. In spite of the differences between them both of these efforts are distinguished by their attempt to resolve the knotty problem posed by the fact that our information on the Pharisees derives from difficult sources which are quite different from one another and in some measure entirely discrete.[5] Neusner and Rivkin are also, in my opinion, the two most original recent scholars making full-scale contributions to resolving the problems of reconstructing the historical Pharisees; hence this article will be devoted to analysis and critical assessment of their constructions.[6]

## Ellis Rivkin

The core of Rivkin's work is contained in his paper "Defining the Pharisees: The Tannaitic Sources."[7] Rather than offering a definition built out of all the available sources, Rivkin proposes to concentrate on one corpus—Tannaitic literature—and to draw a picture of the Pharisees based on that body of material alone.[8] The problem in utilizing the Tannaitic evidence, as Rivkin correctly notes, is that Pharisees (*perushim*) in these texts is a multivalent term. It can mean "Pharisees," but it can also designate "ascetics," usually with derogatory implications, or "heretics." One must therefore devise a technique for filtering out those places in which *perushim* is not used with the proper meaning. The scholar must build, in other words, on those instances in which the word definitively has the desired sense and use that base as a criterion to test other, less certain, occurrences of the term.

Rivkin suggests that the most certain places to begin are the passages in which *perushim* confront Sadducees or Boethusians (terms which he sees as synonymous).[9] Based on this core, he enlarges the number of texts from which he believes he can draw reliable information; using these sources, Rivkin identifies specific disputes in which a Pharisaic position can be discerned. He proposes, however, to go one step further: these disputes allow us to isolate the underlying principle around which specific controversies revolved. The Pharisees were the group that championed the twofold law, the written and the oral. Equally important for Rivkin is what the Pharisees (as he reconstructs them) were not: he does not see them as a group obsessed with narrow concerns of ritual purity or with separating themselves from the *'am-ha-aretz* (in his historical analysis he eliminated *m. Hag.* 2:8 and similar passages from consideration as reliable sources of information on the Pharisees).[10] The picture to be drawn on the basis of Tannaitic texts, Rivkin concludes, is confirmed by Josephus and the New Testament, hence the sources thought to be discordant are in fact in agreement: they all identify the Pharisees as "the scholar class of the twofold law, nothing more, nothing less."[11]

As indicated above, I believe Rivkin has identified a real problem in the Tannaitic evidence and proposed an imaginative solution. In evaluating his proposal I note, on a preliminary terminological level, that the use of oral and written law is problematic for the Pharisees before the destruction of the Temple. I think it has been shown that these terms are characteristic of the reconstruction of Judaism at Yavneh, and are therefore anachronistic when applied to earlier periods.[12] Pharisees of Temple times would have spoken of their MSRT, *paradosis*, or tradition.[13]

Neusner briefly discusses Rivkin's portrait of the Pharisees, concluding with the comment that Rivkin gives the impression of being less critical, more fundamentalistic; Neusner finds too many groundless historical statements in Rivkin's work.[14] The most significant criticism of the heart of Rivkin's approach, however, was written by Jack Lightstone.[15] Reviewing the innermost circle of sources identified by Rivkin — the ones most certain to yield reliable information on the Pharisees — Lightstone asserts that what he finds missing in these passages is precisely the general conclusion Rivkin draws and on which he means to build. That is, Lightstone finds a number of disputes between Sadducees and Pharisees, but nowhere does he see evidence for the larger rubric adduced by Rivkin; nowhere are appeals made to general criteria such as written or oral law, or exegetical vs. literal interpretation of scripture. According to Lightstone, Rivkin has imported a principle from outside and imposed it on the texts without proving that the principle proposed is in fact the correct one for explaining the passages analyzed.[16]

Evidence from Qumran which has been published in the years since the appearance of Lightstone's article provides the basis for even more serious doubts concerning the validity of Rivkin's conclusions. The brilliance of Rivkin's suggestion is in his devising a technique for dealing with the multivalent nature of *perushim*: using the univalent term "Sadducees" as a criterion for determining when *perushim* has the desired sense and building outward from there.[17] If, however, "Sadducees" in Tannaitic sources is also a multivalent term Rivkin's structure is called into question because he no longer has a definite method for discriminating between the various senses of *perushim*. Yet the multiple meaning of "Sadducees" in Tannaitic texts is a possibility increasingly likely as a result of information yielded by new texts from Qumran: I refer to the Temple Scroll and

4QMMT. Joseph Baumgarten has analyzed disputes between Pharisees and Sadducees preserved in Tannaitic sources in the light of
the Temple Scroll.[18] He notes that a number of positions attributed
by the Rabbis to the Sadducees are now known to have been held by
Qumran sectarians. There are two alternatives, as Baumgarten sees
it, for understanding the data: (1) either the Tannaitic sources used
"Sadducees" in a vague and unspecific way, as a general term for
various groups, identifying them at times with the priestly
Jerusalem Sadducees known from Josephus and the New Testament, at other times with the Sons of Sadoq known from Qumran
(cf. the rabbinic use of the term *minim*); or (2) there were in fact
agreements on specific points of law between the Sadducees known
from non-rabbinic sources and the Qumran covenanters. It is
difficult, as Baumgarten recognizes, to choose between these alternatives with certainty. He, nevertheless, prefers the second alternative.[19]

The picture has been amplified further by material found in a
text soon to be published (at last) — 4QMMT. As those who have
access to the scrolls report, it supports the second of J. Baumgarten's alternatives.[20] Later authorities seem to have been unaware
of finer distinctions between groups with similar sounding names
and therefore blurred the lines between them. Serious doubt (at
the very least) has therefore been raised concerning the univalency
of the term "Sadducees" in Tannaitic texts. That word may not
therefore serve as a criterion for distinguishing between uses of
*perushim*: it may itself be too vague to carry that burden of proof. In
other words, Tannaitic texts may be too far removed from the
details of disputes which took place while the Temple was standing
to be used as the primary basis for drawing a portrait of the Pharisees, as proposed by Rivkin.

Rivkin repeated and expanded the thesis proposed in his *HUCA*
article in his monograph *A Hidden Revolution*.[21] The discussion of
the Tannaitic evidence there repeats the earlier treatment but the
picture is expanded by full-length considerations of the testimonies
of Josephus and the New Testament. According to Rivkin, Josephus
viewed the Pharisees as a *hairēsis*, a school of thought noted for its
expert interpretation of the law, its moderation, reason, dedication
to justice, virtue, friendliness and belief in the afterlife. Fundamental to this group was its adherence to the unwritten (oral) law.
Except for a brief interval (from the time when it was abandoned by
John Hyrcanus until its restoration under Salome Alexandra), the
group enjoyed the whole-hearted confidence and support of the
masses. Josephus himself, according to Rivkin, was a Pharisee;
hence he knew the group from the inside, and his comments on the
Pharisees are generally favourable. Some of the sources Josephus

used were hostile to the Pharisees (e.g., *Antiquities* 13. 408-11), but in spite of his personal allegiance he did not tamper with them.[22]

Rivkin's assessment of Josephus's evidence has been subjected to severe criticism by Shaye Cohen,[23] hence I will confine myself to two observations. First, Rivkin reads almost all his sources in a simplistic way, assuming the virtually absolute reliability of Josephus and Tannaitic sources. This conclusion, however, must be proven, not assumed.[24] Second, Rivkin seems so determined to make Josephus's Pharisees likeable that he is reduced to extreme and arbitrary solutions when confronted with evidence uncongenial to his hypothesis. This emerges best from his treatment of *Antiquities* 17. 41-46.[25] This passage, which I have discussed elsewhere and will discuss further below,[26] is a nasty piece of propaganda against the Pharisees, accusing them of all sorts of sordid activities. According to most scholars, Josephus derived it from the work of Nicolas of Damascus, who made these charges against the Pharisees because they opposed Herod, his employer and patron.[27] The contents, however, pose a problem to the idyllic portrait of the Pharisees Rivkin wants to draw. The difficulty could have been avoided by arguing that the information comes from a hostile source (which, as indicated above, most scholars believe to be the case), but Rivkin does not take this course. I can only guess the reason; perhaps he could not accept the assertion made in this passage that there were only 6,000 Pharisees;[28] perhaps he realized that even hostile sources usually attest to at least part of the truth. Whatever the reason, Rivkin is unwilling to grant even the slightest bit of credibility to the information. He takes the extreme step of arguing that the Pharisees are not here the subject; it is a group of ascetic separatists. That is, as *perushim* was a multivalent term in Tannaitic sources and could mean both "Pharisees" and "ascetics," so was it multivalent for Josephus (or his source). In contrast, however, to Tannaitic works where several meanings are found and are widely attested, this text in Josephus is the sole proof for multivalency in Greek sources. Moreover, it is one thing to argue for several meanings for a term in a body of literature edited long after the events, where there are innumerable possibilities for confusion or misunderstanding; it is quite a different matter to argue thus for Josephus or his source. Finally, if most scholars are right in asserting that the ultimate source of the passage was Nicolas of Damascus, is such a usage plausible for him? What seems important for Rivkin, however, is not probability but the overwhelming desire to save his lovable Pharisees from being stained by even the slightest bit of mud slung at them by Josephus or his source. The arbitrariness and tendentiousness of Rivkin's explanation of this key passage seem too obvious to require further comment.

To summarize the discussion of Rivkin, his approach is characterized by an intellectual economy and elegance which I find admirable. When confronted by the complexities of the evidence, however, these assets become liabilities. Thus, as argued above, the reading of Rabbinic sources is somewhat naive while the discussion of Josephus is overly simplistic and determined to reach a favourable conclusion at all costs.[29] The breakthrough Rivkin attempted in understanding the Pharisees is being severely undermined by complications introduced by sources published after the time his contributions were written.

## Jacob Neusner and Morton Smith

Jacob Neusner has devoted many of his extensive scholarly publications to the Pharisees. His views on the subject have changed over the years,[30] thus posing a difficulty to an endeavour such as mine: exactly which stage of Neusner's work is one to analyze? I have chosen to focus on the studies contained in his *From Politics to Piety*,[31] based on previous publications such as *The Rabbinic Traditions about the Pharisees Before 70*.[32] In these books Neusner has recognized (more clearly and effectively than any other scholar, in my opinion) the proper method for dealing with the complexities of reconstructing the historical Pharisees based on the sources available. Employing an approach which (borrowing a term from other disciplines) I have elsewhere called "triangulation,"[33] he attempts to understand the nature of our sources and then proceeds to compare points on which they agree or disagree, while amending the information provided by each source to correct for intentional or accidental distortion.

Before presenting and evaluating Neusner's application of these techniques a few words of introduction are necessary. Much of Neusner's contribution on the Pharisees involves an explicitly acknowledged debt to the published work of his former mentor Morton Smith.[34] Smith's comments on the Pharisees do not constitute a fully developed and thoroughly argued case; his suggestions are made in a few pages in a semi-popular volume of essays and an extensive book review.[35] Neusner acknowledges that at least in part he is doing nothing more than providing detailed proof for the validity of Smith's suggestions.[36] Neusner, of course, goes beyond the work of his mentor, but Smith's contribution to Neusner's effort is so overwhelming that I believe one must distinguish between that part of Neusner's analysis which is directly based on Smith and that part which is independent. I therefore propose to divide the discussion of Neusner into two sections, one in which we are considering the position of Smith/Neusner and one in which Neusner stands on his own.

The breakthrough proposed by Smith/Neusner is in our understanding of Josephus.[37] Rather than reading Josephus on the Pharisees naively they propose a critical assessment of his various comments. Josephus, in his autobiography, clearly makes a number of favourable remarks about the Pharisees (e.g., *Life*, 191).[38] The situation is the same in *Antiquities* (e.g., 18. 15), written at roughly the same time. The crucial difference according to Smith/Neusner is in the attitude displayed towards the group in his earlier work, *War*, where Josephus has much less favourable things to say. Smith/ Neusner propose to explain these differences as a response to the changing political fate of the Pharisees. The more favourable comments in the later works are inspired in some way by the rise to power of R. Gamaliel II (scion of one of the great Pharisaic families) at Yavneh. The evidence of *Antiquities* and *Life* concerning the great popularity and influence of the Pharisees thus loses much if not all of its value for the period before 70, and Josephus's Pharisees before 70 C.E. are thus cut down to more realistic size, facilitating more productive comparison with the Pharisees of rabbinic sources and of the New Testament (after the pictures of the latter sources have been critically analyzed). The Pharisees before 70 C.E. thus emerge as far less influential than one might otherwise conclude.

Josephus's evidence, however, is far too complex to be explained even by a critical theory such as that of Smith/Neusner. Let me begin by noting two pieces of evidence which, each in its own way, does not fit in well with the Smith/Neusner approach. Josephus's autobiography is the starting point for the contention of his late-life "conversion" to Pharisaism, for his rewriting of his own experience as if he had always been a Pharisee. As has been argued recently by Steven Mason,[39] in the heart of the passage in which Josephus seems to be proclaiming his long-term allegiance as a Pharisee he makes a perplexing remark about his own education. Having learned all about the three groups within Judaism in a brief period of time, he was "not content" with this instruction, hence he spent three years in the wilderness with Bannus. There, by contrast, he "accomplished his purpose" (*Life*, 11-12). All this suggests that Josephus's ultimate allegiance was to none of the three groups with which he began but to Bannus,[40] yet these statements are followed by the assertion that Josephus then returned to the city and began to govern his life by the rules of the Pharisees (ibid.). *Life* itself thus seems to contain conflicting valuations of the Pharisees, the perplexing statement we have just discussed and the high praise in *Life*, 191. This complication of the picture, however, could pose a serious problem for Smith/Neusner, as it may undermine the starting point of their interpretation.

Another difficulty arises from a comparison of the descriptions of the Pharisees in *War* 2. 161 and *Life*, 191. As I have noted elsewhere,[41] the very same terms are used in both works. Whether these terms are to be understood as praise or as condemnation, the identity of terms suggests that there was no real change in Josephus's opinion of the Pharisees. What then of Smith/Neusner?

The most damaging criticism of Smith/Neusner to appear thus far was written by Daniel Schwartz.[42] Schwartz shows that detailed examination of Josephus's parallel accounts of events in *War* and *Antiquities* proves that there is little if any rewriting in the latter in praise of the Pharisees. In fact, according to Schwartz, the Pharisees are portrayed in *Antiquities* as having been responsible for failures in the past. Schwartz even toys with the idea of turning the Smith/Neusner hypothesis on its head: Josephus deliberately associated the Pharisees with rebels and failure in his later books in order to condemn them.[43] Schwartz's final suggestion for understanding the evidence is that Josephus's intention in *War* was to portray the Pharisees incorrectly but safely as apolitical and uninvolved in the revolt against Rome. In his later works he remains well disposed towards the group but, since the politics of the past were less pressing, he was also less cautious with his source material and admitted into his account pieces of evidence which were unfavourable to the Pharisees, or he portrayed them as active in the revolt. Consistency, in any case, was never one of Josephus's stronger points.[44]

The Smith/Neusner hypothesis has been defended in a recent article by Goodblatt.[45] Goodblatt distinguishes sharply between Smith's original contribution and those who have tried to expand his line of thought,[46] and argues that the core of Smith's original insight remains valid in spite of the criticism levelled against it by scholars such as Schwartz. Goodblatt concedes that Schwartz has identified passages in *Antiquities* which are hostile to the Pharisees. Josephus's testimony concerning the Pharisees, Goodblatt recognizes, "is more complex than appears from Smith's brief outline or from Neusner's more detailed presentation."[47] This concession, however, is more crucial than Goodblatt would seem to be willing to admit because it further undermines the fundamental point of departure of the Smith/Neusner approach.[48] If so, the Pharisees may have been more prominent in pre-70 C.E. times than Smith/Neusner are willing to conclude, and Goodblatt's other defences of their position are therefore irrelevant.[49]

It would be misleading to end the discussion of Smith/Neusner on this note; for they have, I believe, made one valuable contribution to our understanding of the Pharisees which has stood well the test

of critical reflection. I refer to what Smith described as "the enormous difference which separated this small, exclusive, sectarian
Pharisaic party of the temple period from the rabbinic organization
of the third century."[50] Or, in a slightly different formulation, the
"exceptional rapid change [which took] place in the seventy five
years between A.D. 65 and 140 which separate Pharisaism from
developed Rabbinic Judaism."[51] These ideas, fundamental to the
Smith/Neusner approach, have proved their value in further studies. Pharisees are not now assumed simply to equal Rabbis, and one
no longer claims to have obtained information on the Pharisees simply by reading rabbinic texts; at the very least, one must work to
extract the Pharisaic layer within the rabbinic evidence. Some sort
of transformation—whether as radical as Smith/Neusner maintain,
or more modest in scale—took place in the move from Pharisees to
Rabbis, from being one competing group among many to eventual
dominance. I note two successful applications of this approach:
Neusner's distinction between Pharisaic tradition and rabbinic oral
law mentioned above, and Cohen's attempt to understand the
significance of the change which took place at Yavneh.[52]

What then was the exact status of the Pharisees in pre-70 times?
This question requires further work before a definite answer can be
offered. Josephus's description of the Pharisees is very complex, but
his praise of them in his later works, as we have seen, cannot be
explained as simply as Smith/Neusner propose. It would seem that
Smith/Neusner have overstated the relative unimportance of the
Pharisees before 70. That is, in response to the view of the Pharisees
as normative Smith/Neusner have exaggerated their lack of importance; the more accurate description may lie somewhere between
the extremes. Evidence from Qumran may support this conclusion:
4QMMT is a list of disagreements between the Qumran community
and official Judaism, yet the points of law which characterize official
Judaism also appear in the *halakah* of the Rabbis and would seem to
have very deep roots in the rabbinic tradition, hence are likely to go
back to the Pharisees. Yet these same points of law also are those of
official Judaism. Does this mean that official Judaism and Pharisaism are more or less identical in the eyes of Qumran covenanters? If
so, it would be important testimony to the place of the Pharisees in
the eyes of their contemporaries and should join other Qumran evidence on the preeminence of the Pharisees, such as the description
of their power and authority in 4QpNah. Clearly, the status of the
Pharisees in the eyes of opponents cannot be taken as the final word
on the subject, and we can only hope for additional evidence which
may clarify the picture, yielding data about periods and groups not
covered by the texts from Qumran discussed above. Nevertheless,
the undermining of the Smith/Neusner analysis of Josephus

together with the Qumran sources already available seem to me to increase the likelihood that the Pharisees had considerable power fairly often during the Second Temple period.

The Smith/Neusner approach strikes me, on balance, as a partial success: the reading of Josephus is problematic not because of any inherent fault or apologetic tendency (cf. the discussion of Rivkin above) but because the data may be too complex to be explained by the theory proposed. Qumran sources also raise questions about the validity of certain aspects. The general approach to Pharisees and Rabbis, however, has proven fruitful.

## Jacob Neusner

We can now turn to that part of Neusner's work in which he stands on his own. I propose to concentrate on his description of Hillel, on the account of the change in Pharisaism which Neusner attributed to him. According to Neusner, the rabbinic traditions concerning Hillel teach us very little that is reliable about the man.[53] By contrast, when drawing up his general summary Neusner notes that the most striking result of his survey of rabbinic traditions concerning the Pharisees is that the group is portrayed as entirely inward-looking. The Pharisees under discussion are mostly of the late Herodian period or thereafter. Pharisaism of that time, Neusner concludes, was therefore a non-political movement, and this picture of the group agrees with the evidence of the Synoptics, as Neusner understands them. The Pharisees of Josephus, by contrast, had been a political movement, hence Neusner suggests that we explain the apparent discrepancy by positing a change in the nature of the group: what began as a political party became in time a table fellowship. This leads to a further obvious question: who was responsible for that change? Neusner proposes to credit Hillel. All this, Neusner concedes, is more than conjecture but less than established fact;[54] nevertheless one point should be noted even at this stage of the discussion. In analyzing the information on Hillel in our sources Neusner is very critical in deciding which accounts he will accept as reliable; much of what we could learn from these texts is considered ahistorical at best. In the end, however, Neusner attributes to Hillel actions never even mentioned in the sources. We can see outlines of an odd mixture of hyper-criticism concerning the sources combined with free speculation concerning questions and answers not to be found at all in the texts.[55]

Neusner's thesis about Hillel is probably ultimately unprovable. It will always remain at least in part (as its author concedes) a guess at tying loose pieces together. One point which does seem worthy of extended discussion, however, is the thesis of the transformation of

Pharisaism from a political movement to a table fellowship. This conclusion has been the basis of further research, most notably by Lee Levine.[56] Levine reviews all the sources in which Pharisees are portrayed as politically active during the reign of Herod and the rule of the procurators and concludes that individual Pharisees are certainly described as having political goals and ideals. Nevertheless, he finds that the data confirm Neusner's picture of the movement as a whole; in large part it retreated from the political arena during Herod's reign and became primarily a religious group. The apolitical nature of the Pharisees, Levine guesses, may have had something to do with the group's ability to survive the crisis of the destruction of Jerusalem and may have facilitated the attainment of positions of leadership by their descendants. Levine's role is clear: he is trying to provide more detailed proof for the validity of Neusner's conclusions about the transformation of the Pharisees into a table fellowship around the time of Herod.[57]

This line of argument seems to me to founder irrevocably on one passage, hardly mentioned by Neusner and discussed only partially by Levine. I refer to Josephus, *Antiquities*, 17.41-46. This text, mentioned above, is a nasty piece of anti-Pharisaic propaganda, and probably comes from the pen of Nicolas of Damascus. Nicolas is hardly likely to have had an independent notion of the relative merits of different Jewish groups, so we must presume that the opinion expressed and implied reflects views Nicolas learned in Herod's court, in which he served.

For the sake of convenience, let me cite the passage in full:

There was also a group of Jews priding itself *overmuch* on its adherence to ancestral custom and *pretending* to observe the laws of which the Deity approves, and by these men, called Pharisees, the women (of the court) were ruled. These men were able to help the king greatly because of their foresight, and yet they were obviously intent upon combating and injuring him. At least when the whole Jewish people affirmed by an oath that it would be loyal to Caesar and the King's government, these men, over six thousand in number, refused to take this oath, and when the king punished them with a fine, Pheroras' wife paid the fine for them. In return for her friendliness they foretold — for they were believed to have foreknowledge of things through God's appearances to them — that by God's decree Herod's throne would be taken from him, both from himself and his descendants, and the royal power would fall to her and Pheroras and to any children that they might have. These things, which did not remain unknown to Salome, were reported to the king, as was the news that the Pharisees had corrupted some of the people in court. And the king put to death those of the Pharisees who were most to blame and the eunuch Bagoas and a certain Karos, who was outstanding among his contemporaries for his surpassing beauty and was loved by the king. He also killed all those of his household who approved of what the Pharisee said. Now Bagoas had been carried away by their assurance that he would be called the father and benefactor of him who would some day be set over

the people with the title of king, for all the power would belong to him
and he would give Bagoas the ability to marry and to beget children of his
own.[58]

The passage is full of anti-Pharisaic charges, and they are accused of
all sorts of sordid behaviour. They were particularly influential with
the women, a first sign that the group is not to be taken seriously.[59]
Since Pheroras's wife paid the fine on their behalf, they returned
the favour by making extravagant predictions of Herod's imminent
downfall and of the transfer of power to Pheroras, his wife and their
offspring. They suborned Karos and enticed the eunuch Bagoas
with promises that he would be called "father" and "benefactor" of
the future king, that is by distributing honorary titles in the future
royal (messianic) court.[60] Finally, they took unscrupulous advantage
of Bagoas's physical condition by assuring him that the future king
would give him the power to marry and beget children. All of these
charges are intensified by the introduction to the passage which
accuses the Pharisees (as a group) of priding themselves overly
much on their adherence to ancestral law and of pretending to
observe the laws of which God approves.

Two obscure points, admittedly, remain: (1) why at one place is
the Pharisee (singular) spoken of, when the rest of the time the
Pharisees (plural) are the subject; (2) what is the relationship
between the kingship promised the descendants of Pheroras and the
messianic expectations raised at the end of the passage? I think
these difficulties can be explained by the obvious hatred of the Pharisees which permeates the passage: as a result all sorts of charges are
being thrown together, even if they are not completely consistent
with each other.[61]

Did the Pharisees really do all these dishonourable things; is this
unfavourable portrait of the group accurate? I presume not wholly,
at the very least. Nevertheless, one conclusion seems certain. In
order to have earned the hostility of Nicolas and his Jewish infor-
mants the Pharisees *as a group* must have been working against
Herod.[62] We are not dealing here with actions which can be
dismissed as the work of one or two individuals; enough Pharisees
must have been participating in the plot against Herod to provoke
the general denunciation of the movement. Serious doubt is thus
cast on the validity of Neusner's reconstruction of the Pharisees as a
group that began in politics but then turned aside to table fellowship during Herod's reign. The Pharisees of the Herodian age
were playing an active part in politics, and if the passage we have
analyzed is to be believed, were not above using disreputable means
to achieve their goals.[63]

## Conclusion

It seems appropriate to conclude this chapter with a few remarks on the direction of future studies on the Pharisees. Much remains to be done. We are not (as I once thought) at a point where all that can be known is known, and what is not known is beyond the reach of our evidence. There is an excellent possibility that additional Qumran sources will teach us more about the Pharisees and their relationship to official (i.e., Temple-dominated) Judaism.[64] Josephus's evidence, in my opinion, is a complex created by his conflicting loyalties, tendencies and sources, all further confused by his methods in writing history.[65] The nature of this complex remains to be determined in all its details, and the implications for the study of the Pharisees drawn. Careful work must be done in reconstructing Pharisaic law and determining the group's attitude on the great issues of the day, such as their view of Herod and his house.[66] These are profitable avenues to explore if we hope to build beyond the levels attained by Rivkin and Neusner in understanding the Pharisees and the meaning of their embodiment of Torah.

## Notes

1 I summarize briefly here points discussed more extensively in Albert I. Baumgarten, "Qumran and Jewish Sectarianism," *Proceedings of the Hebrew University Conference: Qumran after Forty Years*, in press (in Hebrew).

2 See further Albert I. Baumgarten, "The Name of the Pharisees," *Journal of Biblical Literature*, 102 (1983): 413-17. In candour, one ought to concede that other groups of that era would have seen themselves similarly.

3 Ralph Marcus, "The Pharisees and Modern Scholarship," *Journal of Religion*, 32 (1952): 153-64.

4 Jacob Neusner, *The Rabbinic Traditions about the Pharisees before 70* (Leiden: Brill, 1971), Vol. 3, p. 320-68. An abbreviated version of the same material appeared as "The Rabbinic Traditions about the Pharisees in Modern Historiography," *Central Conference of American Rabbis Journal*, 19 (1972): 78-108.

5 This formulation of the problem is based on Neusner's comments, *Rabbinic Traditions*, Vol. 3, p. 364.

6 I stress the fact that Neusner and Rivkin have been chosen as the focus of discussion because they have made full-scale, book-length (and more) contributions to the topic. This is not to minimize the importance of the work of other scholars, as will be obvious below.

7 Ellis Rivkin, "Defining the Pharisees: The Tannaitic Sources," *Hebrew Union College Annual*, 40-41 (1969-70): 204-49.

8 Rivkin never explains why he picked Tannaitic literature as the body of material with which to begin. Perhaps it was because his ultimate goal was to discredit *m. Hag.* 2:8 and similar sources as reliable places to find information on the Pharisees. In any case, in his full-length treatment, *A Hidden Revolution* (Nashville: Abingdon, 1978), he discussed Josephus first, then the New Testament, and only thereafter did he turn to Tannaitic literature. He justified

beginning with Josephus by arguing that Josephus viewed the Pharisees from a number of vantage points (p. 32). On Rivkin's analysis of Josephus on the Pharisees see below.

9  Rivkin, "Defining," p. 210, and *Hidden Revolution*, p. 134. This view is far from unanimous. See Moshe D. Herr, "Who Were the Boethusians?" *Proceedings of the Seventh World Congress of Jewish Studies: Studies in the Talmud, Halacha and Midrash* (Jerusalem: World Union of Jewish Studies, 1981), p. 1-20 (in Hebrew).

10  Rivkin, "Defining," p. 234-36.

11  Ibid., p. 249.

12  Neusner, *Rabbinic Traditions*, Vol. 3, p. 163ff. The same conclusion had been reached earlier by Isaac H. Weiss, *Dor Dor Vedorshav* (Vilna: Romm, 1904), Vol. 1, p. 1, n. 1.

13  See further my "The Pharisaic *Paradosis*," *Harvard Theological Review*, 80 (1987): 63-77.

14  Neusner, *Rabbinic Traditions*, Vol. 1, p. 3ff.

15  Jack Lightstone, "Sadducees *versus* Pharisees: The Tannaitic Sources," in J. Neusner, ed., *Christianity, Judaism and Other Greco-Roman Cults: Studies for Morton Smith at Sixty* (Leiden: Brill, 1975), Vol. 3, p. 206-17.

16  This criticism is similar to that levelled by Neusner against a large number of other scholars who have written on the Pharisees. See *Rabbinic Traditions*, Vol. 3, p. 319-22. Lightstone also notes that these Tannaitic sources are highly formulaic in structure, that their *Tendenz* is rhetoric and vilification, and that they are not necessarily early: "Sadducees *versus* Pharisees," p. 217. Compare my discussion of the possible unreliability of these sources in the light of new information from Qumran, which follows.

17  Rivkin assumed the univalency of the meaning of Sadducees, and if one accepts their equation with Boethusians (above, n. 9), there was no reason not to do so at the time he wrote.

18  Joseph M. Baumgarten, "The Pharisaic-Saducean Controversies about Purity and the Qumran Texts," *Journal of Jewish Studies*, 31 (1980): 157-70.

19  According to J. Baumgarten, proofs that the church fathers knew of two kinds of Sadducees are incorrect. Furthermore, he sees the other possibility as "simplistic" ("Pharisaic-Saducean Controversies," p. 167-69). Whether the church fathers, who had little if any independent knowledge on the subject, knew of two kinds of Sadducees is irrelevant. The question is based on a comparison of Qumran texts and Rabbinic evidence. As for "simplistic," I cannot avoid the feeling that J. Baumgarten is reluctant to concede what the evidence suggests: that the later Rabbis were not all that well informed about the details of differences between groups and lumped them under larger headings which simplify but hence distort the picture they present.

20  See Elisha Qimron and John Strugnell, "An Unpublished Halakhic Letter from Qumran," *Israel Museum Journal*, 2 (1984-85): 9-12. My comments are also based on the lecture delivered by Y. Sussman, to be published in the *Proceedings of the Hebrew University Conference: Qumran after Forty Years*.

21  For bibliographic details, see above, n. 8.

22  Rivkin, *Hidden Revolution*, p. 31-75.

23  Shaye J. D. Cohen, Review of Rivkin's *Hidden Revolution*, *Journal of Biblical Literature*, 99 (1980): 627-29. See further Shaye J. D. Cohen, "The Significance of Yavneh: Pharisees, Rabbis and the End of Jewish Sectarianism," *Hebrew Union College Annual*, 55 (1984): 30, n. 6.

24  See above Neusner's assessment of Rivkin as fundamentalistic.

25  Rivkin, *Hidden Revolution*, p. 321-24, n. 3.

26  Baumgarten, "Name," p. 414-16, and A. I. Baumgarten, "The Legitimacy of Herod and His Descendants as Kings of the Jews," in *Samuel Safrai Jubilee Volume*, in press (in Hebrew).

27  Baumgarten, "Name," p. 414-15, n. 15. See also Daniel R. Schwartz, "Nicolaus and Josephus on the Pharisees," *Journal for the Study of Judaism in the Persian, Hellenistic and Roman Period*, 14 (1983): 160, n. 12.

28  Hugo D. Mantel, "The Sadducees and Pharisees," in M. Avi-Yonah and Z. Baras, eds., *World History of the Jewish People*, Vol. 8: *Society and Religion in the Second Temple Period* (New Brunswick, NJ: Rutgers University Press, 1977), p. 117, tries to save the passage from its obvious meaning by explaining that the Pharisees numbered six thousand *heads of families*.

29  In this sense there is a direct line between Rivkin's work and that of 19th- and 20th-century German Jewish scholars analyzed by Daniel R. Schwartz, "History and Historiography: 'A Kingdom of Priests' as a Pharisaic Slogan," *Zion*, 45 (1980): 96-117 (in Hebrew).

30  Neusner concedes this aspect of his work. Thus in a letter to Daniel Schwartz dated July 19, 1989, which Neusner circulated, he wrote: "I don't agree with anything I have written two minutes ago; the key to my working on and on is my own criticism of my own work, and each book or project . . . constitutes a very serious, very rigorous and ordinarily rather unfriendly review of what I did before." Nevertheless, Neusner has often republished essays of differing vintages in the same volume, thus complicating the task of the reader or student. See, for example, E. P. Sanders' review of J. Neusner's *Judaism in the Beginning of Christianity* in *Theology*, 88 (1985): 392-93.

31  Jacob Neusner, *From Politics to Piety* (Englewood Cliffs, NJ: Prentice Hall, 1973).

32  For bibliographic information see above, n. 4. This part of Neusner's work has merited favourable comment in handbooks such as Emil Schürer, *The History of the Jewish People in the Age of Jesus Christ*, revised and edited by Geza Vermes, Fergus Millar and Matthew Black (Edinburgh: T & T Clark, 1979), Vol. 2, p. 388, n. 16. It has also been the basis of further work by other scholars such as Lee I. Levine, "On the Political Involvement of the Pharisees Under Herod and the Procurators," *Cathedra*, 8 (1978): 12-28 (in Hebrew), and David Goodblatt, "The Origins of the Roman Recognition of the Patriarchate," *Studies in the History of the Jewish People and the Land of Israel*, 4 (1978): 89-102 (in Hebrew).

33  Baumgarten, *The Pharisaic Paradosis*," p. 63-64.

34  There may also be a debt to Smith's oral suggestions. As those who know him will attest, Smith is a rich source of original ideas on how to approach virtually any problem connected with the study of antiquity.

35  Morton Smith, "Palestinian Judaism in the First Century," in M. Davis, ed., *Israel: Its Role in Civilization* (New York: Harper & Row, 1956), p. 75-79, and Morton Smith, "A Comparison of Early Christianity and Early Rabbinic Tradition," *Journal of Biblical Literature*, 82 (1963): 169-76.

36  See Jacob Neusner, "Josephus's Pharisees," *Ex Orbe Religionum: Studia Geo Widengren Oblata, Numen Supplement*, 21 (1972), Vol. 1, p. 225.

37  I focus here on the understanding of Josephus because the Smith/Neusner position on the rabbinic evidence is not their discovery. They have the merit, as will be discussed below, of having stated a position taken by others with special clarity.

38  I follow Shaye J. D. Cohen, *Josephus in Galilee and Rome* (Leiden: Brill, 1979), p. 144f., in understanding this passage.

39  Steven Neil Mason, "Josephus on the Pharisees: A Composition-Critical Study" (PhD thesis, Wycliffe College, 1986), p. 574-600. A revised version of

the entire work is due to appear soon, to be published by Brill. For a brief discussion of the relevant evidence, see Mason's article "Was Josephus a Pharisee? A Reexamination of *Life* 10-12," *Journal of Jewish Studies*, 40 (1989): 31-45.
Mason's own proposal for understanding Josephus's comments on the Pharisees is virtually a mirror image of Rivkin's. Josephus, according to Mason, consistently tries to portray the Pharisees in an unfavourable light. Josephus's
position, in my view, is too complex to be explained by any such simple
solution—whether Rivkin's or Mason's. See further above, n. 24.

40 There is one other passage which would seem to support this conclusion.
   When summarizing the doctrines of the Jewish groups in *War* 2, Josephus says
   some very complimentary things about the Essenes: "Such are the theological
   views of the Essenes concerning the soul, whereby they irresistibly attract all
   who have once tasted their philosophy" (*War* 2.158). Bannus and the Essenes
   may well have appealed to the same group of people and it would not be
   surprising for someone who "accomplished his purpose" with Bannus to say
   such favourable things about the Essenes.

   Josephus's remark concerning the Essenes is important for another issue.
   His description of the Jewish sects is also known in a version preserved by the
   Church Father Hippolytus. The literary relationship between these accounts
   has been discussed, and I have proposed that Hippolytus worked from a revi-
   sion of Josephus, one which had been made more pro-Pharisaic than the original in *War* 2. See Albert I. Baumgarten, "Josephus and Hippolytus on the
   Pharisees," *Hebrew Union College Annual*, 55 (1984): 1-25. Of the major differences between Josephus and Hippolytus five are sections in the latter not
   found in the former. There is only one section in Josephus missing in
   Hippolytus's version: *War* 2.156-58. I believe this omission to be confirmation
   of the explanation which I proposed and further proof of the existence of a
   pro-Pharisaic reviser standing between Josephus and Hippolytus. This reviser,
   I suggest, could not let the praise of the Essenes and the great attraction of
   their doctrine stand; hence he eliminated the passage in his version.

41 Albert I. Baumgarten, "The Torah as a Public Document in Judaism" *Studies
   in Religion/Sciences Religieuses*, 14 (1985): 23, n. 27.

42 Schwartz, "Nicolaus and Josephus," p. 157-71. Mason's book contains even
   more detailed examination of Josephus's passages on the Pharisees and
   should, in my opinion, complete the demolition of Smith/Neusner. I say this
   in spite of the fact that I am far from convinced by the alternate proposal
   brought forward by Mason. See above, n. 39.

43 Schwartz, "Nicolaus and Josephus," p. 169.

44 See Cohen, *Josephus*, p. 31-47 and p. 233-34.

45 David Goodblatt, "The Place of the Pharisees in First Century Judaism: The
   State of the Debate," *Journal for the Study of Judaism in the Persian, Hellenistic and
   Roman Period*, 20 (1989): 12-29.

46 This distinction is essentially equivalent to the one I have proposed between
   Smith/Neusner and the points on which Neusner stands on his own.

47 Goodblatt, "Place," p. 19.

48 I leave discussion of Goodblatt's detailed criticism of Schwartz's own account
   of the nature of Josephus's evidence for this note. Goodblatt finds that
   Schwartz does not adequately explain all the twists and turns in Josephus's
   descriptions of the Pharisees ("Place," p. 22-26), and concludes with the comment that Josephus's exact intentions may be beyond our knowledge—unless
   we should one day recover his diary, or personal correspondence (ibid., p. 28).
   To Goodblatt's observations I would add the following: How are we to account

for Josephus's preference for ascetic types, or for his having been very much a priest?

49 It should be noted that Goodblatt wrote his contribution before Mason's first article appeared, and he did not have the advantage of reading Mason's thesis. Mason's conclusion, as noted above, makes Goodblatt's defence of Smith/ Neusner even less convincing.

50 Smith, "Comparison," p. 171. Smith views the Pharisees as a sect. See also Cohen, "Significance of Yavneh," p. 30-31. I would prefer to see them more as a party. See further E. P. Sanders, *Paul and Palestinian Judaism* (London: SCM, 1977), p. 152-56 and 425-26. For a discussion of the place of the Pharisees in the years before 70 C.E. see below.

51 Smith, "Comparison," p. 170, n. 3.

52 Cohen, "Significance of Yavneh," p. 27-54.

53 See the discussion in *From Politics to Piety*, p. 13-44. Compare also the treatment of much of the same material by Yonah Frankel, "Hermeneutical Questions in Research on Aggadic Stories," *Tarbiz*, 47 (1978-79): 139-72 (in Hebrew). The comments of E. E. Halevi in *Tarbiz*, 49 (1980-81): 422-28 (in Hebrew) and Frankel's response in *Tarbiz*, 49 (1980-81): 429 (in Hebrew) illustrate the importance of the point at stake.

54 Neusner, *Rabbinic Traditions*, Vol. 3, p. 304-306.

55 This point has been made as a general criticism of Neusner's work by Hyam Maccoby. See for instance his review of Neusner's *Judaism: The Evidence of the Mishnah* in *Times Literary Supplement*, August 13, 1982, p. 887, or his article "Jacob Neusner's Mishnah," *Midstream*, 30, 5 (1984): 31. In his critical reviews of the work of others on the Pharisees Neusner accused them of importing concepts from the outside and imposing them on the data. See above, n. 14.

56 Levine, "Political Involvement," p. 12-28.

57 Levine's relationship to Neusner is analogous to Neusner's relationship to Smith. Each is trying to provide more detailed proof for an idea advanced but not fully worked out by his predecessor.

58 I have modified the translation in the LCL version, as indicated by italicizing; see further the discussion in my "Name," p. 415, n. 16 and 17. On the meaning of *prospoioumenon* see further Josephus *Antiquities* 18.81, a reference I owe to Mason, "Josephus on the Pharisees," p. 239.

59 See Origen, *contra Celsum* 3.44 and 4.36. See also fragments 4-6 of Porphyry's *Against the Christians*.

60 See Elias J. Bickerman, "The Name of the Christians," *Studies in Jewish and Christian History, Part Three* (Leiden: Brill, 1986), p. 150.

61 Cf. Levine, "Political Involvement," p. 18, n. 27.

62 As a further indication, if one were needed, that all is not straightforward in Josephus's account of the Pharisees compare the role of Pollion the Pharisee and his disciple Samias in *Antiquities* 15.3. This is apparently the same Samias who criticized Herod in *Antiquities* 14.172-76, and who believed that Herod was a punishment sent on the Jews for their sins.

63 If the Pharisees are the ones hiding behind Josephus's account of the actions of those who were "strict in observance of the law," who complained to Agrippa II about the actions of Ananus in executing James (*Antiquities* 20.200-202), this would be another example of political activity on their part. It would also be another example of their use of what might seem to be underhanded means. For a discussion of the possibility that Josephus may intend Pharisees in *Antiquities* 20.200-202 see my "Name," p. 413-14. If the enigmatic *Megillat Taanit* is Pharisaic—I would stress, the Aramaic source only, not the later Hebrew commentary—it too would be evidence for political activity on the

part of at least that group or those groups of Pharisees responsible for the text. On the Pharisaic nature of *Megillat Taanit* see the article questioning that conclusion by Meir Bar-Ilan, "The Character and Origin of *Megillat Taanit*," *Sinai*, 98 (1985-86): 114-37 (in Hebrew).

64 See further the discussion of 4QMMT above.

65 See above n. 38, 39, 42 and 48.

66 Since completing the initial draft of this chapter, I have written a study on this point; see my "Legitimacy."

# Chapter 8

# Sadducees and *Halakah*

## Background

There are no extant Sadducean writings; all attempts to find original Sadducean material in the Apocrypha and Pseudepigrapha have
failed.[1] We are left only with texts about the Sadducees written by
non-Sadducees: the New Testament, the writings of Josephus, and
rabbinic literature. The New Testament gives very little information
about the Sadducees. The evangelists narrate that the Sadducees
disagreed with Jesus in a discussion regarding resurrection.[2] In Acts
the Sadducees are reported to have been behind the imprisonment
of the disciples.[3] Josephus and rabbinic authors depict the Sadducees in a biassed fashion. Josephus presents himself as a Pharisee,[4]
and sometimes is critical of the Sadducees in his description of the
party. The rabbinic literature reflects the Pharisees' disapproval of
the Sadducean position in various questions. This situation makes it
extremely difficult to get an adequate picture of the group and, as
we might expect, the resulting portrayals by scholars vary considerably.

The central issue is Sadducean *halakah* (that is, their legal system)
and the Sadducean attitude toward Torah. The New Testament
contains virtually no material relevant to this issue. Josephus alludes
to halakhic differences between the two groups, but most important
are the halakhic controversies recorded in rabbinic literature
between the Sadducees and the Pharisees. Do these controversies
stem from general disagreements, arising perhaps from social
conflicts? Or are they rooted in different theologies, or different
perceptions of Torah and oral tradition? Do the rabbinic accounts
allow us to answer these questions?

Josephus mentions the Sadducees several times, alongside the

Notes to Chapter 8 appear on pages 142-46. This chapter was prepared by Cecilia
Wassén.

Pharisees and the Essenes, when he describes the different parties of the Jews. The Sadducees are depicted as a small group of people from the upper classes.[5] They do not believe in fate, resurrection, reward or punishment, but stress the importance of free will. While the Pharisees are said to be affectionate to each other the Sadducees are "boorish in their behaviour" and rude to each other as well as to foreigners.[6] With regard to *halakah*, Josephus reports that the Pharisees are able to enforce their practice on the Sadducees, because they are supported by the masses, while the Sadducees have followers only from the upper classes.[7] He states that the Sadducean penalty code is more severe than that of the Pharisees.[8] Furthermore, he claims that the Sadducees accept no laws or rules apart from those in the written Torah.[9] The Pharisees, however, followed oral traditions; according to Josephus this was the heart of the dispute between the Pharisees and the Sadducees.[10]

The rabbinic literature focusses on the halakhic divergences between the Pharisees and the Sadducees. The Boethusians appear as a group closely associated with, or a part of, the Sadducees. Nothing explicit is said about the groups' social positions or their theologies.[11] The Pharisees are described as the winners in the disputes and the Pharisaic *halakah* is said to have been applied in the Temple ritual.[12] In the earliest traditions, the Tannaitic material, we find at least twelve halakhic issues in which the Sadducean or the Boethusian position is distinct from the halakhic point of view of either Mishna or Tosefta. The Pharisees are explicitly mentioned as opponents in five of the debates: immersion of the *menorah*, ritual impurity by handling the Holy Scripture, *nissoq* (the liquid flowing from one vessel into another), owners' responsibility over damages caused by their slaves, and female inheritance.[13] Other opponents to the Sadducees recorded in the halakhic discourses are "the sages" and individual Rabbis.[14] In two additional passages the people at large are portrayed as being opposed to the Boethusians' mode of rituals in the Temple.[15] The opponents' views are generally considered to represent the Pharisaic *halakah*. No distinction is usually made, therefore, between the controversies in which the "Pharisees" are mentioned and those in which they are not explicitly referred to.

The Talmudic literature further explores most of the halakhic debates between the parties which are mentioned in the Tannaitic literature, and the same groups of opponents appear again. A few new controversies are recorded, for example regarding the *tamid* offering, execution by burning and the animal skin used for *tephillin*.[16] Altogether about 20 halakhic disputes may be derived from the rabbinic corpus.[17] The main areas of disagreement concern purity laws, the Temple ritual, civil law, penalty law and the calendar. In these debates both parties usually support their viewpoints by reference to the Torah, even in cases where the specific issue under discussion is not mentioned in it.

The majority of scholars understand the main difference between the Sadducees and the Pharisees to be their different attitudes toward oral halakhic traditions. In general, they hold that the Sadducees considered only the written Torah absolutely authoritative while the Pharisees considered the oral laws to be as binding as the written. But scholars have different views of the Sadducean *halakah*, differing on whether the Sadducees followed oral tradition apart from the written law, whether they interpreted the Torah more literally than the Pharisees, and the background of the controversy. The works of seven scholars on these issues will be considered, divided into three groups; the first group stems from the first half of this century, and the two others from the later part.

## Lauterbach, Finkelstein and Zeitlin

In the early part of the 20th century some influential scholars attempted to clarify the backgrounds of the disputes and to find general principles of disagreement between the Sadducees and the Pharisees. Jacob Lauterbach is significant[18] and his ideas are still current.[19] He described the origin of the parties as resulting from a split between the priests and laymen. The priests, he claimed, struggled to maintain their benefits and power, against laymen, who, religiously motivated, attempted to make Torah accessible to all Israel. The priests later formed the party of the Sadducees, while from the lay teachers the Pharisees developed.[20]

Lauterbach showed full confidence in the reports given in the rabbinic literature and Josephus. These sources show, he claimed, that the fundamental difference between the Sadducees and the Pharisees consisted in their distinctive attitude towards the traditional laws not recorded in Torah. The Pharisees considered such laws to be as authoritative as the written, while the Sadducees did not regard them as obligatory. According to Lauterbach, the Sadducees nonetheless adhered to these traditional laws and kept them as their priestly forefathers had done. He argued that the reason that only a few controversies were recorded in the rabbinic literature is that the Sadducees might have followed all the rest of the traditional laws. He described the Sadducees as highly conservative and claimed that the rabbinic literature shows that the Sadducees held on to the literal meaning of the Torah and to old beliefs.[21]

Lauterbach gave an explanation of the origin of the attitude he perceived among the Sadducees. In Nehemiah 10 it is recorded that the community recognized the Law of Moses as their constitution before Ezra, the priest and scribe, and that the priestly leaders together with the people took an oath to obey the laws forever. Lauterbach argued that the Sadducees—the priestly part— remained true to the oath taken by their fathers. Only those laws included in the oath were therefore binding, and only in their simple literal sense, as they would have been understood in the time when the oath was taken. No other laws could therefore attain the same status. The reason that the Sadducees adhered to the oath was their fear of the curses related to it, according to Lauterbach. He considered this to be superstition. Another reason for their conservatism was the wish to retain the old priestly benefits, as described in the Torah—to be the official interpreters and teachers of the *torah*.[22]

From this basic understanding of the Sadducean attitude to the laws he drew several conclusions. Because the Sadducees obeyed the laws in the Torah out of fear for the oath, they neither respected nor were devoted to the Torah; instead, they became slaves of the letter. In apparent contradiction to this point Lauterbach also held that while the Sadducees were rigid in their observance of the Temple ritual, they transgressed the laws for everyday life. The reason for this, he argued, is that it gradually became impossible to follow the written laws, and the Sadducees would generally not adjust them to new circumstances.

At the same time Lauterbach acknowledged that the Sadducees did create new laws to regulate the ordinary life, which they did not consider as binding as those written in Torah. He claimed that these rules were written down in the "Book of Decrees."[23] In this way, they did adjust somewhat to new needs as circumstances changed. He argued, however, that since the Sadducees created extra-scriptural laws with no connection to Torah they did not conform Torah to a new lifestyle, thereby excluding all possibilities of progress in it. In this way, in fact, they separated the scriptural laws from life and become "blind slaves to the letter of the Law without regard for its spirit."[24] The religion of the Sadducees, according to Lauterbach, became thereby "mere formalism and ritualism."[25] The Pharisees, in contrast, who also added new laws, linked them to the Torah by scriptural argument. Lauterbach argued that the Pharisees thereby injected an element of evolution and progress into their understanding of the written laws, and connected them to life.[26]

Unfortunately, Lauterbach did not give much evidence for his theory about the oath. His main argument was that the Sadducees held on to old beliefs and had a strict literal interpretation of Torah, in which the necessity of obeying the laws was expressed in terms of oaths and curses.[27] His theory is questionable since the oath is never referred to in connection with the Sadducees in any source. Further, he does not show that the Sadducees in actual fact were literal in their interpretation, to the extent that they were like blind slaves. His theory of the oath as the underlying reason for Saducean conservativism has never been widely accepted.

Although Lauterbach's theory of the Sadducees as those who adhered to the literal meaning of Torah because of the oath was never widely accepted, his general portrayal of the Sadducees was. His major contribution to the understanding of the Sadducees in comparison with the Pharisees is the emphasis he put on their different attitudes to extra-scriptural tradition, acknowledging that the Sadducees both kept traditional laws and created their own.

Lauterbach conducted an analysis of a major controversy concerning Yom Kippur between the Sadducees and the Pharisees, in accordance with his general view on the parties.[28] The issue of debate was at what moment the High Priest should put the incense on the coal when entering the Holy of Holies. The Pharisees argued that it should be performed after he had gone through the curtain; this Lauterbach regarded as the proper literal meaning of the scripture. According to the Sadducees the High Priest should perform the ritual before going through the curtain, so that he would enter the Holy of Holies covered with smoke from the incense. Lauterbach claimed that this was the ancient ritual which the Pharisees wanted to reform. The rabbinic texts do not give any reason for the dispute; instead, a variety of scriptural and non-scriptural arguments are used on both sides. Lauterbach acknowledged that the Pharisaic arguments were poor, and he searched for an underlying theological controversy. He brought to light various old and (in his view) superstitious beliefs connected with the Holy of Holies, e.g., that God could be seen there and that the one who saw him would die, that Satan the accuser would follow the High Priest and that an angel would hit and kill the High Priest.[29] These beliefs are recorded in rabbinic literature and were held by some Rabbis. Lauterbach explained that these were old priestly beliefs that had yet not died out in Talmudic times. The Pharisees in their lofty conception of the omnipresent God fought against any superstitious anthropomorphic views of God, and therefore they changed the ritual. While the Sadducees saw the smoke as a protecting barrier for the High Priest, against both the hazard of seeing God and that of being followed by Satan, the Pharisees demonstrated that these beliefs were wrong by insisting that the High Priest should enter without any smoke around him.[30]

Lauterbach demonstrated his anti-Saducean bias by attributing primitive beliefs to the Sadducees, even though these beliefs are found both in Torah and the Talmud, and only developed theological positions are attributed to the Pharisees. Perhaps the Sadducees held on to the old ritual not because of a "primitive" theology but simply out of conservatism.

Lauterbach's explanation of the background of the controversy over Yom Kippur has been well received by other scholars. Jean Le Moyne, for example, considers Lauterbach's interpretation the solution to the problem.[31]

Another scholar who focussed on the rabbinic records of the disputes between the parties was Louis Finkelstein.[32] Like Lauterbach, he thought that the controversies originated in the priestly struggle for benefits and their materialistic and self-serving interests. He found considerable evidence of priestly aristocratic wealth and cynicism — as well as of the desire for prestige — behind the controversies.[33] These priests, he argued, were not Sadducees but an earlier pre-Hasmonean priesthood out of which the Sadducees developed and whose *halakah* they kept.

Finkelstein accepted the rabbinic accounts as factual. For example, he adopted the rabbinic notion that the Sadducees admired the Pharisaic teaching although they formally rejected it. Finkelstein thought that many of the Sadducees in the later part of the Second Temple period were pious and good-willed people because they sided with the Pharisees secretly, unlike their priestly ancestors.[34] He argued that the Sadducean *halakah* did not give evidence of being closer to the literal meaning of the Torah than the Pharisaic. Instead he claimed that the earlier high-priesthood had rejected some of the biblical laws because they were too difficult to follow. He gave ten examples of the Sadducean *halakah* which he classified as contravening the prescriptions of the Torah. One example was the Sadducean position on the issue of incense on Yom Kippur. He agreed with the explanation given by Lauterbach but argued that several factors were involved. The Sadducean way of preparing the incense corresponded to both pagan customs and the procedure by which slaves approached their masters. He acknowledged that a reason for the Sadducees' rejection of the literal sense of the commandment might have been that the Pharisaic prescription for preparing the incense was more difficult to perform in the darkness, and might also have involved a danger of fire. Still, Finkelstein regarded the Sadducean position as a "cynical disregard of the plain command of Scripture."[35]

Finkelstein also gave two examples of how the Sadducees opposed the "spirit of the Biblical Law": their position on the controversy of water libation on Sukkot and Josephus's notion that the Sadducees were stringent in their penalty code.[36] Finkelstein thus had a personal bias in favour of the Pharisees, which shines through his description of the controversies. He sided with the arguments of the Pharisees and was disturbed by the Sadducees' deviation from the literal meaning of Torah.[37]

Finkelstein's *The Pharisees* has been a useful source for anyone interested in the Sadducees, by providing an exhaustive analysis including almost all the rabbinic records on the issue. For a traditional understanding of the disputes between the Sadducees and the Pharisees, his study may be classified as "a standard work."

The third scholar to be considered is Solomon Zeitlin who saw the Sadducees as the party for the wealthy, both laymen and priests.[38] As was usual for any upper class at this time, he argued, they were assimilated into the ruling class and adopted Hellenistic customs. The Pharisees[39] were the people at large who opposed the aristocracy. Zeitlin analyzed 12 halakic controversies between the Sadducees and the Pharisees and found major disagreements behind many of them. He claimed that the rabbinic material shows that the parties had different conceptions of the very essence of the Judean state, in that the Pharisees were concerned with the laity and the Sadducees were primarily concerned with the priests.

Zeitlin concluded that the basic conflict was between the Pharisees' attempts to democratize religion and engage the participation of the whole people in the rituals, and the Sadducees' efforts to maintain the segregation between the common people and the priests. Zeitlin thought that three of the halakhic disputes showed this tendency. Regarding the financing of the daily offering in the Temple, the *tamid*, the Pharisees insisted that money should be taken from public funds while the Sadducees allowed individuals to contribute.[40] Zeitlin interpreted the Sadducean position as aiming to exclude poor people from the offering. In two disputes, regarding the willow-beating ceremony on Sukkot[41] and the cutting of the *omer*,[42] the Sadducean *halakah* was stricter in its insistence on Sabbath observance. It prevented the rituals taking place on a Sabbath, while according to the Pharisees, these rituals should also be performed on the Sabbath. The rituals were a popular event in which lay people participated. Zeitlin argued that the Pharisaic standpoint was taken to eradicate the discrepancy in status between the common people and the priests. Since the priests were allowed to perform rituals during the Sabbath in the Temple, which would normally have meant breaking the Sabbath laws, the lay people should have the same right to perform the ceremonies.[43]

Zeitlin perceived theological motives behind two halakhic controversies regarding the Temple ritual. Concerning the issue of incense on Yom Kippur, he adopted Lauterbach's explanation. The other controversy concerned the libation on Sukkot, in which water was poured on the altar. Rabbinic literature records that a Sadducean priest once poured the water on his feet instead of the altar, and because of that was bombarded by *etrogim* thrown by the people.[44] Zeitlin argued that this showed that the Sadducees opposed the Temple ritual altogether, while the Pharisees accepted it. According to Zeitlin, this was an ancient ritual which had the magical connotation of inducing rainfall. The problem arises as to why the Pharisees agreed to the ritual, while the Sadducees, who according to Zeitlin were supposed to have held ancient beliefs, did not. Zeitlin drew the conclusion that the Pharisees in fact did not sympathize with the performance, since "rain is a divine gift and only through prayer to God can one plea for rain"; but because it was a popular practice, they agreed to it.[45] The reason for the Sadducees' opposition was, according to Zeitlin, that as wealthy landowners they were concerned about proper rainfall and preferred to perform the water libation outside the Temple according to ancient Israelite practice.[46]

Zeitlin's conviction that the Pharisees held the better position in every instance was firm, and he did not hide the fact that he was guided by his prior assumptions in interpreting the halakic controversies.[47]

The views of Lauterbach, Finkelstein and Zeitlin have dominated the field. All three ascribed complete reliability to rabbinic accounts. They concluded that the Sadducees were forced to follow the Pharisaic *halakah* in the Temple and that the Pharisees were victorious in the debates. They also studied Josephus uncritically. These scholars admired the Pharisees in every respect and interpreted the controversies accordingly. They found conflicting interests behind many of the controversies which cast the Sadducees in a bad light. Lauterbach noted that the Sadducees acknowledged oral traditions and created their own laws, and yet he portrayed them as blind slaves of the letter. Finkelstein, on the other hand, considered controversies where the Sadducees contravened the literal meaning, and his conclusion was that they cynically violated the law.

---

### Daube and Lightstone

---

Some recent scholars take positions similar to those of the scholars mentioned above, but others have questioned such an understanding.

David Daube disputes the common view that the Sadducees were literal in their interpretation of the Torah.[48] He considers their interpretation to be reasonable, flexible and far from literal. He acknowledges that the Sadducean laws generally are closer to the scripture, but argues that this is due to Pharisaic deviation from the literal meaning rather than any literalism on the part of the Sadducees. Daube recounts two instances in rabbinic literature which illustrate a liberal interpretation on the part of the Sadducees. First, he points to the controversy over the execution of false witnesses. The Sadducees advocated execution of the witnesses if their testimony led to the killing of the accused, referring to *lex talionis* ("life for life, eye for eye"), which they argued presupposed that the accused was already dead. The Pharisees, according to Daube, held that the witnesses were to be put to death only if their attempt failed, i.e., if the accused was freed.[49] Daube argues that the stricter Pharisaic interpretation corresponds with the literal meaning in the Torah while the Sadducees deviated from it in order to make the law in tune with the general criminal code. He considers their rationalization of the literal meaning to be "a tenable piece of interpretation." The second example is the dispute over owners' responsibility for damages caused by their slaves, a question on which the Torah is silent.[50] The Sadducees supported their case by using an *a fortiori* argument. The reasoning is based on the notion that the Torah imposes duties on owners regarding their slaves (circumcision, etc.) and not concerning their animals.[51] Would not the owner be responsible for damages caused by slaves, they argued, for whom he has duties, considering that he is responsible for damages caused by animals, for whom he has not duties? Daube considers the Sadducean interpretation to be highly liberal.

Daube argues that the Sadducees refused to recognize the huge body of Pharisaic oral laws. Still, both parties upheld oral traditions. The main difference was the status attached to them. Contrary to the Pharisees, the Sadducees assigned no binding authority to the traditions outside the scriptural realm. Therefore, Daube argues, their position in matters outside the Torah could easily be defeated by the Pharisees who regarded their oral traditions as absolute. Daube further argues that the Sadducean emphasis on written authority forced the Pharisees to base their traditions on the Torah as well. He explains that in the time of Hillel the Pharisees adhered to the Sadducean principle that no law was binding if it was not founded on the Torah. They also took over Sadducean hermeneutical principles, such as the principle of *a fortiori* arguments, in order to derive oral traditions from the Torah.

The theories put forward by Daube are innovative and important. He shows that the rabbinic evidence does not always support the general view of the Sadducees as being literal in their interpretation of the Torah; on the contrary, there is evidence that points in the opposite direction. Daube is convinced that the misconception has arisen because historians have looked at Jewish history "through Pharisaic spectacles."[52]

Jack Lightstone also looks for general principles behind the halakhic controversies.[53] He limits his research to the earliest, and what he considers to be the best, rabbinic evidence—the Tannaitic literature. He further limits his study to those pericopes in which both the Sadducees (or Boethusians) and the Pharisees are mentioned. Lightstone presumes that the heart of the controversy is most likely to surface in those texts where both groups appear together. His analysis is therefore confined to seven pericopes only.[54] He finds no general principles of disagreement behind them: "Appeals by either group to general criteria, such as Oral Law *versus* Written Law, or exegetical *versus* literal interpretation of Scripture, are conspicuously absent."[55] Instead, he argues, the pericopes show differences over particular laws, spanning a wide range of legal issues. Lightstone makes some noteworthy points showing that this rabbinic material does not support the common portrayal of the controversies between the two parties. For instance, the Sadducees ridiculed the Pharisees for immersing the *menorah*, saying: "Come and see the Pharisees who are immersing the light of the moon."[56] Lightstone points out that these Pharisees undoubtedly were priests, since they performed the immersion within the sanctuary. This contradicts the usual classification of the Sadducees as the priestly party opposed to the Pharisees, who are usually seen as representatives of the laity. Furthermore, the Sadducees appear to have the less stringent purity law, since no immersion was necessary according to the Sadducean *halakah*. Concerning the question of *nissoq*,[57] the parties were accusing each other of leniency in issues of purity. Further, in the debate whether Holy Scripture renders the hands unclean both groups attempted to prove the inconsistency of their opponents' *halakah*.[58] In one case alone, on the question of female inheritance, is the Sadducean *halakah* closer to the literal meaning of Scripture, but the Sadducees do not appeal to Torah in the text.[59]

Lightstone describes the discussions between the parties as highly rhetorical and mutually abusive ("We cry out against you, Pharisees . . ." and "We cry out against you, Sadducees . . ."). He examines the material from a historical-critical point of view, comparing parallel texts, and tracing the redactional work. One phrase of particular importance, which he rates as later interpolation, is the expression "we (or they) fear the Pharisees" (referring to the Sadducees). Overall, Lightstone is highly sceptical of the historical value of the pericopes. He finds significant evidence of the redactional process, first, in the developed formulaic structure and, second, in the vilification of the Sadducees, which he understands as the result of later rabbinic redaction.[60] Furthermore, the fact that the Pharisaic standpoint is in accordance with that of *Mishnah* in every instance might show that the Tannaim projected their own laws onto the Pharisees.[61] Lightstone concludes that rabbinic material as

a whole provides no help in reconstructing the nature of the controversy between the Sadducean and the Pharisaic parties pre-70 C.E.
His conclusion is based on the assumption that the rest of rabbinic
literature will be no more useful for the task than the earliest evidence which he examined.

---

## Le Moyne and Saldarini

---

Jean Le Moyne makes an important contribution with a thorough
analysis of all available evidence on the Sadducees.[62] He is more
optimistic than Lightstone concerning the possibilities of finding
pre-70 evidence on the Sadducees in rabbinic literature. He acknowledges that rabbinic literature was written in order to justify
the Pharisaic point of view, and advocates, therefore, a careful critical examination of the material. He claims that the depiction of Sadducean *halakah* often is historically accurate, whereas details in the
controversies, such as many of the phrases that are put into the
mouths of Sadducees, are less certain.[63]

Le Moyne stresses that the Sadducees were religious people;
nowhere are they criticized for being impious. On the contrary,
they are portrayed as a group anxious to fulfil the commandments
in the Torah. Le Moyne also disputes the common view that the
Sadducees were primarily a priestly party. True, the High Priests
were generally Sadducees, but there is no evidence showing that the
ordinary members were priests. Josephus does not portray them as
priests, and in Acts 4:1, "the priests" are distinguished from "the
Sadducees." Further, he argues that the existence of Sadducean laymen is attested in Acts 23:14, where the elders mentioned are Sadducees.[64]

According to Le Moyne the Sadducees were characterized by
their fidelity towards the Torah, which they interpreted in its literal
sense. In contrast to Lauterbach he argues that it was out of devotion for the Torah that the Sadducees observed the commandments
according to the letter. Le Moyne presents a rabbinic saying which,
he argues, shows the Sadducees' fundamental view on the Torah:
Rabbi Ishmael (d. 135 C.E.) says in opposition to Rabbi Akiba's complex method of interpreting every detail in the text, "The Torah
speaks in human language." According to Le Moyne the saying
makes the point that no interpretation by scholars, or any tradition,
is necessary for an understanding of the Torah. Le Moyne explains
that Rabbi Ishmael is the last representative of the older *halakah*,
which he thinks corresponds with the Sadducean view.[65] Le Moyne
points out several controversies in which the Sadducees stick to the
letter of the *torah*, as opposed to the Pharisees. For example, the
Sadducees interpreted the *lex talionis* literally,[66] and the Sadducean

conviction that the High Priest should wait until sunset to become purified at the burning of the Red Heifer is closer to the *torah* than the view of the Pharisees.[67]

Le Moyne argues that due to their fidelity to the letter of the *torah*, the Sadducees were hostile toward new rituals, laws and beliefs not recorded in the Torah. The beliefs in resurrection, and reward and punishment after death, are examples of popular ideas rejected by the Sadducees. They did not accept the feast of Purim or the water libation on Sukkot either, since these popular practices lacked scriptural legitimation.[68] Their literal interpretation of the Torah also brought about a major divergence over purity, which, according to Le Moyne, was a fundamental halakhic controversy between the Sadducees and the Pharisees. The Pharisees imposed the purity rules prescribed for the Temple rituals on the common people outside the Temple, while the Sadducees continued to regard them as applicable only within the sanctuary.[69] As a matter of fact, there is no explicit evidence that proves that this was the actual view of the Sadducees. Le Moyne argues, however, that the debate over the burning of the Red Heifer is not intelligible if we do not presuppose this basic controversy.[70] That purity rules in general were the subject of arguments between the two parties is shown by the fact that many controversies on this matter are recorded in rabbinic literature.[71]

Besides the emphasis on the written Torah, the Sadducees also upheld certain traditions not recorded in Torah. Le Moyne argues, however, that these traditions did not acquire the same status of obligatory law as they did in the Pharisaic system. This is clearly illustrated in one specific controversy, the willow-beating ceremony on Sukkot. During six days on Sukkot there was a daily procession in the Temple with people carrying branches which they laid down around the altar. If the seventh day fell on the Sabbath the ceremony continued for one day extra. On the sixth day, or on the seventh (if the seventh fell on the Sabbath), the people beat the soil around the holocaust with the branches in accordance with the Pharisaic *halakah*. The Boethusians repudiated the beating only if it fell on a Sabbath. It happened once on a Sabbath, according to *Tosefta*, that the Boethusians tried to hide the willows in order to prevent the people from using them. The ritual was a popular practice, but was not mentioned in the Torah. Le Moyne explains that, for the Pharisees, the tradition (as in this case) had obligatory status and thus had precedence over the Sabbath, while the Boethusians rejected the ritual according to the principle that the Sabbath takes primacy over rituals not commanded in the Torah.[72]

Le Moyne points out that the Sadducees also created their own *halakah* on issues where the Torah was silent. He distinguishes between instances when the Sadducees support their *halakah* by scriptural arguments and arguments in which the scripture is not used. In the first category we have four cases: concerning *tamid, omer,* owners' responsibility for slaves and the execution of false witnesses. Le Moyne believes that Sadducees' attempt to support their practice by scripture demonstrates their belief that they were following the letter of the law. In the second category we find among others the controversy on female inheritance and *nissoq*.[73] Le Moyne, like Daube, argues that the Sadducees, by emphasizing the written Torah, may have forced the Pharisees to justify their new practices with scripture.

Regarding the reasons behind the controversies, it is apparent that the split derived to a great extent from conflicting attitudes towards Torah and traditions. Le Moyne points out that, in many cases, there were also other motives. This is evident in controversies where the parties are not arguing over scriptural exegesis, and in cases where they are forcing the meaning of the text to prove their case. Le Moyne concludes that we can not know what the original rationale might have been. In a few controversies, however, he still suggests underlying motives. Concerning Yom Kippur, Le Moyne presumes a theological conflict and sympathizes with Lauterbach's theory. He also considers it feasible that an aristocratic tendency is shown in one instance, the dispute over the *tamid* offering, but he is not thereby saying that the Sadducees generally were aristocrats.

Anthony Saldarini presents a study on the Sadducees and the Pharisees using sociological and text-critical methods.[74] He is highly sceptical of the historicity of the information on the Sadducees that is provided in rabbinic literature, including both the early and the later sources. Rabbinic authors in general, he claims, perceived the Sadducees as opponents of the Pharisees, but apart from that possessed no knowledge of the details of the controversies. He gives as an example of the *Talmud*'s ignorance of this historical reality the fact that the Sadducees are sometimes not even portrayed as legitimate Jews but as heretics. In the narrative on the controversy on the burning of the Red Heifer the Pharisees are said to have deliberately rendered the High Priest unclean in order to force him to purify himself according to the Pharisaic norm. Saldarini rejects the account as fiction.[75] He argues that *Mishnah* and *Tosefta* provide us with only a few historical remarks, and give no information on the exact teaching of the Sadducees. Since the Sadducees opposed the Pharisaic *halakah* and accordingly the Mishnaic as well. It follows that *Mishnah* recounts the controversies in order to ridicule the arguments that are challenging its position. He sides with Lightstone in arguing that the early sources do not provide any clear picture of a general disagreement between the two parties. The sources merely show that the Sadducees had different laws from those of the Pharisees, especially in the area of purity rules. Further, he rejects as unhistorical the notion that the Pharisees were in charge of the Temple.[76]

Saldarini presents a sociological understanding of features related to the Sadducees. He considers it to be certain that the Sadducees were generally more conservative, and negatively disposed toward new customs and beliefs. This, he explains, fits the general pattern for upper classes and governing bodies, among whom he reckons the Sadducees. As a rule, they strive to preserve the status quo. Saldarini understands the controversy over purity in similar terms. If the Pharisees imposed purity rules on all Israel, the Sadducees would certainly have been against it. He argues that the Sadducees, who generally were priests, would strongly have disliked seeing common people observing rules especially designated for themselves, and would not have allowed the laws to be diluted.[77]

Saldarini argues that there is no justification for differentiating the Sadducees from the Pharisees on the basis of their rejection of the oral Torah, or the supposed literalness of their interpretation of the Torah. He accuses scholars who attribute such characteristics to the Sadducees of using the sources uncritically.[78] Instead, he argues, no interpretation of either group is to be considered as particularly literal, since both are trying to link their laws to the Torah. Further, all post-exilic groups were engaged in the processes of adaptation to new circumstances and had their own "oral Torah," i.e., customs and traditions beyond the Torah for how to live.

## Conclusion

Many important questions are at stake in the study of the Sadducean *halakah*, and there is a diversity of opinions among scholars in the area. First, how may we describe their *halakah*? Earlier scholars tended to interpret the halakhic disputes by accepting the generally negative portrayal of the Sadducees presented in the sources. They argued that the *halakah* reflected the Sadducees' social status as well as theological standpoints, showing that they were wealthy, superstitious and power-seeking, and that they held ancient beliefs combined with a literal interpretation of the Torah. They were generally considered to be a primarily priestly party, struggling against the lay movement and its Pharisaic leaders. The optimism shown by these scholars about the possibility of characterizing Sadducean *halakah* conclusively was due to the fact that historical criticism had not yet become a major concern. Occasionally they were guided in their interpretation of the sources by their personal bias toward the Pharisees.

In the last several decades there has been a growing awareness of the need for critical analysis of the sources. The adoption of a critical and more objective approach has made more difficult the attempt to characterize the Saducean *halakah* and its differences from Pharisaic positions, since the sources do not easily allow us to classify their respective *halakah* in terms of contrasts and polarities. The fundamental issue today that has to be dealt with more extensively is how to evaluate the sources. The degree of scepticism regarding the historical value of rabbinic reports on the Saducees varies considerably among scholars. Lightstone and Saldarini argue that there is hardly any historical information in rabbinic literature on the Saducean *halakah* pre-70 C.E. Le Moyne on the other hand argues that the parties' halakic standpoints are generally accurately recorded, although the details are often unhistorical.

In order to comprehend the Saducean *halakah*, the question of their attitude toward Torah and tradition must be resolved. This is a complex problem, as is shown by the variety of opinions presented by scholars. The discussion is often confusing; some of the confusion would be avoided if scholars could agree on the definition of "conservative," and on what a "literal" or "liberal" interpretation of Torah would entail, in the study of the Saducees and the Pharisees. Lauterbach argued that the Pharisees, who connected their extra-scriptural laws with the Torah, were liberal in contrast to the Saducees, who did not connect their unwritten laws to scripture at all. Saldarini argues that none of the parties' interpretations are to be considered as literal, since they obviously supported their views by intentionally interpreting the Torah to favour their own positions. Le Moyne, on the other hand, considers the scriptural support given by the Saducees, even in cases where the Torah was silent, to prove their fidelity to the Torah. Both Daube and Le Moyne argue that the emphasis on scripture on the part of the Saducees forced the Pharisees to support their new laws with scripture. The question of the Saducean attitude toward the Torah is closely related to the question of their attitude to tradition, these are two aspects of the same problem. Both aspects of the problem should, therefore, be dealt with together, in order to obtain a coherent picture of the Saducean *halakah*. It is difficult to find any consistency in the portrayal of the Saducees given by Lauterbach, for example, who argued that the Saducees were slaves of the letter and at the same time claimed that they created their own laws.

It is evident that the Saducees created their own *halakah* in matters where the Torah was silent, for example concerning owners' responsibility for damages caused by their slaves. Further, they accepted traditions not recorded in the Torah, such as willow-beating on Sukkot. This makes it impossible to uphold the stereotypical image of the Sadducees as the strict keepers of the literal meaning of the Torah. Instead, the Sadducees must be recognized as bearers and creators of oral traditions. Certainly, their tradition differed from the Pharisaic, as is well attested in the sources. The difference consisted, first, in that the Sadducees possessed a different tradition from that of the Pharisees and probably did not recognize the huge body of new laws which the Pharisees embraced. Secondly, the Sadducees held a different attitude toward traditional laws than did the Pharisees, as many scholars have observed. While the Pharisees understood these laws as absolute, the Sadducees did not. This is shown in the rabbinic literature on the divergent attitudes toward the status of Sabbath laws when the strict observance was challenged by popular rituals. Josephus, who obviously was aware of the difference in acceptance of traditional laws between the Sadducees and the Pharisees, points toward a similar conclusion.

The Sadducean laws and traditions should be recognized as different from those of the Pharisees, but any contrasts should not be made too extreme. The question is whether the Sadducees would have been characterized as strictly literal in their interpretation of the Torah and as highly conservative, had they been studied on their own terms, and not in comparison with the Pharisees.

## Notes

1 Jean Le Moyne, *Les Sadducéens* (Paris: Études Bibliques, 1972), p. 67-85.
2 Matthew 22:23-33, Mark 12:18-27 and Luke 20:27-40.
3 Acts 4:1-3 and 5:17-18.
4 Flavius Josephus, *Life*, 10-12. References are to The Loeb Classical Library, 9 vols., translated by H. St. Thackeray et al. (Cambridge, MA: Harvard University Press; London: William Heinemann, 1926-65).
5 "There are but few men to whom this doctrine [the Sadducean] has been made known, but these are men of the highest standing" (*Antiquities* 18.17).
6 *War* 2.164-66.
7 *Antiquities* 13.298, 18.17.
8 *Antiquities* 13.294, 20.199.
9 "The Pharisees had passed on to the people certain regulations handed down by former generations and not recorded in the Laws of Moses, for which reason they are rejected by the Sadducaean group, who hold that only those regulations should be considered valid which were written down (in Scripture), and that those which had been handed down by former generations need not be observed" (*Antiquities* 13.297). "They [the Sadducees] own no observance of any sort apart from the laws; in fact, they reckon it a virtue to dispute with the teachers of the path of wisdom that they pursue" (*Antiquities* 18.16).
10 *Antiquities* 13.298.
11 In one case only is the High Priest explicitly reported to be a Sadducee, namely, Ishmael; *b. Ber.* 29a. During the Roman period at least six High Priests belonged to the Boethos family, who presumably were members of the Boethusians (Le Moyne, *Les Sadducéens*, p. 347).

12  Ibid., p. 110-12.
13  Immersion of the *menorah, t. Hag.* 3:35 (238, 23), *j. Hag.* 3.8, 79d 31; whether Holy Scripture render the hands unclean, *m. Yad.* 4:6, *nissoq, m. Yad.* 4:7a; owners' responsibility over damages caused by their slaves, *m. Yad.* 4:7b; female inheritance, *t. Yad.* 2:20 (684, 3), *j. B. Bat.* 8.1, 16a 5.
14  Controversies in the Tannaitic material in which the "Pharisees" are not mentioned are for example: the date for Pentecost, *t. Ros. Has.* 1:15 (210, 10); execution of false witnesses, *m. Mak.* 1:6, *t. Sanh.* 6:6 (424, 29); the burning of the Red Heifer, *m. Para* 3:7-8, *t. Para* 3:7 (623, 17); menstrual uncleanness, *t. Nid.* 5:2 (645, 23); preparation of incense on Yom Kippur, *t. Yoma* 1:8 (181, 1). The "Pharisees" appear in some of the Talmudic records concerning these disputes.
15  The rituals are willow-beating on the Sabbath at Sukkot, *t. Sukk.* 3:1 (195, 19), and water libation at Sukkot, *t. Sukk.* 3:16 (197, 22).
16  *Tephillin, b. Sabb.* 108a. The issue of dispute is whether the skin from *neboloth* and *terefoth* (animals which have not been ritually slaughtered) could be used for the making of *tephillin.* Execution by burning; according to *b. Sanh.* 52b a Sadducean court effected the execution by burning the condemned (a daughter of a priest) at the stake. The position of *Mishnah (Sanh.* 7.2) is that the convicted should be burned internally by a kindled wick forced into the mouth. *Tamid, b. Men.* 65a, see above, p. 133. Le Moyne, *Les Sadducéens,* p. 195-97, 236-38.
17  See Le Moyne, *Les Sadducéens,* p. 177-312.
18  Jacob Z. Lauterbach, "The Sadducees and Pharisees: A Study of Their Respective Attitude Toward the Law," in *Rabbinical Essays* (Cincinnati: Hebrew Union College Press, 1951), p. 23-48; originally published in *Studies in Jewish Literature, Issued in Honor of Prof. K. Kohler* (Berlin, 1913), p. 176-98.
19  For example, Lauterbach's theory of the background to the argument over preparation of incense on Yom Kippur is adopted among others by Le Moyne, *Les Sadducéens,* p. 259.
20  Lauterbach, *Rabbinic Essays,* p. 27-29.
21  Ibid., p. 23-27.
22  Ibid., p. 27-39, and Deut. 17:8-13.
23  Ibid., p. 35. Jean Le Moyne rejects the notion that the "Book of Decrees," which is mentioned in *Megillat Taanit* 12, refers to a Sadducean lawcode. The connection of the "Book of Decrees" with Sadducean laws is first posited in the medieval Hebrew commentary to *Megillat Taanit* 12. Le Moyne argues that the "Book of Decrees" originally referred to gentile laws that were forced on the Jews. He recognizes the possibility that the Sadducees kept their *halakah* in written form (*Les Sadducéens,* p. 219-23).
24  Lauterbach, *Rabbinic Essays,* p. 38.
25  Ibid., p. 39.
26  Ibid., p. 34-39, 47-48.
27  Ibid., p. 35, n. 16.
28  Lauterbach, "A Significant Controversy Between the Sadducees and the Pharisees," in *Rabbinic Essays,* p. 51-83; originally published in *Hebrew Union College Annual,* 4 (1927): 273-205; Lev. 16:12-13; *m. Yoma* 1:5; *j. Yoma* 1.5, 39a; *t. Yoma* 1.8 (181,1); *b. Yoma* 19b, 53a; *Sifra* Lev. 16:13, 68a.
29  Lauterbach, *Rabbinic Essays,* p. 60-76.
30  Ibid., p. 73-78, 83.
31  Le Moyne, *Les Sadducéens,* p. 259. Louis Finkelstein and Solomon Zeitlin adhered to Lauterbach's explanation as well.
32  Louis Finkelstein, *The Pharisees: The Sociological Background of Their Faith,*

2 vols., 3rd ed. (Philadelphia: The Jewish Publication Society of America, 1962), p. 637-753.

33 Ibid., p. 637-39. Finkelstein gave as examples: the *omer*, p. 641-54, incense on Yom Kippur, p. 654-60, willow-beating ceremony and water libation on Sukkoth, p. 700-708, the *nissoq*, p. 716-18.

34 Finkelstein, *The Pharisees*, p. 637-39.

35 Ibid., p. 654-60.

36 Ibid., p. 700-10.

37 Ibid., p. 638, 652, 660.

38 Solomon Zeitlin, "The Sadducees and the Pharisees—A Chapter in the Development of the Halakah," translated by Mordekai Shapiro, in *Studies in the Early History of Judaism*, 3 vols. (New York: KTAV Publishing, 1974), p. 259-91; originally published in Hebrew in *Horeb*, 62 (1936).

39 According to Solomon Zeitlin, the Pharisees never existed as a party, instead the name "Pharisees" was given by the Sadducees to their adversaries. Zeitlin still employs the term in its usual sense (ibid., p. 259).

40 *b. Men.* 65a.

41 *b. Sukk.* 43b, and *t. Sukk.* 3:1 (195, 19).

42 *b. Men.* 65a. *Omer*; the cutting and offering of the first fruit. The date of *omer* determined the date of Pentecost which fell on the 50th day after *omer* (Lev. 23:15).

43 Jean Le Moyne describes at length the complexity of the dating for cutting the *omer*. The differences concerning the calendars derive from an ancient period. The basic problem concerned the understanding of the description in Lev. 23; how to interpret "sabbath" in 23:11, and "seven full weeks" in 23:15. There were four different modes of calculating, which suggests that the whole problem might have been more complex than Zeitlin proposes (Le Moyne, *Les Sadducéens*, p. 177-92).

44 *b. Sukk.* 48b. In one instance the priest is said to have been Boethusian; *t. Sukk.* 3:16 (197, 22). Josephus reports that Alexander Jannai was the officiating high priest. Further, the accusation was that he was unfit for high priesthood (*Antiquities* 13.372).

45 Zeitlin, *Studies in Early History*, p. 276-77.

46 Le Moyne argues that the Sadducees probably rejected the ritual of the water libation, but on the basis that it lacked biblical ground (*Les Sadducéens*, p. 283-89).

47 For example, Zeitlin's comment on the issue of execution of false witnesses. According to the rabbinic report, the Sadducees appear to have held the most lenient position. Zeitlin cannot accept this as a possibility: "It would appear on the surface that the Pharisees had a more stringent attitude on this matter than did the Sadducees. This contradicts what we know about these sects [from Josephus], namely, that the Sadducees were rigid in judging offenders but that the Pharisees were more lenient in matters of punishment." Then he argues that the Pharisees in reality were the lenient part in this dispute (Zeitlin, *Studies in Early History*, p. 278-80). According to Le Moyne, the Pharisaic *halakah* was the stricter in this case (*Les Sadducéens*, p. 243).

48 David Daube, "Texts and Interpretation in Roman and Jewish Law," in *The Jewish Journal of Sociology*, 3 (1969): 3-28.

49 *m. Mak.* 1:6; *b. Mak.* 56b; *t. Sanh.* 6.6 (424, 29); *Sifre* Deut. 19.19 (231, 4). Daube rejects the suggestion made by Finkelstein and Geiger that the Pharisees advocated punishment of the false witnesses regardless of the outcome of the trial ("Text and Interpretation," p. 11). According to Le Moyne the divergence regarded the basis for execution of false witnesses. The Pharisees held

that it was enough if the sentence of condemnation had been pronounced while the Sadducees claimed that the execution of the accused must have taken place, before the false witness was eligible for a death sentence (*Les Sadducéens*, p. 228).

50  *m. Yad.* 4:7.

51  Exodus 21:35-36.

52  Daube, "Text and Interpretation," p. 10.

53  Jack N. Lightstone, "Sadducees *versus* Pharisees: The Tannaitic Sources," in Jacob Neusner, ed., *Christianity, Judaism and Other Greco-Roman Cults: Studies for Morton Smith at Sixty*, 4 vols. (Leiden: Brill, 1975), p. 206-17.

54  Lightstone includes two records of controversy in which the "Pharisees" are not mentioned in the Tannaitic versions but appear in Talmud — the issues of incense on Yom Kippur and menstrual uncleanness. In his choice of Tannaitic references to the Sadducean and Pharisaic controversy, Lightstone excludes other passages in which the Sadducean (or Boethusian) halakhic views conflict with those of the "sages" (execution of false witnesses, dating of the Pentecost), and individual Rabbis (burning of the Red Heifer), who are generally considered to represent the Pharisees. See above, n. 14.

55  Ibid., p. 216.

56  *t. Hag.* 3:35 (238, 23).

57  *m. Yad.* 4:7a. *Nissoq* is the stream of liquid running from one vessel into another. The issue of controversy was the following; if a liquid is poured from a clean into an unclean vessel would the former become unclean as well; i.e., did *nissoq* communicate uncleanness into the clean vessel? The Sadducees claimed that it did, while the Pharisees refuted the idea.

58  *m. Yad.* 4:6.

59  *t. Yad.* 2:20 (684, 3).

60  As examples of the tendency to slander the Sadducees, Lightstone notes that they are described as obeying, out of fear of the Pharisees, the Pharisaic *halakah* concerning the ritual on Yom Kippur and the regulations for menstruating women ("Sadducees *versus* Pharisees," p. 211-17).

61  Lightstone seems to prefer this explanation to the other possibility, which is that the Tannaim adopted the Pharisaic *halakah* in every instance (ibid., p. 216).

62  Le Moyne, *Les Sadducéens*.

63  Ibid., p. 325-26.

64  Ibid., p. 344-48, 350-52.

65  *Sifre* Num. 112; *Les Sadducéens*, p. 363. Lauterbach presents a similar interpretation of the saying (*Rabbinic Essays*, p. 31, n. 11).

66  *Les Sadducéens*, p. 223-24, and Exod. 21:24.

67  *Les Sadducéens*, p. 263-80, 371, and Num. 19:7.

68  *Les Sadducéens*, p. 363-70.

69  Ibid., p. 368-69. This is a widespread theory: Finkelstein, *The Pharisees*, p. 664; Joachim Jeremias, *Jerusalem in the Time of Jesus* (London: SCM Press, 1969), p. 231.

70  Le Moyne, *Les Sadducéens*, p. 269.

71  The controversies on purity rules involve at least the following issues: the burning of the Red Heifer, purification of the *Menorah*, the time period of women's ritual impurity after menstruation and childbirth, purifications of hands, the question whether the Holy Scriptures render the hands unclean, and *nissoq* (ibid., p. 369-72).

72  *t. Sukk.* 3:1 (195, 19), and Le Moyne, *Les Sadducéens*, p. 192-95, 374-75.

73  Ibid., p. 370-72.

74 Anthony J. Saldarini, *Pharisees, Scribes and Sadducees in Palestinian Society: A Sociological Approach* (Wilmington, DE: Michael Glazier, 1988).

75 *m. Para* 3:7-8; *b. Hag.* 23a; *t. Para* 3:8 (632, 18); and Saldarini, *Pharisees, Scribes and Sadducees*, p. 234-35, 301.

76 Ibid., p. 231-34.

77 Ibid., p. 298-308.

78 Saldarini's major target is Ellis Rivkin who is criticized for using the sources uncritically in his work *A Hidden Revolution: The Pharisees Search for the Kingdom Within* (Nashville: Abingdon, 1978), and Saldarini, *Pharisees, Scribes and Sadducees*, p. 228-31. Saldarini thinks that also Le Moyne sometimes is too uncritical in his use of rabbinic material (p. 298, n. 1).

# Chapter 9

# *Torah* and *Nomos* in Post-Biblical Judaism and Early Christianity

---

## Background

The seminar on *torah* and *nomos*, a part of the formal activities of the Canadian Society of Biblical Studies from 1983 to 1988, sought to focus on four main features: (1) the relation of *torah* as understood in a Jewish cultural setting to *nomos* as understood in a Greek-speaking environment — whether that milieu be Jewish, Christian or "pagan"; (2) the sociological and societal roles of "law," especially in Judaism, from the Hellenistic period to the time of the *Mishnah*; (3) the development within early Christianity of negative and positive understandings of "law"; and (4) the influence of the understanding of *torah-nomos* upon the relation between Judaism and Christianity as these religious groups developed along different lines.

The exercise has been comparative. It started from the conviction that legal structures reflect underlying social structures and organizations, and that, by studying understandings of "law," scholars can shed light on social and religious understandings of communities that hold those views.

It is not altogether accidental that this ongoing seminar picked up where an earlier seminar had left off. The earlier activities of the Canadian Society of Biblical Studies had focussed on anti-Judaism in early Christianity.[1] The reason for the study of *torah* and *nomos* as a sensible follow-up topic to anti-Judaism is not far to seek, for many of the same motivations impelling a polemical view by Christians of Jews also contributed to early Christianity's negative evaluation of *torah*. By some ironic twist — though probably also for some deeply rooted psychological reasons — at the very same time that the

---

Notes to Chapter 9 appear on pages 155-56. This chapter was prepared by Peter Richardson.

church was carrying on its polemic against the synagogue it was itself developing a notion of Christianity as the "new law." In this way it could denigrate Judaism and assert the ongoing validity of law, an obvious displacement technique.

It is, however, noteworthy that little has been done to study law in Judaism and Christianity on a comparative basis and in equivalent terms. Dictionary articles rarely tell the full story; but it is evident from a perusal of various classical and modern dictionaries that the question is neglected. It is worth noting two examples. The recent edition of the *Encyclopedia Britannica* has headings in the summary volume for "Egyptian Law," "Cuneiform Law," "Chinese Law," "Greek Law," "Hellenistic Law," "Roman Law," "Germanic Law," "Medieval European Law" and so on, but nothing on "Jewish Law."[2] And in its articles there are treatments of primitive law and comparative law, Greek and Hellenistic and Roman Law, Western philosophy of Law, but nothing on Jewish Law, Torah, or Christian law, except insofar as they are buried in other more general articles.

And in the *Encyclopedia of Religion*, edited by Mircea Eliade, one finds a disappointing treatment of "Law and Religion" which presents an "Overview," "Law and Religion in South Asia," ". . . in East Asia," ". . . in the West" and—in the longest section—"Religion and the Constitution of the United States." There is hardly a reference to Judaism and Law in this section and only the briefest description of Christianity and law, despite the claim in the header that "This entry concerns the interactions between religious traditions and legal systems, and it explores the ways in which religion has influenced the development of law in several of the world's major cultural areas." These absences are made up in two other entries, on "Israelite Law" and on "Halakah" (and also by an entry on "Islamic Law"). But in a dictionary stressing a comparative approach, the decision to leave these important topics out of the entry on Law and Religion is regrettable.[3] And still there is nothing dealing properly with Christianity and Law.

The point is twofold: first, that *torah* as developed in and characteristic of Judaism is undervalued in comparative treatments, or else is considered to be so particular to Judaism that it is simply dealt with as an indistinguishable part of the fabric of Jewish history and religion. And second, that Law in Christianity is thought of almost entirely in terms of later canonical law and not as a factor in the earliest development of social and ethical attitudes. From this double failure has come a pervasive tendency to avoid the study of *torah* and *nomos* in a comparative setting during the early period.

It is obvious from the previous eight chapters that questions of *torah* and *nomos* have been much discussed over the last century and more by Jewish and Christian scholars. But the examinations have been limited, and have not attempted very often to look at the role of "law" in the religious *structures* of Christianity and Judaism. There is still a need for substantial studies, mutually informing each other, that show more of the similarities and differences between Jewish and Christian notions of law, the striving for a given in each, the way they have influenced each other, the influence on the relations of the two religious communities, and — perhaps especially — the semantic relation of the words *torah* and *nomos*.

## Semantic Considerations

Some studies have already been published on the linguistic and semantic question in *Studies in Religion/Sciences Religieuses*.[4] In its first year, the seminar was presented a paper by Alan F. Segal[5] in which Sandmel's claim (that the separation between Judaism and Christianity was the fault of a Hellenistic translation of *torah* by *nomos*) was subjected to critical scrutiny. The influence of Sandmel's view that all western culture has been misled by an essentially non-rabbinic understanding of Judaism was reinforced by Dodd's strong argument that Paul was misled by the LXX translation. This inherited view, Segal argues from a study of Philo, is wrong. *Nomos* is not a bad translation for *torah*, especially if one removes the Platonic framework, since Philo understands and makes use of the ambiguities of the term *nomos* quite well.

Later, Stephen Westerholm went further in demonstrating how this semantic question has been shaped by Wellhausen and Schechter.[6] Wellhausen did not like law, even in ancient Judaism; he saw it as a regression following the creative developments in the prophetic period. For Wellhausen the post-exilic period was narrow-minded and legalistic. Schechter, however, argued that *torah* does not mean "law" and that Second Temple Judaism was under a night of legalism. But he argued this without an adequate semantic study of *torah*. Dodd sought to supply such a study but his study was not adequate; the effect has been a shaping of Christian attitudes that identify Judaism as legalistic and that show a condescending attitude to Judaism. Westerholm, on the other hand, stresses the semantic range of words for "law"; he argues that sometimes *torah* is well translated by *nomos*, and that while Paul's view of law is different from the rabbi's views it is not because of his use of *nomos*.

Adele Reinhartz has argued in a somewhat similar but more limited way.[7] In analyzing one treatise of Philo's she demonstrates convincingly that Philo departs from a narrow definition of *nomos*; he depicts the Pentateuch as a law code providing specific injunctions but he also sees it as pointing to the ideal life, life according to nature. For Philo what is special about the law of Moses is that it breaks out of a narrow legal definition of *nomos* to cover territory not covered by other law codes. The translation of *torah* by *nomos* did not lead to misunderstandings by Hellenistic readers—nor by Paul.

One of these points had earlier been very helpfully tackled head-on by Harold Remus.[8] *Nomoi* belong to the givens of particular cultures, to their social worlds. The striving for a given was not limited to Jews and Christians but was found in paganism as well, and where it was found it touched sensitive nerves. Philo, however, when he used the phrase *nomos physeōs* was evidencing a strong desire to transcend cultural relativity and to locate somewhere a given beyond his own people's *nomos*. That *nomos* was a Hellenistic transmutation of materials from a culture distant from his own. When he weds *nomos* and *physis* into another given, he develops a pairing that wins consent through its ingenuousness and ingenuity.

On a different tack, William Klassen examined how, in Musonius Rufus, the king is viewed as animate law, as *empsychos nomos*.[9] This concept, widely discussed in the Hellenistic period, leads to a corollary: not only is the good king a philosopher but the philosopher is a kingly person. The animate law—the King—then stands alongside the inanimate—the written law. This notion, argues Klassen, informs a number of passages in the New Testament that are often interpreted wrongly without reference to this concept.

These papers just described all too briefly expanded the horizons of the seminar and began to form a new consensus. That consensus focussed on the damage done by a too narrow range of meanings that had been attached to *nomos* in Jewish and Christian circles. The assumption that *torah* had been wrongly translated by *nomos* was itself inadequate (perhaps even wrong), and that it caused subsequent misunderstandings that could have been avoided itself was responsible for shaping contemporary attitudes towards Judaism and its *torah*.

## Community Considerations

Another theme that has emerged in the papers published to date and that deserves brief exposure here is the way "law" comes to be interpreted. I have in mind the fact that, while "law" (*torah*, *nomos*) serves as the basic constitutional document of Judaism, its various communities have tended to develop secondary or subordinate documents that come to take precedence in understanding the primary documents. I also have in mind the insights from the social scientific study of religion that have enhanced substantially our understanding of religious groups and communities through a fresh re-reading of the literary and archeological evidence. And I think of the helpful approaches of a sociology of knowledge used by Harold Remus in the paper just described and again by John Corbett (below).

The role of a subordinate standard comes most clearly to view, as Wayne McCready has shown,[10] in Qumran. Building upon, but going beyond, the view of Schiffmann that the laws of the Bible fall into two categories, revealed laws (*niglot*) for all and hidden laws (*nistarot*) for the community, McCready argues that the product of exegesis of the Dead Sea Scrolls was a corpus that controlled the inherited texts and reworked views of ancient heroes and acts. So the scrolls function as a counterpart of inherited *torah*, as an authority. McCready also goes beyond the views of Wacholder on the Temple Scroll (who retitles it 11QTorah!) by arguing that sectarian *torah* brings new or renewed conditions of righteousness. The result of this is that the sectarian writings come effectively to be the primary documents, even if the *torah* of Moses is still viewed as a unit and as authoritative, setting up conflict between the community writings and the Mosaic *torah*.

In a somewhat similar vein Alan Segal examines a little used part of the Jewish materials to illuminate the contest between Judaism and Christianity over the covenant.[11] There is not much literary evidence, apart from Qumran, for first-century Jewish views of covenant. E. P. Sanders includes *midrash* as part of the evidence, but it is not clear that *midrash* is first-century. So Segal investigates liturgy and ritual and concludes that the emphatic use in ritual of covenant-renewal ceremonies allows rabbinic Judaism to pass over the covenant in silence. His evidence is drawn from the liturgy associated with circumcision, from the daily service, from the Sabbath service (where the conception that *torah* is the sign of the covenant underlies the use of the Torah as a covenant ratification), from the fact that tefillin in the first century contain the decalogue and from the Shema.

Jack Lightstone has argued for a homological "fit" between the idea of *torah*, the Deuteronomic priestly document and the socio-cultic form of organization of the Jewish community.[12] In the Greco-Roman diaspora there are also homological relations, so that while the Temple could not blur ethnic boundaries, the synagogue could. The cult of Torah, as in the Herodian Temple, produces a single unique order with respect to which the whole world is oriented—an Israel-centric universe. But in the Greco-Roman diaspora the synagogue decentralizes the laws of sacredness and denationalizes *torah*. The Torah in the diaspora serves as an authoritative sourcebook of *nomoi*, appropriating an ethnic past, mediating the power of the deity, reinforcing religio-ethnic identity in a highly varied Hellenistic society.

A closely related piece by Lightstone argues in a similar fashion about *Mishnah*.[13] By looking at the larger systemic contexts, he shows how the canon is a structured whole: closed in Hebrew, containing only ancient documents — a reflection of an ideal national territorial state of affairs. There is a homological relationship between scripture and sacred space and sacred time. Likewise *Mishnah* is a structured whole: it is in Hebrew but not biblical Hebrew, all rabbis speak in the same "voice" without individuality, the subject matter is closed, with each tractate a coherent essay. The same circles that fixed the canon were responsible for *Mishnah*; each structurally mirrors the other. And both mirror the social institutions and experiences of the second century C.E., where (in the wake of the revolts of 66-70 and 132-135 C.E. and the attendant dissolution of the fabric of society) there is no need for a messianic fulfillment but there is a need for order, holiness and purity.

John Corbett adopted a sociology of knowledge perspective, using varied evidence and arguing for a different point.[14] When the Pharisees arose as a scholarly elite, their techniques of exegesis created a sophisticated and literate scholarship that allowed them eventually to control the Temple cult through a creative application of the laws of purity. By contrast, the Cynics attacked law and debated the relationship of *nomos* (law) and *physis* (nature). It is relatively unnoticed that one centre of Cynic teaching was located in Gadara in the Decapolis. Paul's radical rejection of law, Corbett claims, reminds us of the Cynics though his authoritarianism sounds more like the Stoics. In any event, a literate revolution took place in the ancient Mediterranean world which resulted in oral traditions being frozen in texts, subject to a literate craft guild. Pharisees, Cynics and Christians — each in different ways — attacked illegitimate authority and aimed to reappropriate Law as the foundation of liberty. Ultimately there could be no alliance between Cynics, Jews and Christians after the second revolt; and this is tragic, because they all had in common the view of (internalized) law as realized liberty.

In a careful exegetical study Michel Desjardins has examined two Jewish writings from the late first century C.E.[15] He has shown how "law" functions in both 2 Baruch and 4 Ezra, how law is for each considered to be divinely provided and how adherence to it guarantees eternal life. Both writings arise in communities reflecting on dreadful experience of the revolts. Suffering will peak soon, and then will come the Messianic kingdom and judgment. In the life of these communities, the Law served to sustain them after the destruction of the Temple.

Torah is the possession of all Jews.[16] That all Jews should know the laws and that this general knowledge is distinctive of Judaism is confirmed by non-Jewish authors such as Juvenal, Seneca and

Tacitus. A. I. Baumgarten goes on from these statements to claim that the Bible then becomes the common property of all humanity. Nevertheless, Jews were different, as Greco-Roman writers argued, because the Bible was a public document for them. One significance of this is that the Pharisees, lacking an appeal to priestly traditions, utilized the shared belief in *torah* (the national heritage of all Jews) as part of the basis for arguing for *their* tradition as part of the patrimony of all.

Steve Mason has published an important article that bears on the subject matter of A. I. Baumgarten's contribution to this present volume; see "Josephus on the Pharisees Reconsidered: A Critique of Smith/Neusner," *Studies in Religion/Sciences Religieuses*, 17, 4 (1988): 455-69. He concludes that in *Antiquities* Josephus has radically redrawn the picture of Alexandra Salome's reign, but in doing so he has altered everything except the picture of the Pharisees, *contra* Smith/Neusner.

This universal dimension of *torah* has been argued in a more theological way by Sidney Greidanus; his point is to show that the Hebrew scriptures teach that they have a universal validity, applicable to all people.[17] God's law is in agreement with nature but it is not to be identified with nature, nor can it be known by reason. Nature is not the lawgiver; God is the source of all laws.

One small aspect of the functional use of law in Judaism in the Second Temple period is assessed by the present writer.[18] The prohibition against figurative representation in the second commandment was debated in the period of Herod the Great. In his vast building program, Herod appears to have consistently maintained the second commandment in his buildings within Israel, even in those that were essentially private and where his piety was not on display. In his buildings outside the Holy Land, however, he uses figurative representations. Overall, his building program is an outworking of various "pieties"—to the God of Israel, to his patron Augustus, to his family and to the well-being of the Jewish diaspora.

## Further Work

The seminar has held back from going very far afield, but two important contributions beyond its usual boundaries have been published. Ira Robinson has analyzed medieval debates on the extent of Torah and whether non-rabbinic disciplines could be considered integral parts of Torah.[19] Though Ashkenazic culture is more insular than Sephardic, even in Torah-centred Ashkenaz there were protests against a Talmudic monopoly in the curriculum. Torah as codified in the Talmud contained only a part of the commandments, and arguments were made for including astronomy, physics, metaphysics and others. Once it was accepted that the concept of Torah extended beyond *nomos* the battle was joined to see which of the major rivals, kabbala or philosophy, would emerge as the goal of the Jewish intellectual effort.

The analysis has been brought up to today by Moshe Amon in a study of reactions to the Jewishness of the state of Israel.[20] The question is how to link the Jewish mode of existence with Torah. The analysis shows the tensions that arise from a variety of viewpoints when basic conceptions of *torah* differ as fundamentally as those of the *Agudat Israel*, Rabbi Abraham Kook and the *Gush Emmunim*, and Rabbi Meir Kahane.

The seminar in its first several years also tried to stay away from tackling Christian materials, preferring to concentrate on the early church towards the end of its mandate. These papers will appear in other volumes. But two important analyses of Pauline problems have been published to date. Lloyd Gaston, in characteristic fashion, attacks the difficult problem of the phrase *erga nomou*.[21] He begins from Lohmeyer's claim that the phrase, despite its natural meaning, means "works which the law prescribes." Gaston argues cogently for its natural meaning, "works worked by the law," primarily from the two cases that gave Lohmeyer trouble—Galatians 3:10 and Romans 2:15. He concludes that "works of law" is a subjective genitive, not a Jewish commonplace but a peculiar Pauline notion: law works in the gentile world to create a situation from which redemption is needed. Law exercises retribution from human sinfulness in a process called "wrath."

Alan Segal proposes a different solution to another *crux interpretum* in Romans 7.[22] Paul is speaking personally, describing his experience with *torah* after conversion. In Romans 7:9 he has given up serious allegiance to *torah* but he still returns to it as a courtesy to others (as he also describes in 1 Corinthians 9:19-22). Romans 7 is not psychoanalytic or existential, it is the apologia of one who compromised when his radical solution was not accepted by conservatives. Paul's reflections in Romans 7 are a natural aspect of a strongly debated issue of Jewish law in Christianity. His experience was relevant to the legal point because he was counselling tolerance of antinomian Christians. His own behaviour prompted a new understanding of the value of Torah. In the shared experiences of this behaviour he was trying to meld the two communities together; this led to danger and the stuff of tragedy.

The papers described above are those that have been published to date. This review of where to find the early work of the seminar in printed form may indicate sufficiently the rich fare and the broad mandate that has been developed. What is needed now are studies that compare the various ways in which law functions within groups in pre- and post-destruction Judaism; similarly there is a need for comparative studies of the development of law in various Christian groups in the first and second centuries. The Jewish and Christian developments are discrete but more or less parallel. The variety is substantial. Yet the importance of law in both religious communities is enormous.

## Notes

1  See the two volumes of papers produced by that earlier seminar: Peter Richardson, ed., with David Granskou, *Anti-Judaism in Early Christianity*, Vol. 1: *Paul and the Gospels* (Waterloo: Wilfrid Laurier University Press, 1985), and S. G. Wilson, ed., Vol. 2: *Separation and Polemic* (Waterloo: Wilfrid Laurier University Press, 1985).

2  *Encyclopedia Britannica*, 15th ed. (Chicago: Encyclopaedia Britannica, 1979), Propaedia: 354-55.

3  Mircea Eliade, ed. in chief, *The Encyclopedia of Religion* (New York: Macmillan, 1987), 8:463-85; 6:158-73; 7:466-81; 7:431-53.

4  The CSBS is indebted to the editors of *Studies in Religion/Sciences Religieuses* for devoting much of issues 13, 1 (1984); 14, 1 (1985); and 15, 3 (1986) to papers from the *Torah-nomos* seminar. Some of these papers will be summarized in what follows.

5  Alan F. Segal, "Torah and *Nomos* in Recent Scholarly Discussion," *Studies in Religion/Sciences Religieuses*, 13, 1 (1984): 19-27.

6  Stephen Westerholm, "*Torah, Nomos*, and Law: A Question of Meaning," *Studies in Religion/Sciences Religieuses*, 15, 3 (1985): 327-36. See also his more programmatic comments above in Chapters 2 and 3.

7  Adele Reinhartz, "The Meaning of *Nomos* in Philo's *Exposition of the Law*," *Studies in Religion/Sciences Religieuses*, 15, 3 (1986): 337-45.

8  Harold Remus, "Authority, Consent, Law: *Nomos, Physis*, and the Striving for a Given," *Studies in Religion/Sciences Religieuses*, 13, 1 (1984): 5-18.

9  William Klassen, "The King as 'Living Law' with Particular Reference to Musonius Rufus," *Studies in Religion/Sciences Religieuses*, 14, 1 (1985): 63-71.

10  Wayne McCready, "A Second Torah at Qumran," *Studies in Religion/Sciences Religieuses* 14, 1 (1985): 5-15.

11  Alan F. Segal, "Covenant in Rabbinic Writings," *Studies in Religion/Sciences Religieuses*, 14, 1 (1985): 53-62. See also his *Rebecca's Children: Judaism and Christianity in the Roman World* (Cambridge, MA: Harvard University Press, 1986).

12  Jack N. Lightstone, "Torah Is *Nomos* — Except When It Is Not: Prolegomena to the Study of the Law in Late Antique Judaism," *Studies in Religion/Sciences Religieuses*, 13, 1 (1984): 29-37.

13  Jack N. Lightstone, "Scripture and Mishnah in Earliest Rabbinic Judaism," *Studies in Religion/Sciences Religieuses*, 15, 3 (1986): 317-25. See also his full-scale study, *Society, The Sacred, and Scripture in Ancient Judaism: A Sociology of Knowledge* (Waterloo: Wilfrid Laurier University Press, 1988).

14  John Corbett, "The Pharisaic Revolution and Jesus as Embodied Torah," *Studies in Religion/Sciences Religieuses*, 15, 3 (1986): 375-91.

15  Michel Desjardins, "Law in 2 Baruch and 4 Ezra," *Studies in Religion/Sciences Religieuses*, 14, 1 (1985): 25-37.

16 A. I. Baumgarten, "The Torah as a Public Document in Judaism," *Studies in Religion/Sciences Religieuses*, 14, 1 (1985): 17-24. See also his contribution on Rivkin and Neusner in Chapter 7 above.

17 Sidney Greidanus, "The Universal Dimension of Law in the Hebrew Scriptures," *Studies in Religion/Sciences Religieuses*, 14, 1 (1985): 39-51.

18 Peter Richardson, "Law and Piety in Herod's Architecture," *Studies in Religion/Sciences Religieuses*, 15, 3 (1986): 347-60.

19 Ira Robinson, "Torah and Halakha in Mediaeval Judaism," *Studies in Religion/Sciences Religieuses*, 13, 1 (1984): 47-55.

20 Moshe Amon, "Jewish Law in Israel Today: A Conundrum for Messianic Times," *Studies in Religion/Sciences Religieuses*, 13, 1 (1984): 57-63.

21 Lloyd Gaston, "Works of Law as a Subjective Genitive," *Studies in Religion/Sciences Religieuses*, 13, 1 (1984): 39-46; this has also appeared in revised form in his important book *Paul and the Torah* (Vancouver: University of British Columbia Press, 1987), especially chap. 6.

22 Alan F. Segal, "Romans 7 and Jewish Dietary Law," *Studies in Religion/Sciences Religieuses*, 15, 3 (1986): 361-74. See also his recent book, *Paul the Convert: The Apostolate and Apostasy of Saul the Pharisee* (New Haven CN: Yale, 1990).

# Index of Authors*

Indexes prepared by Barry W. Henaut

# Index of References

# SR SUPPLEMENTS

Note: Nos. 1, 3, 4, 5, 6, 7, 8, 10, 15 and 20 in this series are out of print.

# EDITIONS SR

Note: Nos. 1 and 3 in this series are out of print.

# STUDIES IN CHRISTIANITY AND JUDAISM / ETUDES SUR LE CHRISTIANISME ET LE JUDAISME

# THE STUDY OF RELIGION IN CANADA / SCIENCES RELIGIEUSES AU CANADA

# COMPARATIVE ETHICS SERIES / COLLECTION D'ÉTHIQUE COMPARÉE

Available from / en vente chez:

*Wilfrid Laurier University Press*
Wilfrid Laurier University
Waterloo, Ontario, Canada   N2L 3C5


Published for the
Canadian Corporation for Studies in Religion/
Corporation Canadienne des Sciences Religieuses
by Wilfrid Laurier University Press